To B,

May your search be fruitful...
Christmas 2001

Love
D

D0015605

THE ART OF HAPPINESS

The ART of
HAPPINESS

A Handbook for Living

HIS HOLINESS
THE DALAI LAMA
and
HOWARD C. CUTLER, M.D.

Riverhead Books

a member of Penguin Putnam Inc.

New York   1998

Riverhead Books
a member of
Penguin Putnam Inc.
375 Hudson Street
New York, NY 10014

Excerpt from "Eight Verses of the Training on the Mind" by Geshe Langri
Thangpa on page 182 is from the Four Essential Buddhist Commentaries by His
Holiness the Dalai Lama. Reprinted by permission of the Library of
Tibetan Works and Archives, Dharamsala (H.P.), India.

Copyright © 1998 by HH Dalai Lama and Howard C. Cutler, M.D.
All rights reserved. This book, or parts thereof, may not
be reproduced in any form without permission.
Published simultaneously in Canada

Library of Congress Cataloging-in-Publication Data

Bstan-'dzin-rgya-mtsho, Dalai Lama XIV, date.
The art of happiness : a handbook for living / by the Dalai Lama
and Howard C. Cutler.
p.   cm.
ISBN 1-57322-111-2 (alk. paper)
1. Religious life—Buddhism.   2. Happiness—Religious
aspects—Buddhism.   3. Buddhism—Doctrines.   I. Cutler, Howard C.
II. Title
BQ7935.B774A78   1998   98-20431 CIP
294.3'444—dc21

Printed in the United States of America

45 47 49 50 48 46

This book is printed on acid-free paper. ⊚

Book design by Chris Welch

Dedicated to the Reader:
May you find happiness.

CONTENTS

AUTHOR'S NOTE

In this book, extensive conversations with the Dalai Lama have been recounted. The private meetings with the Dalai Lama in Arizona and India, which form the basis of this work, took place with the express purpose of collaborating on a project that would present his views on leading a happier life, augmented by my own observations and commentary from the perspective of a Western psychiatrist. The Dalai Lama generously allowed me to select whatever format for the book I felt would most effectively convey his ideas. I felt that the narrative format found in these pages would be most readable and at the same time impart a sense of how the Dalai Lama incorporates his ideas into his own daily life. With the Dalai Lama's approval, I have organized this book according to subject matter, and thus at times I have chosen to combine and integrate material that may have been taken from several different conversations. Also, with the Dalai Lama's permission, where I deemed necessary for clarity or comprehensiveness, I have woven in material from some of his public talks in Arizona. The Dalai Lama's interpreter, Dr. Thupten Jinpa, kindly reviewed the final manuscript to assure that there were no inadvertent distortions of the Dalai Lama's ideas as a result of the editorial process.

A number of case histories and personal anecdotes have been presented to illustrate the ideas under discussion. In order to maintain confidentiality and protect personal privacy, in every instance I have changed names and altered details and other distinguishing characteristics so as to prevent identification of particular individuals.

—Howard C. Cutler, M.D.

INTRODUCTION

I found the Dalai Lama alone in an empty basketball locker room moments before he was to speak before a crowd of six thousand at Arizona State University. He was calmly sipping a cup of tea, in perfect repose. "Your Holiness, if you're ready . . ."

He briskly rose, and without hesitation he left the room, emerging into the thick backstage throng of local reporters, photographers, security personnel, and students—the seekers, the curious, and the skeptical. He walked through the crowd smiling broadly and greeting people as he passed by. Finally passing through a curtain, he walked on stage, bowed, folded his hands, and smiled. He was greeted with thunderous applause. At his request, the house lights were not dimmed so he could clearly see his audience, and for several moments he simply stood there, quietly surveying the audience with an unmistakable expression of warmth and goodwill. For those who had never seen the Dalai Lama before, his maroon and saffron monk's robes may have created a somewhat exotic impression, yet his remarkable ability to establish rapport with his audience was quickly revealed as he sat down and began his talk.

"I think that this is the first time I am meeting most of you. But to me, whether it is an old friend or new friend, there's not much difference anyway, because I always believe we are the same; we are all human beings. Of course, there may be differences in cultural background or way of life, there may be differences in our faith, or we may be of a different color, but we are human beings, consisting of the human body and the human mind. Our physical structure is the same, and our mind and our emotional nature are also the same. Wherever I meet people, I always have the feeling that I am encountering another human being, just like myself. I find it is much easier to communicate with others on that level. If we emphasize specific characteristics, like I am Tibetan or I am Buddhist, then there are differences. But those things are secondary. If we can leave the differences aside, I think we can easily communicate, exchange ideas, and share experiences."

With this, in 1993 the Dalai Lama began a week-long series of public talks in Arizona. Plans for his visit to Arizona had first been set into motion over a decade earlier. It was at that time that we first met, while I was visiting Dharamsala, India, on a small research grant to study traditional Tibetan medicine.

Dharamsala is a beautiful and tranquil village, perched on a hillside in the foothills of the Himalayas. For almost forty years, this has been the home of the Tibetan government-in-exile, ever since the Dalai Lama, along with one hundred thousand other Tibetans, fled Tibet after the brutal invasion by Chinese forces. During my stay in Dharamsala I had gotten to know several members of the Dalai Lama's family, and it was through them that my first meeting with him was arranged.

In his 1993 public address, the Dalai Lama spoke of the importance of relating as one human being to another, and it was this very same quality that had been the most striking feature of our first conversation at his home in 1982. He seemed to have an uncommon ability to put one completely at ease, to quickly create a simple and direct connection with a fellow human being. Our first meeting had lasted around forty-five minutes, and like so many other people, I came away from that meeting in great spirits, with the impression that I had just met a truly exceptional man.

As my contact with the Dalai Lama grew over the next several years, I gradually came to appreciate his many unique qualities. He has a penetrating intelligence, but without artifice; a kindness, but without excessive sentimentality; great humor, but without frivolousness; and, as many have discovered, the ability to inspire rather than awe.

Over time I became convinced that the Dalai Lama had learned how to live with a sense of fulfillment and a degree of serenity that I had never seen in other people. I was determined to identify the principles that enabled him to achieve this. Although he is a Buddhist monk with a lifetime of Buddhist training and study, I began to wonder if one could identify a set of his beliefs or practices that could be utilized by non-Buddhists as well—practices that could be directly applied to our lives to simply help us become happier, stronger, perhaps less afraid.

Eventually, I had an opportunity to explore his views in greater depth, meeting with him daily during his stay in Arizona and following up these discussions with more extensive conversations at his home in India. As we conversed, I soon discovered that we had some hurdles to overcome as we struggled to reconcile our different perspectives: his as a Buddhist monk, and mine as a Western psychiatrist. I began one of our first sessions, for example, by posing to him certain common human problems, illustrating with several lengthy case histories. Having described a woman who persisted in self-destructive behaviors despite the tremendous negative impact on her life, I asked him if he had an explanation for this behavior and what advice he could offer. I was taken aback when after a long pause and reflection, he simply said, "I don't know," and shrugging his shoulders, laughed good-naturedly.

Noting my look of surprise and disappointment at not receiving a more concrete response, the Dalai Lama said, "Sometimes it's very difficult to explain why people do the things they do . . . You'll often find that there are no simple explanations. If we were to go into the details of individual lives, since a human being's mind is so complex, it would be quite difficult to understand what is going on, what exactly is taking place."

I thought that he was being evasive. "But as a psychotherapist, my task is to find out why people do the things that they do . . ."

Once again, he broke into the laugh that many people find so extraordinary—a laugh saturated with humor and goodwill, unaffected, unembarrassed, beginning with a deep resonance and effortlessly climbing several octaves to end in a high pitch of delight.

"I think that it would be extremely difficult to try and figure out how the minds of five billion people work," he said, still laughing. "It would be an impossible task! From the Buddhist viewpoint, there are many factors contributing to any given event or situation . . . There can be so many factors at play, in fact, that sometimes you may never have a full explanation of what's going on, at least not in conventional terms."

Sensing some discomfort on my part, he observed, "In trying to determine the source of one's problems, it seems that the Western approach differs in some respects from the Buddhist approach. Underlying all Western modes of analysis is a very strong rationalistic tendency—an assumption that everything can be accounted for. And on top of that, there are constraints created by certain premises that are taken for granted. For example, recently I met with some doctors at a university medical school. They were talking about the brain and stated that thoughts and feelings were the result of different chemical reactions and changes in the brain. So, I raised the question: Is it possible to conceive the reverse sequence, where the thought gives rise to the sequence of chemical events in the brain? However, the part that I found most interesting was the answer that the scientist gave. He said, 'We start from the premise that all thoughts are products or functions of chemical reactions in the brain.' So it is simply a kind of rigidity, a decision not to challenge their own way of thinking."

He was silent for a moment, then went on: "I think that in modern Western society, there seems to be a powerful cultural conditioning that is based on science. But in some instances, the basic premises and parameters set up by Western science can limit your ability to deal with certain realities. For instance, you have the constraints of the idea that everything can be explained within the framework of a single lifetime, and you combine this with the notion that everything can and must be explained and accounted for. But when you encounter phenomena that you cannot account for, then there's a kind of a tension created; it's almost a feeling of agony."

Even though I sensed there was truth in what he said, I found it difficult to accept at first. "Well, in Western psychology when we come across human behaviors that on the surface are difficult to explain, there are certain approaches that we can use to understand what's going on. For example, the idea of the unconscious or subconscious part of the mind plays a prominent role. We feel that sometimes behavior can be a result of psychological processes that we aren't consciously aware of—for instance, one might act in a certain way so as to avoid an underlying fear. Without being aware of it, certain behaviors may be motivated by the desire to not allow those fears to surface in the conscious mind, so we don't have to feel the discomfort associated with them."

Reflecting for a moment, the Dalai Lama said, "In Buddhism there is the idea of dispositions and imprints left by certain types of experiences, which is somewhat similar to the idea of the unconscious in Western psychology. For instance, a certain type of event may have occurred in an earlier part of your life which has left a very strong imprint on your mind which can remain hidden, and then later affect your behavior. So, there is this idea of something that can be unconscious—imprints that one may not be consciously aware of. Anyway, I think that Buddhism can accept many of the factors that the Western theorists can come up with, but on top of that it would add additional factors. For example, it would add the conditioning and imprints from previous lives. In Western psychology, however, I think that there may be a tendency to overemphasize the role of the unconscious in looking for the source of one's problems. I think that this stems from some of the basic assumptions that Western psychology starts with: for instance, it does not accept the idea of imprints being carried over from a past life. And at the same time there is an assumption that everything must be accounted for within this lifetime. So, when you can't explain what is causing certain behaviors or problems, the tendency is to always attribute it to the unconscious. It's a bit like you've lost something and you decide that the object is in this room. And once you have decided this, then you've already fixed your parameters; you've precluded the possibility of its being outside the room or in another room. So you keep on searching and searching, but you are not finding it, yet you continue to assume that it is still hidden somewhere in the room!"

When I initially conceived of this book, I envisioned a conventional self-help format in which the Dalai Lama would present clear and simple solutions to all life's problems. I felt that, using my background in psychiatry, I could codify his views in a set of easy instructions on how to conduct one's daily life. By the end of our series of meetings I had given up on that idea. I found that his approach encompassed a much broader and more complex paradigm, incorporating all the nuance, richness, and complexity that life has to offer.

Gradually, however, I began to hear the single note he constantly sounded. It is one of hope. His hope is based on the belief that while attaining genuine and lasting happiness is not easy, it nevertheless can be done. Underlying all the Dalai Lama's methods there is a set of basic beliefs that act as a substrate for all his actions: a belief in the fundamental gentleness and goodness of all human beings, a belief in the value of compassion, a belief in a policy of kindness, and a sense of commonality among all living creatures.

As his message unfolded, it became increasingly clear that his beliefs are not based on blind faith or religious dogma but rather on sound reasoning and direct experience. His understanding of the human mind and behavior is based on a lifetime of study. His views are rooted in a tradition that dates back over twenty-five hundred years yet is tempered by common sense and a sophisticated understanding of modern problems. His appreciation of contemporary issues has been forged as a result of his unique position as a world figure, which has allowed him to travel the world many times, exposing himself to many different cultures and people from all walks of life, exchanging ideas with top scientists and religious and political leaders. What ultimately emerges is a wise approach to dealing with human problems that is at once optimistic and realistic.

In this book I have sought to present the Dalai Lama's approach to a primarily Western audience. I have included extensive excerpts from his public teachings and our private conversations. In keeping with my purpose of trying to emphasize the material that is most readily applicable to our daily lives, I have at times chosen to omit portions of the Dalai Lama's discussions that concern some of the more philosophical aspects of Tibetan Buddhism. The Dalai Lama has already written a number of excellent books on various aspects of the Buddhist path. Selected titles can be found at the end of this book, and those interested in more in-depth exploration of Tibetan Buddhism will find much of value in these books.

Part I

THE PURPOSE
OF LIFE

Chapter 1

THE RIGHT TO
HAPPINESS

I believe that the very purpose of our life is to seek happiness. That is clear. Whether one believes in religion or not, whether one believes in this religion or that religion, we all are seeking something better in life. So, I think, the very motion of our life is towards happiness . . ."

With these words, spoken before a large audience in Arizona, the Dalai Lama cut to the heart of his message. But his claim that the purpose of life was happiness raised a question in my mind. Later, when we were alone, I asked, "Are *you* happy?"

"Yes," he said. He paused, then added, "Yes . . . definitely." There was a quiet sincerity in his voice that left no doubt—

a sincerity that was reflected in his expression and in his eyes.

"But is happiness a reasonable goal for most of us?" I asked. "Is it really possible?"

"Yes. I believe that happiness can be achieved through training the mind."

On a basic human level, I couldn't help but respond to the idea of happiness as an achievable goal. As a psychiatrist, however, I had been burdened by notions such as Freud's belief that "one feels inclined to say that the intention that man should be 'happy' is not included in the plan of 'Creation.' " This type of training had led many in my profession to the grim conclusion that the most one could hope for was "the transformation of hysteric misery into common unhappiness." From that standpoint, the claim that there was a clearly defined path to happiness seemed like quite a radical idea. As I looked back over my years of psychiatric training, I could rarely recall having heard the word "happiness" even mentioned as a therapeutic objective. Of course, there was plenty of talk about relieving the patient's symptoms of depression or anxiety, of resolving internal conflicts or relationship problems, but never with the expressly stated goal of becoming happy.

The concept of achieving true happiness has, in the West, always seemed ill defined, elusive, ungraspable. Even the word "happy" is derived from the Icelandic word *happ*, meaning luck or chance. Most of us, it seems, share this view of the mysterious nature of happiness. In those moments of joy that life brings, happiness feels like something that comes out of the blue. To my Western mind, it didn't seem the sort of thing that one could develop, and sustain, simply by "training the mind."

When I raised that objection, the Dalai Lama was quick to explain. "When I say 'training the mind,' in this context I'm not referring to 'mind' merely as one's cognitive ability or intellect. Rather, I'm using the term in the sense of the Tibetan word *Sem*, which has a much broader meaning, closer to 'psyche' or 'spirit'; it includes intellect and feeling, heart and mind. By bringing about a certain inner discipline, we can undergo a transformation of our attitude, our entire outlook and approach to living.

"When we speak of this inner discipline, it can of course involve many things, many methods. But generally speaking, one begins by identifying those factors which lead to happiness and those factors which lead to suffering. Having done this, one then sets about gradually eliminating those factors which lead to suffering and cultivating those which lead to happiness. That is the way."

The Dalai Lama claims to have found some measure of personal happiness. And throughout the week he spent in Arizona, I often witnessed how this personal happiness can manifest as a simple willingness to reach out to others, to create a feeling of affinity and goodwill, even in the briefest of encounters.

One morning after his public lecture the Dalai Lama was walking along an outside patio on the way back to his hotel room, surrounded by his usual retinue. Noticing one of the hotel housekeeping staff standing by the elevators, he paused to ask her, "Where are you from?" For a moment she appeared taken aback by this foreign-looking man in the maroon robes and seemed puzzled by the deference of the entourage. Then she smiled and answered shyly, "Mexico." He paused briefly to chat with her a few moments and then walked on, leaving her with a look of excitement and pleasure on her face. The next morning at the same time, she appeared at the same spot with another of the housekeeping staff, and the two of them greeted him warmly as he got into the elevator. The interaction was brief, but the two of them appeared flushed with happiness as they returned to work. Every day after that, they were joined by a few more of the housekeeping staff at the designated time and place, until by the end of the week there were dozens of maids in their crisp gray-and-white uniforms forming a receiving line that stretched along the length of the path that led to the elevators.

Our days are numbered. At this very moment, many thousands are born into the world, some destined to live only a few days or weeks, and then tragically succumb to illness or other misfortune. Others are destined to push through to the century mark, perhaps even a bit beyond, and savor every taste life has to offer: triumph, despair, joy, hatred, and love. We never know. But whether we live a day or a century, a central question always remains: What is the purpose of our life? What makes our lives meaningful?

The purpose of our existence is to seek happiness. It seems like common sense, and Western thinkers from Aristotle to William James have agreed with this idea. But isn't a life based on seeking personal happiness by nature self-centered, even self-indulgent? Not necessarily. In fact, survey after survey has shown that it is *unhappy* people who tend to be most self-focused and are often socially withdrawn, brooding, and even antagonistic. Happy people, in contrast, are generally found to be more sociable, flexible, and creative and are able to tolerate life's daily frustrations more easily than unhappy people. And, most important, they are found to be more loving and forgiving than unhappy people.

Researchers have devised some interesting experiments demonstrating that happy people exhibit a certain quality of openness, a willingness to reach out and help others. They managed, for instance, to induce a happy mood in a test subject by arranging to have the person unexpectedly find money in a phone booth. Posing as a stranger, one of the experimenters then walked by and "accidentally" dropped a load of papers. The investigators wanted to see whether the subject would stop to help the stranger. In another scenario, the subjects' spirits were lifted by listening to a comedy album, and then they were approached by someone in need (also in cahoots with the experimenter) wanting to borrow money. The investigators discovered that the subjects who were feeling happy were more likely to help someone or to lend money than another "control group" of individuals who were presented with the same opportunity to help but whose mood had not been boosted ahead of time.

While these kinds of experiments contradict the notion that the pursuit and achievement of personal happiness somehow lead to selfishness and self-absorption, we can all conduct our own experiment in the laboratory of our own daily lives. Suppose, for instance, we're stuck in traffic. After twenty minutes it finally begins moving again, at around parade speed. We see someone in another car signaling that she wants to pull into our lane ahead of us. If we're in a good mood, we are more likely to slow down and wave them on ahead. If we're feeling miserable, our response may be simply to speed up and close the gap. "Well, I've been stuck here waiting all this time; why shouldn't they?"

We begin, then, with the basic premise that the purpose of our life is to seek happiness. It is a vision of happiness as a real objective, one that we can take positive steps toward achieving. And as we begin to identify the factors that lead to a happier life, we will learn how the search for happiness offers benefits not only for the individual but for the individual's family and for society at large as well.

Chapter 2

THE SOURCES
OF HAPPINESS

Two years ago, a friend of mine had an unexpected wind-fall. Eighteen months before that time, she had quit her job as a nurse to go to work for two friends who were starting a small health-care company. The company enjoyed meteoric success, and within the eighteen months they were bought out by a large conglomerate for a huge sum. Having gotten in on the ground floor of the company, my friend emerged from the buyout dripping with stock options—enough to be able to retire at the age of thirty-two. I saw her not long ago and asked how she was enjoying her retirement. "Well," she said, "it's great being able to travel and do the things that I've always wanted to do. But," she added, "it's strange; after I got over all the excitement of making all that money, things kinda returned to normal. I mean things are different—I bought a new house and stuff—but overall I don't think I'm much happier than I was before."

Just around the time that my friend was cashing in on her windfall profits, I had another friend of the same age who found out he was HIV positive. We spoke about how he was dealing with his HIV status. "Of course, I was devastated at first," he said. "And it took me almost a year just to come to terms with the fact that I had the virus. But over the past year things have changed. I seem to get more out of each day than I ever did before, and on a moment-to-moment basis, I feel happier than I ever have. I just seem to appreciate everyday things more, and I'm grateful that so far I haven't developed any severe AIDS symptoms and I can really enjoy the things I have. And even though I'd rather not be HIV positive, I have to admit that in some ways it has transformed my life . . . in positive ways . . ."

"In what ways?" I asked.

"Well, for instance, you know that I've always tended to be a confirmed materialist. But over the past year coming to terms with my mortality has opened up a whole new world. I've started exploring spirituality for the first time in my life, reading a lot of books on the subject and talking to people . . . discovering so many things that I've never even thought about before. It makes me excited about just getting up in the morning, about seeing what the day will bring."

Both these people illustrate the essential point that *happiness is determined more by one's state of mind than by external events*. Success may result in a temporary feeling of elation, or tragedy may send us into a period of depression, but sooner or later our overall level of happiness tends to migrate back to a certain baseline. Psychologists call this process *adaptation*, and we can see how this principle operates in our everyday life; a pay raise, a new car, or recognition from our peers may lift our mood for a while, but we soon return to our customary level of happiness. In the same way, an argument with a friend, a car in the repair shop, or a minor injury may put us in a foul mood, but within a matter of days our spirits rebound.

This tendency isn't limited to trivial, everyday events but persists even under more extreme conditions of triumph or disaster. Researchers surveying Illinois state lottery winners and British pool winners, for instance, found that the initial high eventually wore off and the winners returned to their usual range of moment-to-moment happiness. And other studies have demonstrated that even those who are struck by catastrophic events such as cancer, blindness, or paralysis typically recover their normal or near-normal level of day-to-day happiness after an appropriate adjustment period.

So, if we tend to return to our characteristic baseline level of happiness no matter what our external conditions are, what determines this baseline? And, more important, can it be modified, set at a higher level? Some researchers have recently argued that an individual's characteristic level of happiness or well-being is genetically determined, at least to some degree. Studies such as one that found that identical twins (sharing the same genetic constitution) tend to have very similar levels of well-being—regardless of whether they were raised together or apart—have led these investigators to postulate a biological set point for happiness, wired into the brain at birth.

But even if genetic makeup plays a role in happiness—and the verdict is still out on how large that role is—there is general agreement among psychologists that no matter what level of happiness we are endowed with by nature, there are steps we can take to work with the "mind factor," to enhance our feelings of happiness. This is because our moment-to-moment happiness is largely determined by our outlook. In fact, whether we are feeling happy or unhappy at any given moment often has very little to do with our absolute conditions but, rather it is a function of *how we perceive our situation, how satisfied we are with what we have.*

THE COMPARING MIND

What shapes our perception and level of satisfaction? *Our feelings of contentment are strongly influenced by our tendency to compare.* When we compare our current situation to our past and find that we're better off, we feel happy. This happens, for instance, when our income suddenly jumps from $20,000 to $30,000 a year, but it's not the *absolute* amount of income that makes us happy, as we soon find out when we get used to our new income and discover that we won't be happy again unless we're making $40,000 a year. We also look around and compare ourselves to others. No matter how much we make, we tend to be dissatisfied with our income if our neighbor is making more. Professional athletes complain bitterly about annual salaries of $1 million, $2 million, or $3 million, citing the higher salary of a teammate as justification for their unhappiness. This tendency seems to support H. L. Mencken's definition of a wealthy man: one whose income is $100 a year higher than his wife's sister's husband.

So we can see how our feeling of life satisfaction often depends on who we compare ourselves to. Of course, we compare other things besides income. Constant comparison with those who are smarter, more beautiful, or more successful than ourselves also tends to breed envy, frustration, and unhappiness. But we can use this same principle in a positive way; we can *increase* our feeling of life satisfaction by comparing ourselves to those who are less fortunate than us and by reflecting on all the things we have.

Researchers have conducted a number of experiments demonstrating that one's level of life satisfaction can be enhanced simply by shifting one's perspective and contemplating how things could be worse. In one study, women at the University of Wisconsin at Milwaukee were shown images of the extremely harsh living conditions in Milwaukee at the turn of the century or were asked to visualize and write about going through personal tragedies such as being burned or disfigured. After completing this exercise, the women were asked to rate the quality of their own lives. The exercise resulted in an increased sense of satisfaction with their lives. In another experiment at the State University of New York at Buffalo, subjects were asked to complete the sentence "I'm glad I'm not a . . ." After five repetitions of this exercise, the subjects experienced a distinct elevation in their feelings of life satisfaction. Another group of subjects was asked by the experimenters to complete the sentence "I wish I were a . . ." This time, the experiment left the subjects feeling more dissatisfied with their lives.

These experiments, which show that we can increase or decrease our sense of life satisfaction by changing our perspective, clearly point to the supremacy of one's mental outlook in living a happy life.

The Dalai Lama explains, "Although it is possible to achieve happiness, happiness is not a simple thing. There are many levels. In Buddhism, for instance, there is a reference to the four factors of fulfillment, or happiness: wealth, worldly satisfaction, spirituality, and enlightenment. Together they embrace the totality of an individual's quest for happiness.

"Let us leave aside for a moment ultimate religious or spiritual aspirations like perfection and enlightenment and deal with joy and happiness as we understand them in an everyday or worldly sense. Within this context, there are certain key elements that we conventionally acknowledge as contributing to joy and happiness. For example, good health is considered to be one of the necessary factors for a happy life. Another factor that we regard as a source of happiness is our material facilities, or the wealth that we accumulate. An additional factor is to have friendship, or companions. We all recognize that in order to enjoy a fulfilled life, we need a circle of friends with whom we can relate emotionally and trust.

"Now, all of these factors are, in fact, sources of happiness. But in order for an individual to be able to fully utilize them towards the goal of enjoying a happy and fulfilled life, *your state of mind is key*. It's crucial.

"If we utilize our favorable circumstances, such as our good health or wealth, in positive ways, in helping others, they can be contributory factors in achieving a happier life. And of course we enjoy these things—our material facilities, success, and so on. But without the right mental attitude, without attention to the mental factor, these things have very little impact on our long-term feelings of happiness. For example, if you harbor hateful thoughts or intense anger somewhere deep down within yourself, then it ruins your health; thus it destroys one of the factors. Also, if you are mentally unhappy or frustrated, then physical comfort is not of much help. On the other hand, if you can maintain a calm, peaceful state of mind, then you can be a very happy person even if you have poor health. Or, even if you have wonderful possessions, when you are in an intense moment of anger or hatred, you feel like throwing them, breaking them. At that moment your possessions mean nothing. Today there are societies that are very developed materially, yet among them there are many people who are not very happy. Just underneath the beautiful surface of affluence there is a kind of mental unrest, leading to frustration, unnecessary quarrels, reliance on drugs or alcohol, and in the worst case, suicide. So there is no guarantee that wealth alone can give you the joy or fulfillment that you are seeking. The same can be said of your friends too. When you are in an intense state of anger or hatred, even a very close friend appears to you as somehow sort of frosty, or cold, distant, and quite annoying.

"All of this indicates the tremendous influence that the mental state, the mind factor, has on our experience of daily life. Naturally, then, we have to take that factor very seriously.

"So leaving aside the perspective of spiritual practice, even in worldly terms, in terms of our enjoying a happy day-to-day existence, the greater the level of calmness of our mind, the greater our peace of mind, the greater our ability to enjoy a happy and joyful life."

The Dalai Lama paused for a moment as if to let that idea settle, then added, "I should mention that when we speak of a calm state of mind or peace of mind, we shouldn't confuse that with a totally insensitive, apathetic state of mind. Having a calm or peaceful state of mind doesn't mean being totally spaced out or completely empty. Peace of mind or a calm state of mind is rooted in affection and compassion. There is a very high level of sensitivity and feeling there."

Summarizing, he said, "As long as there is a lack of the inner discipline that brings calmness of mind, no matter what external facilities or conditions you have, they will never give you the feeling of joy and happiness that you are seeking. On the other hand, if you possess this inner quality, a calmness of mind, a degree of stability within, then even if you lack various external facilities that you would normally consider necessary for happiness, it is still possible to live a happy and joyful life."

INNER CONTENTMENT

Crossing the hotel parking lot on my way to meet with the Dalai Lama one afternoon, I stopped to admire a brand-new Toyota Land Cruiser, the type of car I had been wanting for a long time. Still thinking of that car as I began my session, I asked, "Sometimes it seems that our whole culture, Western culture, is based on material acquisition; we're surrounded, bombarded, with ads for the latest things to buy, the latest car and so on. It's difficult not to be influenced by that. There are so many things we want, things we desire. It never seems to stop. Can you speak a bit about desire?"

"I think there are two kinds of desire," the Dalai Lama replied. "Certain desires are positive. A desire for happiness. It's absolutely right. The desire for peace. The desire for a more harmonious world, a friendlier world. Certain desires are very useful.

"But at some point, desires can become unreasonable. That usually leads to trouble. Now, for example, sometimes I visit supermarkets. I really love to see supermarkets, because I can see so many beautiful things. So, when I look at all these different articles, I develop a feeling of desire, and my initial impulse might be, 'Oh, I want this; I want that.' Then, the second thought that arises, I ask myself, 'Oh, do I really need this?' The answer is usually no. If you follow after that first desire, that initial impulse, then very soon your pockets will empty. However, the other level of desire, based on one's essential needs of food, clothing, and shelter, is something more reasonable.

"Sometimes, whether a desire is excessive or negative depends on the circumstances or society in which you live. For example, if you live in a prosperous society where a car is required to help you manage in your daily life, then of course there's nothing wrong in desiring a car. But if you live in a poor village in India where you can manage quite well without a car but you still desire one, even if you have the money to buy it, it can ultimately bring trouble. It can create an uncomfortable feeling among your neighbors and so on. Or, if you're living in a more prosperous society and have a car but keep wanting more expensive cars, that leads to the same kind of problems."

"But," I argued, "I can't see how wanting or buying a more expensive car leads to problems for an individual, as long as he or she can afford it. Having a more expensive car than your neighbors might be a problem for them—they might be jealous and so on—but having a new car would give you, yourself, a feeling of satisfaction and enjoyment."

The Dalai Lama shook his head and replied firmly, "No. . . . Self-satisfaction alone cannot determine if a desire or action is positive or negative. A murderer may have a feeling of satisfaction at the time he is committing the murder, but that doesn't justify the act. All the nonvirtuous actions—lying, stealing, sexual misconduct, and so on—are committed by people who may be feeling a sense of satisfaction at the time. The demarcation between a positive and a negative desire or action is not whether it gives you a immediate feeling of satisfaction but whether it ultimately results in positive or negative consequences. For example, in the case of wanting more expensive possessions, if that is based on a mental attitude that just wants more and more, then eventually you'll reach a limit of what you can get; you'll come up against reality. And when you reach that limit, then you'll lose all hope, sink down into depression, and so on. That's one danger inherent in that type of desire.

"So I think that this kind of excessive desire leads to greed—an exaggerated form of desire, based on overexpectation. And when you reflect upon the excesses of greed, you'll find that it leads an individual to a feeling of frustration, disappointment, a lot of confusion, and a lot of problems. When it comes to dealing with greed, one thing that is quite characteristic is that although it arrives by the desire to obtain something, it is not satisfied by obtaining. Therefore, it becomes sort of limitless, sort of bottomless, and that leads to trouble. One interesting thing about greed is that although the underlying motive is to seek satisfaction, the irony is that even after obtaining the object of your desire, you are still not satisfied. *The true antidote of greed is contentment.* If you have a strong sense of contentment, it doesn't matter whether you obtain the object or not; either way, you are still content."

So, how can we achieve inner contentment? There are two methods. One method is to obtain everything that we want and desire—all the money, houses, and cars; the perfect mate; and the perfect body. The Dalai Lama has already pointed out the disadvantage of this approach; if our wants and desires remain unchecked, sooner or later we will run up against something that we want but can't have. The second, and more reliable, method is not to have what we want but rather to want and appreciate what we have.

The other night, I was watching a television interview with Christopher Reeve, the actor who was thrown from a horse in 1994 and suffered a spinal cord injury that left him completely paralyzed from the neck down, requiring a mechanical ventilator even to breathe. When questioned by the interviewer about how he dealt with the depression resulting from his disability, Reeve revealed that he had experienced a brief period of complete despair while in the intensive care unit of the hospital. He went on to say, however, that these feelings of despair passed relatively quickly, and he now sincerely considered himself to be a "lucky guy." He cited the blessings of a loving wife and children but also spoke gratefully about the rapid advances of modern medicine (which he estimates will find a cure for spinal cord injury within the next decade), stating that if he had been hurt just a few years earlier, he probably would have died from his injuries. While describing the process of adjusting to his paralysis, Reeve said that while his feelings of despair resolved rather quickly, at first he was still troubled by intermittent pangs of jealousy that could be triggered by another's innocent passing remark such as, "I'm just gonna run upstairs and get something." In learning to deal with these feelings, he said, "I realized that the only way to go through life is to look at your assets, to see what you can still do; in my case, fortunately I didn't have any brain injury, so I still have a mind I can use." Focusing on his resources in this manner, Reeve has elected to use his mind to increase awareness and educate the public about spinal cord injury, to help others, and has plans to continue speaking as well as to write and direct films.

INNER WORTH

We've seen how working on our mental outlook is a more effective means of achieving happiness than seeking it through external sources such as wealth, position, or even physical health. Another internal source of happiness, closely linked with an inner feeling of contentment, is a sense of self-worth. In describing the most reliable basis for developing that sense of self-worth, the Dalai Lama explained:

"Now in my case, for instance, suppose I had no depth of human feeling, no capacity for easily creating good friends. Without that, when I lost my own country, when my political authority in Tibet came to an end, becoming a refugee would have been very difficult. While I was in Tibet, because of the way the political system was set up, there was a certain degree of respect given to the office of the Dalai Lama and people related to me accordingly, regardless of whether they had true affection towards me or not. But if that was the only basis of people's relation towards me, then when I lost my country, it would have been extremely difficult. But there is another source of worth and dignity from which you can relate to other fellow human beings. *You can relate to them because you are still a human being, within the human community. You share that bond. And that human bond is enough to give rise to a sense of worth and dignity. That bond can become a source of consolation in the event that you lose everything else.*"

The Dalai Lama stopped for a moment to take a sip of tea, then shaking his head he added, "Unfortunately, when you read history, you'll find cases of emperors or kings in the past who lost their status due to some political upheaval and were forced to leave the country, but the story afterwards wasn't that positive for them. I think without that feeling of affection and connection with other fellow human beings, life becomes very hard.

"Generally speaking, you can have two different types of individuals. On the one hand, you can have a wealthy, successful person, surrounded by relatives and so on. If that person's source of dignity and sense of worth is only material, then so long as his fortune remains, maybe that person can sustain a sense of security. But the moment the fortune wanes, the person will suffer because there is no other refuge. On the other hand, you can have another person enjoying similar economic status and financial success, but at the same time, that person is warm and affectionate and has a feeling of compassion. Because that person has another source of worth, another source that gives him or her a sense of dignity, another anchor, there is less chance of that person's becoming depressed if his or her fortune happens to disappear. Through this type of reasoning you can see the very practical value of human warmth and affection in developing an inner sense of worth."

HAPPINESS VERSUS PLEASURE

Several months after the Dalai Lama's talks in Arizona, I visited him at his home in Dharamsala. It was a particularly hot and humid July afternoon, and I arrived at his home drenched in sweat after only a short hike from the village. Coming from a dry climate, I found the humidity to be almost unbearable that day, and I wasn't in the best of moods as we sat down to begin our conversation. He, on the other hand, seemed to be in great spirits. Shortly into our conversation, we turned to the topic of pleasure. At one point in the discussion, he made a crucial observation:

"Now sometimes people confuse happiness with pleasure. For example, not long ago I was speaking to an Indian audience at Rajpur. I mentioned that the purpose of life was happiness, so

◆

one member of the audience said that Rajneesh teaches that our happiest moment comes during sexual activity, so through sex one can become the happiest," the Dalai Lama laughed heartily. "He wanted to know what I thought of that idea. I answered that from my point of view, the highest happiness is when one reaches the stage of Liberation, at which there is no more suffering. That's genuine, lasting happiness. True happiness relates more to the mind and heart. Happiness that depends mainly on physical pleasure is unstable; one day it's there, the next day it may not be."

On the surface, it seemed like a fairly obvious observation; of course, happiness and pleasure were two different things. And yet, we human beings are often quite adept at confusing the two. Not long after I returned home, during a therapy session with a patient, I was to have a concrete demonstration of just how powerful that simple realization can be.

Heather was a young single professional working as a counselor in the Phoenix area. Although she enjoyed her job working with troubled youth, for some time she had become increasingly dissatisfied with living in that area. She often complained about the growing population, the traffic, and the oppressive heat in the summer. She had been offered a job in a beautiful small town in the mountains. In fact, she had visited that town many times and had always dreamed of moving there. It was perfect. The only problem was the fact that the job she was offered involved an adult clientele. For weeks, she had been struggling with the decision whether to accept the new job. She just couldn't make up her mind. She tried making up a list of pros and cons, but the list was annoyingly even.

She explained, "I know I wouldn't enjoy the work as much as my job here, but that would be more than compensated for by the pure pleasure of living in that town! I really love it there. Just being there makes me feel good. And I'm so sick of the heat here. I just don't know what to do."

Her mention of the term "pleasure" reminded me of the Dalai Lama's words, and, probing a bit, I asked, "Do you think that moving there would bring you greater happiness or greater pleasure?"

She paused for a moment, uncertain what to make of the question. Finally she answered, "I don't know . . . You know, I think it would bring me more pleasure than happiness . . . Ultimately, I don't think I'd really be happy working with that clientele. I really *do* get a lot of satisfaction working with the kids at my job. . . ."

Simply reframing her dilemma in terms of "Will it bring me happiness?" seemed to provide a certain clarity. Suddenly it became much easier to make her decision. She decided to remain in Phoenix. Of course, she still complained about the summer heat. But, having made the conscious decision to remain there on the basis of what she felt would ultimately make her happier, somehow made the heat more bearable.

Everyday we are faced with numerous decisions and choices. And try as we may, we often don't choose the thing that we know is "good for us." Part of this is related to the fact that the "right choice" is often the difficult one—the one that involves some sacrifice of our pleasure.

◆

In every century, men and women have struggled with trying to define the proper role that pleasure should play in their lives— a legion of philosophers, theologists, and psychologists, all exploring our relationship with pleasure. In the third century B.C., Epicurus based his system of ethics on the bold assertion that "pleasure is the beginning and end of the blessed life." But even Epicurus acknowledged the importance of common sense and moderation, recognizing that unbridled devotion to sensual pleasures could sometimes lead to pain instead. In the closing years of the nineteenth century, Sigmund Freud was busy formulating his own theories about pleasure. According to Freud, the fundamental motivating force for the entire psychic apparatus was the wish to relieve the tension caused by unfulfilled instinctual drives; in other words, our underlying motive is to seek pleasure. In the twentieth century, many researchers have chosen to sidestep more philosophical speculations, and, instead, a host of neuroanatomists have taken to poking around the brain's hypothalamus and limbic regions with electrodes, searching for the spot that produces pleasure when electrically stimulated.

None of us really need dead Greek philosophers, nineteenth-century psychoanalysts, or twentieth-century scientists to help us understand pleasure. We know it when we feel it. We know it in the touch or smile of a loved one, in the luxury of a hot bath on a cold rainy afternoon, in the beauty of a sunset. But many of us also know pleasure in the frenetic rhapsody of a cocaine rush, the ecstasy of a heroin high, the revelry of an alcohol buzz, the bliss of unrestrained sexual excess, the exhilaration of a winning streak in Las Vegas. These are also very real pleasures— pleasures that many in our society must come to terms with.

Although there are no easy solutions to avoiding these destructive pleasures, fortunately we have a place to begin: the simple reminder that what we are seeking in life is happiness. As the Dalai Lama points out, that is an unmistakable fact. If we approach our choices in life keeping that in mind, it is easier to give up the things that are ultimately harmful to us, even if those things bring us momentary pleasure. The reason why it is usually so difficult to "Just say no!" is found in the word "no"; that approach is associated with a sense of rejecting something, of giving something up, of denying ourselves.

But there is a better approach: framing any decision we face by asking ourselves, "Will it bring me happiness?" That simple question can be a powerful tool in helping us skillfully conduct all areas of our lives, not just in the decision whether to indulge in drugs or that third piece of banana cream pie. It puts a new slant on things. Approaching our daily decisions and choices with this question in mind shifts the focus from what we are denying ourselves to what we are seeking—ultimate happiness. A kind of happiness, as defined by the Dalai Lama, that is stable and persistent. A state of happiness that remains, despite life's ups and downs and normal fluctuations of mood, as part of the very matrix of our being. With this perspective, it's easier to make the "right decision" because we are acting to give ourselves something, not denying or withholding something from ourselves—an attitude of moving toward rather than moving away, an attitude of embracing life rather than rejecting it. This underlying sense of moving toward happiness can have a very profound effect; it makes us more receptive, more open, to the joy of living.

◆

Chapter 3

TRAINING THE MIND
FOR HAPPINESS

THE PATH TO HAPPINESS

In identifying one's mental state as the prime factor in achieving happiness, of course that doesn't deny that our basic physical needs for food, clothing, and shelter must be met. But once these basic needs are met, the message is clear: *we don't need more money, we don't need greater success or fame, we don't need the perfect body or even the perfect mate—right now, at this very moment, we have a mind, which is all the basic equipment we need to achieve complete happiness.*

In presenting his approach to working with the mind, the Dalai Lama began, "When we refer to 'mind' or 'consciousness,' there are many different varieties. Just like external conditions or objects, some things are very useful, some are very harmful, and some are neutral. So when dealing with external matter, usually we first try to identify which of these different substances or chemicals are helpful, so we can take care to cultivate, increase, and use them. And those substances which are harmful, we get rid of. So similarly, when we talk about mind, there are thousands of different thoughts or different 'minds.' Among them, some are very helpful; those, we should take and nourish. Some are negative, very harmful; those, we should try to reduce.

"So, the first step in seeking happiness is learning. We first have to learn how negative emotions and behaviors are harmful to us and how positive emotions are helpful. And we must realize how these negative emotions are not only very bad and harmful to one personally but harmful to society and the future of the whole world as well. That kind of realization enhances our determination to face and overcome them. And then, there is the realization of the beneficial aspects of the positive emotions and behaviors. Once we realize that, we become determined to cherish, develop, and increase those positive emotions no matter how difficult that is. There is a kind of spontaneous willingness from within. So through this process of learning, of analyzing which thoughts and emotions are beneficial and which are harmful, we gradually develop a firm determination to change, feeling, 'Now the secret to my own happiness, my own good future, is within my own hands. I must not miss that opportunity!'

"In Buddhism, the principle of causality is accepted as a natural law. In dealing with reality, you have to take that law into

◆

account. So, for instance, in the case of everyday experiences, if there are certain types of events that you do not desire, then the best method of ensuring that that event does not take place is to make sure that the causal conditions that normally give rise to that event no longer arise. Similarly, if you want a particular event or experience to occur, then the logical thing to do is to seek and accumulate the causes and conditions that give rise to it.

"This is also the case with mental states and experiences. If you desire happiness, you should seek the causes that give rise to it, and if you don't desire suffering, then what you should do is to ensure that the causes and conditions that would give rise to it no longer arise. An appreciation of this causal principle is very important.

"Now, we have spoken of the supreme importance of the mental factor in achieving happiness. Our next task, therefore, is to examine the variety of mental states that we experience. We need to clearly identify different mental states and make a distinction, classifying them according to whether they lead to happiness or not."

"Can you give some specific examples of different mental states and describe how you would classify them?" I asked.

The Dalai Lama explained, "Now for instance, hatred, jealousy, anger, and so on are harmful. We consider them negative states of mind because they destroy our mental happiness; once you harbor feelings of hatred or ill feeling towards someone, once you yourself are filled by hatred or negative emotions, then other people appear to you as also hostile. So as a result there is more fear, greater inhibition and hesitation, and a sense of insecurity.

◆

These things develop, and also loneliness in the midst of a world perceived as hostile. All these negative feelings develop because of hatred. On the other hand, mental states such as kindness and compassion are definitely very positive. They are very useful . . ."

"I'm just curious," I interrupted. "You mention that there are thousands of different states of mind. What would be your definition of a psychologically healthy or well-adjusted person? We might use such a definition as a guideline in determining which mental states to cultivate and which ones to eliminate."

He laughed, then with his characteristic humility he responded, "As a psychiatrist, you might have a better definition of a psychologically healthy person."

"But I mean from your standpoint."

"Well, I would regard a compassionate, warm, kindhearted person as healthy. *If you maintain a feeling of compassion, loving kindness, then something automatically opens your inner door. Through that, you can communicate much more easily with other people. And that feeling of warmth creates a kind of openness. You'll find that all human beings are just like you, so you'll be able to relate to them more easily.* That gives you a spirit of friendship. Then there's less need to hide things, and as a result, feelings of fear, self-doubt, and insecurity are automatically dispelled. Also, it creates a feeling of trust from other people. Otherwise, for example, you might find someone who is very competent, and you know that you can trust that person's competence. But if you sense that person is not kind, then you have to hold something back. You feel that 'Oh, I know that person can do things, but can I really trust him?' so you will always have a certain apprehension which creates a kind of distance from him.

◆

"So, anyway, I think that cultivating positive mental states like kindness and compassion definitely leads to better psychological health and happiness."

MENTAL DISCIPLINE

As he spoke, I found something very appealing about the Dalai Lama's approach to achieving happiness. It was absolutely practical and rational: Identify and cultivate positive mental states; identify and eliminate negative mental states. Although his suggestion to begin by systematically analyzing the variety of mental states that we experience initially struck me as being a bit dry, I gradually became carried away by the force of his logic and reasoning. And I liked the fact that rather than classifying mental states, emotions, or desires on the basis of some externally imposed moral judgment such as "Greed is a sin" or "Hatred is evil," he categorizes emotions as positive or negative simply on the basis of whether they lead to our ultimate happiness.

Resuming our conversation the next afternoon, I asked, "If happiness is simply a matter of cultivating more positive mental states like kindness and so on, why are so many people unhappy?"

"Achieving genuine happiness may require bringing about a transformation in your outlook, your way of thinking, and this is not a simple matter," he said. "It requires the application of so many different factors from different directions. You shouldn't have the notion, for instance, that there is just one key, a secret, and if you can get that right, then everything will be okay. It is similar to taking proper care of the physical body; you need a variety of vitamins and nutrients, not just one or two. In the same way, in order to achieve happiness, you need a variety of approaches and methods to deal with and overcome the varied and complex negative mental states. And if you are seeking to overcome certain negative ways of thinking, it is not possible to accomplish that simply by adopting a particular thought or practicing a technique once or twice. Change takes time. Even physical change takes time. For instance, if you're moving from one climate to another, the body needs time to adapt to the new environment. And in the same way, transforming your mind takes time. There are a lot of negative mental traits, so you need to address and counteract each one of these. That isn't easy. It requires the repeated application of various techniques and taking the time to familiarize yourself with the practices. It's a process of learning.

"But I think that as time goes on, you can make positive changes. Everyday as soon as you get up, you can develop a sincere positive motivation, thinking, 'I will utilize this day in a more positive way. I should not waste this very day.' And then, at night before bed, check what you've done, asking yourself, 'Did I utilize this day as I planned?' If it went accordingly, then you should rejoice. If it went wrong, then regret what you did and critique the day. So, through methods such as this, you can gradually strengthen the positive aspects of the mind.

"Now, for example, in my own case, as a Buddhist monk, I

believe in Buddhism and through my own experience I know that these Buddhist practices are very helpful to me. However, because of habituation, through many previous lifetimes, certain things may arise, like anger or attachment. So now what I do is: first learn about the positive value of the practices, then build up determination, and then try to implement them. At the beginning, the implementation of the positive practices is very small, so the negative influences are still very powerful. However, eventually, as you gradually build up the positive practices, the negative behaviors are automatically diminished. So, actually the practice of *Dharma** is a constant battle within, replacing previous negative conditioning or habituation with new positive conditioning."

Continuing he said, "No matter what activity or practice we are pursuing, there isn't anything that isn't made easier through constant familiarity and training. Through training, we can change; we can transform ourselves. Within Buddhist practice there are various methods of trying to sustain a calm mind when

*The term *Dharma* has many connotations but no precise English equivalent. It is most often used to refer to the teachings and doctrine of the Buddha, including the scriptural tradition as well as the way of life and spiritual realizations that result from the application of the teachings. Sometimes Buddhists use the word in a more general sense to signify spiritual or religious practices in general, universal spiritual law, or the true nature of phenomena—and use the term *Buddhadharma* to refer more specifically to the principles and practices of the Buddhist path. The Sanskrit word *Dharma* is derived from the etymological root meaning "to hold," and in this context the word has a broader meaning: any behavior or understanding that serves "to hold one back" or protect one from experiencing suffering and its causes.

some disturbing event happens. Through repeated practice of these methods we can get to the point where some disturbance may occur but the negative effects on our mind remain on the surface, like the waves that may ripple on the surface of an ocean but don't have much effect deep down. And, although my own experience may be very little, I have found this to be true in my own small practice. So, if I receive some tragic news, at that moment I may experience some disturbance within my mind, but it goes very quickly. Or, I may become irritated and develop some anger, but again, it dissipates very quickly. There is no effect on the deeper mind. No hatred. This was achieved through gradual practice; it didn't happen overnight."

Certainly not. The Dalai Lama has been engaged in training his mind since he was four years old.

The systematic training of the mind—the cultivation of happiness, the genuine inner transformation by deliberately selecting and focusing on positive mental states and challenging negative mental states—is possible because of the very structure and function of the brain. We are born with brains that are genetically hardwired with certain instinctual behavior patterns; we are predisposed mentally, emotionally, and physically to respond to our environment in ways that enable us to survive. These basic sets of instructions are encoded in countless innate nerve cell activation patterns, specific combinations of brain cells that fire in response to any given event, experience, or thought. But the wiring in our brains is not static, not irrevocably fixed. Our brains are also adaptable. Neuroscientists have documented the fact that the brain can design new patterns, new combinations of nerve cells and neurotransmitters (chemicals that transmit messages between nerve cells) in response to new input. In fact, our brains are malleable, ever changing, reconfiguring their wiring according to new thoughts and experiences. And as a result of learning, the function of individual neurons themselves change, allowing electrical signals to travel along them more readily. Scientists call the brain's inherent capacity to change "plasticity."

This ability to change the brain's wiring, to grow new neural connections, has been demonstrated in experiments such as one conducted by Doctors Avi Karni and Leslie Underleider at the National Institutes of Mental Health. In that experiment, the researchers had subjects perform a simple motor task, a finger-tapping exercise, and identified the parts of the brain involved in the task by taking a MRI brain scan. The subjects then practiced the finger exercise daily for four weeks, gradually becoming more efficient and quicker at it. At the end of the four-week period, the brain scan was repeated and showed that the area of the brain involved in the task had expanded; this indicated that the regular practice and repetition of the task had recruited new nerve cells and changed the neural connections that had originally been involved in the task.

This remarkable feature of the brain appears to be the physiological basis for the possibility of transforming our minds. By mobilizing our thoughts and practicing new ways of thinking, we can reshape our nerve cells and change the way our brains

◆

work. It is also the basis for the idea that inner transformation begins with learning (new input) and involves the discipline of gradually replacing our "negative conditioning" (corresponding with our present characteristic nerve cell activation patterns) with "positive conditioning" (forming new neural circuits). Thus, the idea of training the mind for happiness becomes a very real possibility.

ETHICAL DISCIPLINE

In a later discussion related to training the mind for happiness, the Dalai Lama pointed out, "I think that ethical behavior is another feature of the kind of inner discipline that leads to a happier existence. One could call this ethical discipline. Great spiritual teachers like the Buddha advise us to perform wholesome actions and avoid indulging in unwholesome actions. Whether our action is wholesome or unwholesome depends on whether that action or deed arises from a disciplined or undisciplined state of mind. It is felt that a disciplined mind leads to happiness and an undisciplined mind leads to suffering, and in fact it is said that *bringing about discipline within one's mind is the essence of the Buddha's teaching*.

"When I speak of discipline, I'm referring to self-discipline, not discipline that's externally imposed on you by someone else. Also, I'm referring to discipline that's applied in order to overcome your negative qualities. A criminal gang may need discipline to perform a successful robbery, but that discipline is useless."

The Dalai Lama stopped speaking for a moment and seemed to be reflecting, gathering his thoughts. Or, perhaps he was simply searching for a word in English. I don't know. But thinking about our conversation as he paused that afternoon, something about all this talk concerning the importance of learning and discipline began to strike me as being rather tedious when contrasted with the lofty goals of true happiness, spiritual growth, and complete internal transformation. It seemed that the quest for happiness should somehow be a more spontaneous process.

Raising this issue, I interjected, "You describe the negative emotions and behaviors as being 'unwholesome' and the positive behaviors as 'wholesome.' Further, you've said that an untrained or undisciplined mind generally results in negative or unwholesome behaviors, so we have to learn and train ourselves to increase our positive behaviors. So far, so good.

"But the thing that bothers me is that your very definition of negative or unwholesome behaviors is those behaviors which lead to suffering. And you define a wholesome behavior as one that leads to happiness. You also start with the basic premise that all beings naturally want to avoid suffering and gain happiness—that desire is innate; it doesn't have to be learned. The question then is: If it's natural for us to want to avoid suffering, why aren't we spontaneously and naturally more and more repulsed by the negative or unwholesome behaviors as we grow older? And if it is natural to want to gain happiness, why aren't we spontaneously and naturally more and more drawn to wholesome behaviors and thus become happier as our life progresses? I mean, if these wholesome behaviors naturally lead to happiness and we want happiness, shouldn't that occur as a natural

◆

process? Why should we need so much education, training, and discipline for that process to occur?"

Shaking his head, the Dalai Lama replied, "Even in conventional terms, in our everyday life, we consider education as a very important factor for ensuring a successful and happy life. And knowledge does not come by naturally. We have to train; we have to go through a kind of systematic training program and so forth. And we consider this conventional education and training to be quite hard; otherwise why would students look forward so much to vacations? Still, we know that this type of education is quite vital for ensuring a happy and successful life.

"In the same way, doing wholesome deeds may not come naturally, but we have to consciously train towards it. This is so, particularly in modern society, because there is a tendency to accept that the question of wholesome deeds and unwholesome deeds—what to do and what is not to be done—is something that is considered to be within the purview of religion. Traditionally, it has been considered the responsibility of religion to prescribe what behaviors are wholesome and what are not. However, in today's society, religion has lost its prestige and influence to some degree. And at the same time, no alternative, such as a secular ethics, has come up to replace it. So there seems to be less attention paid to the need to lead a wholesome way of life. It is because of this that I think we need to make some special effort and consciously work towards gaining that kind of knowledge. For example, although I personally believe that our human nature is fundamentally gentle and compassionate, I feel it is not enough that this is our underlying nature; *we must also develop an appreciation and awareness of that fact. And changing how we perceive ourselves, through learning and understanding, can have a very real impact on how we interact with others and how we conduct our daily lives.*"

Playing devil's advocate, I countered, "Still, you use the analogy of conventional academic education and training. That is one thing. But if you are talking about certain behaviors that you call 'wholesome' or positive, leading to happiness, and other behaviors leading to suffering, why does it take so much learning to identify which behaviors are which and so much training to implement the positive behaviors and eliminate the negative? I mean, if you put your hand in a fire, you get burned. You pull your hand back, and you've learned that this behavior leads to suffering. You don't need extensive learning or training to learn not to touch the fire again.

"So, why aren't all behaviors or emotions that lead to suffering like that? For instance, you claim that anger and hatred are clearly negative emotions and ultimately lead to suffering. But why does one have to be educated about the harmful effects of anger and hatred in order to eliminate them? Since anger immediately causes an uncomfortable emotional state in oneself, and it is certainly easy to feel that discomfort directly, why doesn't one just naturally and spontaneously avoid it in the future?"

As the Dalai Lama listened intently to my arguments, his intelligent eyes widened slightly, as if he were mildly surprised, or even amused, at the naïveté of my questions. Then, with a hardy laugh, full of goodwill, he said:

"When you talk of knowledge leading to freedom or resolution of a problem, you have to understand that there are many different levels. For example, let's say that human beings in the Stone Age didn't know how to cook meat but they still had the biological need to eat, so they just ate like a wild animal. As humans progressed, they learned how to cook and then how to put in different spices to make the food more tasty and then they came up with more diverse dishes. And even up to our present age, if we are suffering from a particular illness and through our knowledge we learn that a certain type of food is not good for us, even though we might have the desire to eat it, we restrain ourselves from eating it. So it is clear that the more sophisticated the level of our knowledge is, the more effective we will be in dealing with the natural world.

"You also need the ability to judge the long-term and short-term consequences of your behaviors and weigh the two. For example, in overcoming anger, although animals may experience anger, they cannot understand that anger is destructive. In the case of human beings, however, there is a different level, where you have a kind of self-awareness that allows you to reflect and observe that when anger arises, it hurts you. Therefore, you can make a judgment that anger is destructive. You need to be able to make that inference. So it's not as simple as putting your hand in a fire, and then being burned and just learning in the future never to do it again. The more sophisticated your level of education and knowledge about what leads to happiness and what causes suffering, the more effective you will be in achieving happiness. So, it is because of this that I think education and knowledge are crucial."

Sensing, I suppose, my continued resistance to the idea of simple education as a means of internal transformation, he observed, "One problem with our current society is that we have an attitude towards education as if it is there to simply make you more clever, make you more ingenious. Sometimes it even seems as if those who are not highly educated, those who are less sophisticated in terms of their educational training, are more innocent and more honest. Even though our society does not emphasize this, the most important use of knowledge and education is to help us understand the importance of engaging in more wholesome actions and bringing about discipline within our minds. The proper utilization of our intelligence and knowledge is to effect changes from within to develop a good heart."

Chapter 4

RECLAIMING OUR INNATE STATE OF HAPPINESS

OUR FUNDAMENTAL NATURE

Now, we are made to seek happiness. And it is clear that feelings of love, affection, closeness, and compassion bring happiness. I believe that every one of us has the basis to be happy, to access the warm and compassionate states of mind that bring happiness," the Dalai Lama asserted. "In fact, it is one of my fundamental beliefs that not only do we inherently possess the potential for compassion but I believe that the basic or underlying nature of human beings is gentleness."

"What do you base that belief on?"

"The Buddhist doctrine of 'Buddha Nature' provides some grounds for the belief that the fundamental nature of all sentient beings is essentially gentle and not aggressive.* But one can adopt this view without having to resort to the Buddhist doctrine of 'Buddha Nature.' There are also other grounds on which I base this belief. I think the subject of human affection or compassion isn't just a religious matter; it's an indispensable factor in one's day-to-day life.

"So, first, if we look at the very pattern of our existence from an early age until our death, we can see the way in which we are fundamentally nurtured by other's affection. It begins at birth. Our very first act after birth is to suck our mother's or someone else's milk. That is an act of affection, of compassion. Without that act, we cannot survive. That's clear. And that action cannot be fulfilled unless there is a mutual feeling of affection. From the child's side, if there is no feeling of affection, no bond, towards the person who is giving the milk, then the child may not suck the milk. And without affection on the part of the mother or someone else, then the milk may not come freely. So that's the way of life. That's reality.

"Then, our physical structure seems to be more suited to feelings of love and compassion. We can see how a calm, affectionate, wholesome state of mind has beneficial effects on our health and physical well-being. Conversely, feelings of frustration, fear, agitation, and anger can be destructive to our health.

*In Buddhist philosophy, "Buddha Nature" refers to an underlying, basic, and most subtle nature of mind. This state of mind, present in all human beings, is completely untainted by negative emotions or thoughts.

◆

"We can also see that our emotional health is enhanced by feelings of affection. To understand this, we need only to reflect on how we feel when others show us warmth and affection. Or, observe how our own affectionate feelings or attitudes automatically and naturally affect us from within, how they make us feel. These gentler emotions and the positive behaviors that go with them lead to a happier family and community life.

"So, I think that we can infer that our fundamental human nature is one of gentleness. And if this is the case, then it makes all the more sense to try to live a way of life that is more in accordance with this basic gentle nature of our being."

"If our essential nature is kind and compassionate," I asked, "I'm just wondering how you account for all the conflicts and aggressive behaviors that are all around us."

The Dalai Lama nodded thoughtfully for a moment before replying, "Of course we can't ignore the fact that conflicts and tensions do exist, not only within an individual mind but also within the family, when we interact with other people, and at the societal level, the national level, and the global level. So, looking at this, some people conclude that human nature is basically aggressive. They may point to human history, suggesting that compared to other mammals', human behavior is much more aggressive. Or, they may claim, 'Yes, compassion is a part of our mind. But anger is also a part of our mind. They are equally a part of our nature; both are more or less at the same level.' Nonetheless," he said firmly, leaning forward in his chair, straining with alertness, *"it is still my firm conviction that human nature is essentially compassionate, gentle. That is the predominant feature of human nature.* Anger, violence, and aggression may certainly arise, but I

◆

think it's on a secondary or more superficial level; in a sense, they arise when we are frustrated in our efforts to achieve love and affection. They are not part of our most basic, underlying nature.

"So, although aggression can occur, I believe that these conflicts aren't necessarily because of human nature but rather a result of the human intellect—unbalanced human intelligence, misuse of our intelligence, our imaginative faculty. Now in looking at human evolution, I think that compared to some other animals', our physical body may have been very weak. But because of the development of human intelligence, we were able to use many instruments and discover many methods to conquer adverse environmental conditions. As human society and environmental conditions gradually became more complex, this required a greater and greater role of our intelligence and cognitive ability to meet the ever-increasing demands of this complex environment. So, I believe that our underlying or fundamental nature is gentleness, and intelligence is a later development. And I think that if that human ability, that human intelligence, develops in an unbalanced way, without being properly counterbalanced with compassion, then it can become destructive. It can lead to disaster.

"But, I think it's important to recognize that if human conflicts are created by misuse of human intelligence, we can also utilize our intelligence to find ways and means to overcome these conflicts. When human intelligence and human goodness or affection are used together, all human actions become constructive. When we combine a warm heart with knowledge and education, we can learn to respect other's views and other's rights. This

◆

becomes the basis of a spirit of reconciliation that can be used to overcome aggression and resolve our conflicts."

The Dalai Lama paused and glanced at his watch. "So," he concluded, "no matter how much violence or how many bad things we have to go through, I believe that the ultimate solution to our conflicts, both internal and external, lies in returning to our basic or underlying human nature, which is gentle and compassionate."

Looking again at his watch, he began to laugh in a friendly way. "So . . . we'll stop here . . . It's been a long day!" He gathered up his shoes which he had slipped off during our conversation and retired to his room.

THE QUESTION OF HUMAN NATURE

Over the past few decades, the Dalai Lama's view of the underlying compassionate nature of human beings seems to be slowly gaining ground in the West, although it has been a struggle. The notion that human behavior is essentially egoistic, that fundamentally we are all out for ourselves, is deeply ingrained in Western thought. The idea that not only are we inherently selfish but also that aggression and hostility are part of basic human nature has dominated our culture for centuries. Of course, historically there were plenty of people with the opposite view. For instance, in the mid-1700s David Hume wrote a lot about the "natural benevolence" of human beings. And a century later, even Charles Darwin himself attributed an "instinct of sympathy" to our species. But for some reason the more pessimistic view of humanity has taken root in our culture, at least since the seventeenth century, under the influence of philosophers like Thomas Hobbes, who had a pretty dark view of the human species. He saw the human race as being violent, competitive, in continual conflict, and concerned only with self-interest. Hobbes, who was famous for discounting any notion of basic human kindness, was once caught giving money to a beggar on the street. When questioned about this generous impulse, he claimed, "I'm not doing this to help him. I'm just doing this to relieve my own distress at seeing the man's poverty."

Similarly, in the earlier part of this century, the Spanish-born philosopher George Santayana wrote that generous, caring impulses, while they may exist, are generally weak, fleeting, and unstable in human nature but, "dig a little beneath the surface and you'll find a ferocious, persistent, profoundly selfish man." Unfortunately, Western science and psychology grabbed hold of ideas like that, then sanctioned, and even encouraged, this egoistic view. Beginning in the earliest days of modern scientific psychology, there was a general underlying assumption that all human motivation is ultimately egoistic, based purely on self-interest.

After implicitly accepting the premise of our essential selfishness, a number of very prominent scientists over the past hundred years have added to this a belief in the essential aggressive nature of humans. Freud claimed that, "the inclination to aggression is an original, self-subsisting, instinctual disposition." In the latter half of this century, two writers in particular, Robert Ardrey and Konrad Lorenz, looked at patterns of animal behavior in certain predator species and concluded that humans were basically predators as well, with an innate or instinctive drive to fight over territory.

In recent years, however, the tide appears to be turning on this profoundly pessimistic view of humanity, coming closer to the Dalai Lama's view of our underlying nature as gentle and compassionate. Over the past two or three decades, there have been literally hundreds of scientific studies indicating that aggression is *not* essentially innate and that violent behavior is influenced by a variety of biological, social, situational, and environmental factors. Perhaps the most comprehensive statement on the latest research was summarized in the 1986 Seville Statement on Violence that was drawn up and signed by twenty top scientists from around the world. In that statement, they of course acknowledged that violent behavior does occur, but they categorically stated that *it is scientifically incorrect to say that we have an inherited tendency to make war or act violently. That behavior is not genetically programmed into human nature.* They said that even though we have the neural apparatus to act violently, that behavior isn't automatically activated. There's nothing in our neurophysiology that compels us to act violently. In examining the subject of basic human nature, most researchers in the field currently feel that fundamentally we have the potential to develop into gentle, caring people or violent, aggressive people; the impulse that gets emphasized is largely a matter of training.

Contemporary researchers have refuted not only the idea of humanity's innate aggression, but the idea that humans are innately selfish and egoistic has also come under attack. Investigators such as C. Daniel Batson or Nancy Eisenberg at Arizona State University have conducted numerous studies over the past few years that demonstrate that humans have a tendency toward altruistic behavior. Some scientists, such as sociologist Dr. Linda Wilson, seek to discover why this is so. She has theorized that altruism may be part of our basic survival instinct—the very opposite to ideas of earlier thinkers who theorized that hostility and aggression were the hallmark of our survival instinct. Looking at over a hundred natural disasters, Dr. Wilson found a strong pattern of altruism among disaster victims, which seemed to be part of the recovery process. She found that working together to help each other tended to ward off later psychological problems that might have resulted from the trauma.

The tendency to closely bond with others, acting for the welfare of others as well as oneself, may be deeply rooted in human nature, forged in the remote past as those who bonded together and became part of a group had an increased chance of survival. This need to form close social ties persists up to the present day. In studies, such as one conducted by Dr. Larry Scherwitz, examining the risk factors for coronary heart disease, it has been found that the people who were most self-focused (those who referred to themselves using the pronouns "I," "me," and "my" most often in an interview) were more likely to develop coronary heart disease, even when other health-threatening behaviors were controlled. Scientists are discovering that those who lack close social ties seem to suffer from poor health, higher levels of unhappiness, and a greater vulnerability to stress.

Reaching out to help others may be as fundamental to our nature as communication. One could draw an analogy with the development of language which, like the capacity for compassion and altruism, is one of the magnificent features of the human race. Particular areas of the brain are specifically devoted to the *potential* for language. If we are exposed to the correct environmental conditions, that is, a society that speaks, then those discreet areas of the brain begin to develop and mature and our capacity for language grows. In the same way, all humans may be endowed with the "seed of compassion." When exposed to the right conditions—at home, in society at large, and later perhaps through our own pointed efforts—that "seed" will flourish. With this idea in mind, researchers are now seeking to discover the optimal environmental conditions that will allow the seed of caring and compassion to ripen in children. They have identified several factors: having parents who are able to regulate their own emotions, who model caring behavior, who set appropriate limits on the children's behavior, who communicate that a child is responsible for her or his own behavior, and who use reasoning to help direct the child's attention to affective or emotional states and the consequences of her or his behavior on others.

Revising our basic assumptions about the underlying nature of human beings, from hostile to helpful, can open up new possibilities. If we begin by assuming the self-interest model of all human behavior, then an infant serves as a perfect example, as "proof," of that theory. At birth, infants appear to be programmed with only one thing on their minds: *the gratification of their own needs*—food, physical comfort, and so on. But if we suspend that basic egoistic assumption, a whole new picture begins to emerge. We could just as easily say that an infant is born programmed for only one thing: *the capacity and purpose of bringing plea-sure and joy to others.* By just observing a healthy infant, it would be hard to deny the underlying gentle nature of human beings. And from this new vantage point, we could make a good case that the capacity to bring pleasure to another, the caregiver, is inborn. For example, in a newborn infant the sense of smell is developed to perhaps only 5 percent that of an adult, and the sense of taste is developed very little. But what does exist of these senses in the newborn is geared toward the smell and taste of breast milk. The act of nursing not only provides nutrients for the baby; it also serves to relieve tension in the breast. So, we could say that the infant is born with an innate capacity to bring pleasure to the mother, by relieving the tension in the breast.

An infant is also biologically programmed to recognize and respond to faces, and there are few people who fail to find genuine pleasure in having a young baby gazing innocently into their eyes and smile. Some ethologists have formulated this into a theory, suggesting that when an infant smiles at the caregiver or looks directly into his eyes, the infant is following a deeply ingrained "biological blueprint," instinctively "releasing" gentle, tender, caring behaviors from the caregiver, who is also obeying an equally compelling instinctual mandate. As more investigators strike out to objectively discover the nature of human beings, the notion of the infant as a little bundle of selfishness, an eating and sleeping machine, is yielding to a vision of a being that comes into the world with an innate mechanism to please others, requiring only the proper environmental conditions to allow the underlying and natural "seed of compassion" to germinate and grow.

◆

Once we conclude that the basic nature of humanity is compassionate rather than aggressive, our relationship to the world around us changes immediately. Seeing others as basically compassionate instead of hostile and selfish helps us relax, trust, live at ease. It makes us happier.

MEDITATION ON THE PURPOSE OF LIFE

As the Dalai Lama sat in the Arizona desert that week, exploring human nature and examining the human mind with the scrutiny of a scientist, one simple truth seemed to shine through and illuminate every discussion: *the purpose of our life is happiness.* That simple statement can be used as a powerful tool in helping us navigate through life's daily problems. From that perspective, our task becomes one of discarding the things that lead to suffering and accumulating the things that lead to happiness. The method, the daily practice, involves gradually increasing our awareness and understanding of what *truly* leads to happiness and what doesn't.

When life becomes too complicated and we feel overwhelmed, it's often useful just to stand back and remind ourselves of our overall purpose, our overall goal. When faced with a feeling of stagnation and confusion, it may be helpful to take an hour, an afternoon, or even several days to simply reflect on what it is that will truly bring us happiness, and then reset our priorities on the basis of that. This can put our life back in proper context, allow a fresh perspective, and enable us to see which direction to take.

From time to time we are faced with pivotal decisions that can affect the entire course of our lives. We may decide, for instance, to get married, to have children, or to embark on a course of study to become a lawyer, an artist, or an electrician. The firm resolve to become happy—to learn about the factors that lead to happiness and take positive steps to build a happier life—can be just such a decision. *The turning-toward happiness as a valid goal and the conscious decision to seek happiness in a systematic manner can profoundly change the rest of our lives.*

The Dalai Lama's understanding of the factors that ultimately lead to happiness is based on a lifetime of methodically observing his own mind, exploring the nature of the human condition, and investigating these things within a framework first established by The Buddha over twenty-five centuries ago. And from this background, the Dalai Lama has come to some definite conclusions about which activities and thoughts are most worthwhile. He summarized his beliefs in the following words that can be used as a meditation.

Sometimes when I meet old friends, it reminds me how quickly time passes. And it makes me wonder if we've utilized our time properly or not. Proper utilization of time is so important. While we have this body, and especially this amazing human brain, I think every minute is something precious. Our day-to-day existence is very much alive with hope, although there is no guarantee of our future. There is no guarantee that tomorrow at this time we will be here. But still we are working for that purely on the basis of hope. So, we need to make the best use of our time.

◆

I believe that the proper utilization of time is this: if you can, serve other people, other sentient beings. If not, at least refrain from harming them. I think that is the whole basis of my philosophy.

"So, let us reflect on what is truly of value in life, what gives meaning to our lives, and set our priorities on the basis of that. The purpose of our life needs to be positive. We weren't born with the purpose of causing trouble, harming others. For our life to be of value, I think we must develop basic good human qualities—warmth, kindness, compassion. Then our life becomes meaningful and more peaceful—happier."

◆

Part II

HUMAN WARMTH
AND COMPASSION

Chapter 5

A NEW MODEL
FOR INTIMACY

LONELINESS AND CONNECTION

I entered the sitting room of the Dalai Lama's hotel suite, and he motioned for me to sit down. As tea was poured, he slipped off a pair of butterscotch-colored Rockports and settled comfortably into an oversized chair.

"So?" he asked in a casual tone but with an inflection that said he was ready for anything. He smiled, but remained silent. Waiting.

Moments before, while sitting in the hotel lobby waiting for our session to begin, I had absently picked up a copy of a local alternative newspaper that had been turned to the "Personals" section. I had briefly scanned the densely packed ads, page after page of people searching, desperately hoping to connect with another human being. Still thinking about those ads as I sat down to begin my meeting with the Dalai Lama, I suddenly decided to set aside my list of prepared questions and asked, "Do you ever get lonely?"

"No," he said simply. I was unprepared for this response. I assumed that his response would be along the lines of, "Of course . . . every once in a while everyone feels some loneliness. . . ." Then I was planning on asking him how he deals with loneliness. I never expected to confront anyone who *never* felt lonely.

"No?" I asked again, incredulous.

"No."

"What do you attribute that to?"

He thought for a moment. "I think one factor is that I look at any human being from a more positive angle; I try to look for their positive aspects. This attitude immediately creates a feeling of affinity, a kind of connectedness.

"And it may partly be because on my part, there is less apprehension, less fear, that if I act in a certain way, maybe the person will lose respect or think that I am strange. So because that kind of fear and apprehension is normally absent, there is a kind of openness. I think it's the main factor."

Struggling to comprehend the scope and difficulty of adopting such an attitude, I asked, "But how would you suggest that a person achieve the ability to feel that comfortable with people, not have that fear or apprehension of being disliked or judged by other people? Are there specific methods that an average person could use to develop this attitude?"

"My basic belief is that you first need to realize the usefulness of compassion," he said with a tone of conviction. "That's the key factor. Once you accept the fact that compassion is not something childish or sentimental, once you realize that compassion is something really worthwhile, realize it's deeper value, then you immediately develop an attraction towards it, a willingness to cultivate it.

"And once you encourage the thought of compassion in your mind, once that thought becomes active, then your attitude towards others changes automatically. If you approach others with the thought of compassion, that will automatically reduce fear and allow an openness with other people. It creates a positive, friendly atmosphere. With that attitude, you can approach a relationship in which you, yourself, initially create the possibility of receiving affection or a positive response from the other person. And with that attitude, even if the other person is unfriendly or doesn't respond to you in a positive way, then at least you've approached the person with a feeling of openness that gives you a certain flexibility and the freedom to change your approach as needed. That kind of openness at least allows the possibility of having a meaningful conversation with them. But *without* the attitude of compassion, if you are feeling closed, irritated, or indifferent, then you can even be approached by your best friend and you just feel uncomfortable.

"I think that in many cases people tend to expect the other person to respond to them in a positive way first, rather than

◆

taking the initiative themselves to create that possibility. I feel that's wrong; it leads to problems and can act as a barrier that just serves to promote a feeling of isolation from others. So, if you wish to overcome that feeling of isolation and loneliness, I think that your underlying attitude makes a tremendous difference. And approaching others with the thought of compassion in your mind is the best way to do this."

My surprise about the Dalai Lama's claim that he was never lonely was in direct proportion to my belief in the pervasiveness of loneliness in our society. This belief wasn't born merely from an impressionistic sense of my own loneliness or the thread of loneliness that seemed to run as an underlying theme throughout the fabric of my psychiatric practice. In the past twenty years, psychologists have begun to study loneliness in a scientific manner, conducting a fair number of surveys and studies on the subject. One of the most striking findings of these studies is that virtually *all* people report that they do experience loneliness, either currently or in the past. In one large survey, one-fourth of U.S. adults reported that they had felt extremely lonely at least once within the previous two weeks. Although we often think of chronic loneliness as an affliction particularly widespread among the elderly, isolated in empty apartments or in the back wards of nursing homes, research suggests that teenagers and young adults are just as likely to report they are lonely as the elderly.

Because of the widespread occurrence of loneliness, investigators have begun to examine the complex variables that may contribute to loneliness. For instance, they have found that lonely individuals often have problems with self-disclosure, have difficulty communicating with others, are poor listeners, and lack certain social skills such as picking up conversational cues (knowing when to nod, to respond appropriately, or to remain silent). This research suggests that one strategy for over-coming loneliness would be to work on improving these social skills. *The Dalai Lama's strategy, however, seemed to bypass working on social skills or external behaviors, in favor of an approach that cut directly to the heart—realizing the value of compassion and then cultivating it.*

Despite my initial surprise, as I listened to him speak with such conviction, I came to firmly believe that he was never lonely. And there was evidence to support his claim. Often enough, I had witnessed his first interaction with a stranger, which was invariably positive. It started to become clear that these positive interactions weren't accidental or simply the result of a naturally friendly personality. I sensed that he had spent a great deal of time thinking about the importance of com-passion, carefully cultivating it, and using it to enrich and soften the ground of his everyday experience, making that soil fertile and receptive to positive interactions with others—a method that can, in fact, be used by anyone who suffers from loneliness.

DEPENDENCE ON OTHERS
VERSUS SELF-RELIANCE

"Within all beings there is the seed of perfection. However, compassion is required in order to activate that seed which is inherent in our hearts and minds. . . ." With this, the Dalai Lama introduced the topic of compassion to a hushed assembly. Addressing an audience of fifteen hundred people, counting among them a fair proportion of dedicated students of Buddhism, he then began to discuss the Buddhist doctrine of the Field of Merit.

In the Buddhist sense, Merit is described as positive imprints on one's mind, or "mental continuum," that occur as a result of positive actions. The Dalai Lama explained that a Field of Merit is a source or foundation from which a person can accumulate Merit. According to Buddhist theory, it is a person's stores of Merit that determine favorable conditions for one's future rebirths. He explained that Buddhist doctrine specifies two Fields of Merit: the field of the Buddhas and the field of other sentient beings. One method of accumulating Merit involves generating respect, faith, and confidence in the Buddhas, the Enlightened beings. The other method involves practicing actions like kindness, generosity, tolerance, and so on and conscious restraint from negative actions like killing, stealing, and lying. That second method of acquiring Merit requires interaction with other people, rather than interaction with the Buddhas. On that basis, the Dalai Lama pointed out, other people can be of great help to us in accumulating Merit.

The Dalai Lama's description of other people as a Field of Merit had a beautiful, lyrical quality to it that seemed to lend itself to a richness of imagery. His lucid reasoning and the conviction behind his words combined to give special power and impact to his talk that afternoon. As I looked around the room, I could see that many members of the audience were visibly

◆

moved. I, myself, was less enthralled. As a result of our earlier conversations, I was in the rudimentary stages of appreciating the profound importance of compassion, yet I was still heavily influenced by years of rational, scientific conditioning that made me regard any talk of kindness and compassion as being a bit too sentimental for my taste. As he spoke, my mind began to wander. I started furtively looking around the room, searching for famous, interesting, or familiar faces. Having eaten a big meal just before the talk, I started to get sleepy. I drifted in and out. At one point in the talk, my mind tuned in to hear him say ". . . the other day I spoke about the factors necessary to enjoy a happy and joyful life. Factors such as good health, material goods, friends, and so on. If you closely investigate, you'll find that all of these depend on other people. To maintain good health, you rely on medicines made by others and health care provided by others. If you examine all of the material facilities that you use for the enjoyment of life, you'll find that there are hardly any of these material objects that have had no connection with other people. If you think carefully, you'll see that all of these goods come into being as a result of the efforts of many people, either directly or indirectly. Many people are involved in making those things possible. Needless to say, when we're talking about good friends and companions as being another necessary factor for a happy life, we are talking about interaction with other sentient beings, other human beings.

"So you can see that all of these factors are inextricably linked with other people's efforts and cooperation. Others are indispensable. So, despite the fact that the process of relating to others might involve hardships, quarrels, and cursing, we have to try to maintain an attitude of friendship and warmth in order to lead a way of life in which there is enough interaction with other people to enjoy a happy life."

As he spoke, I felt an instinctive resistance. Although I've always valued and enjoyed my friends and family, I've considered myself to be an independent person. Self-reliant. Prided myself on this quality in fact. Secretly, I've tended to regard overly dependent people with a kind of contempt—a sign of weakness.

Yet that afternoon, as I listened to the Dalai Lama, something happened. As "Our Dependence on Others" was not my favorite topic, my mind started to wander again, and I found myself absently removing a loose thread from my shirt sleeve. Tuning in for a moment, I listened as he mentioned the many people who are involved in making all our material possessions. As he said this, I began to think about how many people were involved in making my shirt. I started by imagining the farmer who grew the cotton. Next, the salesperson who sold the farmer the tractor to plow the field. Then, for that matter, the hundreds or even thousands of people involved in manufacturing that tractor, including the people who mined the ore to make the metal for each part of the tractor. And all the designers of the tractor. Then, of course, the people who processed the cotton, the people who wove the cloth, and the people who cut, dyed, and sewed that cloth. The cargo workers and truck drivers who delivered the shirt to the store and the salesperson who sold the shirt to me. It occurred to me that virtually every aspect of my life came about as the results of others' efforts. My precious self-reliance was a complete illusion, a fan-

◆

tasy. As this realization dawned on me, I was overcome with a profound sense of the interconnectedness and interdependence of all beings. I felt a softening. Something. I don't know. It made me want to cry.

INTIMACY

Our need for other people is paradoxical. At the same time that our culture is caught up in the celebration of fierce independence, we also yearn for intimacy and connection with a special loved one. We focus all our energy on finding the one person who we hope will heal our loneliness yet prop up our illusion that we are still independent. Though this connection is difficult to achieve with even one person, I would find out that the Dalai Lama is capable of and recommends maintaining closeness with as many people as possible. In fact, his aim is to connect with everyone.

Meeting with him in his hotel suite in Arizona late one afternoon, I began, "In your public talk yesterday afternoon you spoke of the importance of others, describing them as a Field of Merit. But in examining our relationship with others, there are really so many different ways in which we can relate to one another, different kinds of relationships . . ."

"That's very true," said the Dalai Lama.

"For instance, there's a certain type of relationship that's highly valued in the West," I observed. "That is a relationship that's characterized by a deep level of intimacy between two people, having one special person with whom you can share your deepest feelings, fears, and so on. People feel that unless they have a relationship of this kind that there is something missing in their lives . . . In fact, Western psychotherapy often seeks to help people learn how to develop that type of intimate relationship . . ."

"Yes, I believe that kind of intimacy can be seen as something positive," the Dalai Lama agreed. "I think if someone is deprived of that kind of intimacy then it can lead to problems . . ."

"I'm just wondering then . . .," I continued, "when you were growing up in Tibet, you were not only considered to be like a king but you were also considered to be a deity. I assume that people were in awe of you, perhaps even a bit nervous or frightened to be in your presence. Didn't that create a certain emotional distance from others, a feeling of isolation? Also, being separated from your family, being raised as a monk from an early age, and as a monk never marrying and so on—didn't all these things contribute to a feeling of separation from others? Do you ever feel that you missed out on developing a deeper level of personal intimacy with others or with one special person, such as a spouse?"

Without hesitation, he replied, "No. I never felt a lack of intimacy. Of course my father passed away many years ago, but I felt quite close to my mother, my teachers, my tutors, and others. And with many of these people I could share my deepest feelings, fears, and concerns. When I was in Tibet, on state occasions and at public events there was a certain formality, a certain protocol was observed, but that wasn't always the case. At other times, for example, I used to spend time in the kitchen and I became quite close with some of the kitchen staff and we could

◆

joke or gossip or share things and it would be quite relaxed, without that sense of formality or distance.

"So, when I was in Tibet or since I've become a refugee, I've never felt a lack of people with whom I can share things. I think a lot of this has to do with my nature. It's easy for me to share things with others; I'm just not good at keeping secrets!" He laughed. "Of course sometimes this can be a negative trait. For example, there may be some discussion in the Kashag* about confidential things, and then I'll immediately discuss these things with others. But on a personal level, being open and sharing things can be very useful. Because of this nature I can make friends more easily, and it's not just a matter of knowing people and having a superficial exchange but of really sharing my deepest problems and suffering. And it's the same thing when I hear good news; I immediately share it with others. So, I feel a sense of intimacy and connection with my friends. Of course it's sometimes easier for me to establish a connection with others because they're often very happy to share their suffering or joy with the 'Dalai Lama,' 'His Holiness the Dalai Lama.'" He laughed again, making light of his title. "Anyway, I feel this sense of connection, of sharing, with many people. For instance, in the past, if I felt disappointed or unhappy with Tibetan government policy or I was concerned with other problems, even the threat of Chinese invasion, then I would return to my rooms and share this with the person who sweeps the floor. From one point of view it may seem quite silly to some that the Dalai Lama, the head of the Tibetan government, facing some international or

*The Cabinet of the Tibetan government-in-exile.

◆

national problems, would share them with a sweeper." He laughed once again. "But personally I feel it is very helpful, because then the other person participates and we can face the problem or suffering together."

EXPANDING OUR DEFINITION OF INTIMACY

Virtually all researchers in the field of human relationships agree that intimacy is central to our existence. The influential British psychoanalyst John Bowlby wrote that "intimate attachments to other human beings are the hub around which a person's life revolves . . . From these intimate attachments a person draws his strength and enjoyment of life and, through what he contributes, he gives strength and enjoyment to others. These are matters about which current science and traditional wisdom are at one."

It is clear that intimacy promotes both physical and psychological well-being. In looking at the health benefits of intimate relationships, medical researchers have found that people who have close friendships, people whom they can turn to for affirmation, empathy, and affection, are more likely to survive health challenges such as heart attacks and major surgery and are less likely to develop diseases such as cancer and respiratory infections. For example, one study of over a thousand heart patients at Duke University Medical Center found that those who lacked a spouse or close confidant were three times more likely to die within five years of the diagnosis of heart disease as those who were married or had a close friend. Another study of thousands of residents in Alameda County, California, over a nine-year period showed that those with more social support and intimate relationships had lower death rates overall and lower rates of cancer. And a study at the University of Nebraska School of Medicine of several hundred elderly people found that those with an intimate relationship had better immune function and lower cholesterol levels. Over the course of the past several years there have been at least a half-dozen massive investigations conducted by a number of different researchers looking at the relationship between intimacy and health. After interviewing thousands of people, the various investigators all seem to have reached the same conclusion: close relationships do, in fact, promote health.

Intimacy is equally as important in maintaining good emotional health. The psychoanalyst and social philosopher Erich Fromm claimed that humankind's most basic fear is the threat of being separated from other humans. He believed that the experience of separateness, first encountered in infancy, is the source of all anxiety in human life. John Bowlby agreed, citing a good deal of experimental evidence and research to support the idea that separation from one's caregivers—usually the mother or father—during the latter part of the first year of life, inevitably creates fear and sadness in babies. He felt that separation and interpersonal loss are at the very roots of the human experiences of fear, sadness, and sorrow.

So, given the vital importance of intimacy, how do we set about achieving intimacy in our daily lives? Following the Dalai Lama's approach outlined in the last section, it would seem reasonable to begin with learning—with understanding what intimacy is, seeking a workable definition and model of

◆

intimacy. In looking to science for the answer, however, it seems that despite the universal agreement among researchers about the importance of intimacy, that seems to be where the agreement ends. Perhaps the most striking feature of even a cursory review of the various studies on intimacy is the wide diversity of definitions and theories about exactly what intimacy is.

At the most concrete end of the spectrum is the author Desmond Morris, who writes about intimacy from the perspective of a zoologist trained in ethology. In his book, *Intimate Behavior*, Morris defines intimacy: "To be intimate means to be close . . . In my terms, the act of intimacy occurs whenever two individuals come into bodily contact." After defining intimacy in terms of purely physical contact, he then goes on to explore the countless ways in which humans come into physical contact with one another, from a simple pat on the back to the most erotic sexual embrace. He sees touch as the vehicle through which we comfort one another and are comforted, via hugs or clasps of the hand and, when those avenues are not available to us, more indirect means of physical contact such as a manicure. He even theorizes that the physical contacts we have with objects in our environment, from cigarettes to jewelry to waterbeds, act as substitutes for intimacy.

Most investigators are not so concrete in their definitions of intimacy, agreeing that intimacy is more than just physical closeness. Looking at the root of the word intimacy, from the Latin *intima* meaning "inner" or "innermost," they most often subscribe to a broader definition, such as the one offered by Dr. Dan McAdams, author of several books on the subject of intimacy:

"The desire for intimacy is the desire to share one's innermost self with another."

But definitions of intimacy don't stop there. On the opposite end of the spectrum from Desmond Morris stand experts such as the father/son psychiatrist team, Drs. Thomas Patrick Malone and Patrick Thomas Malone. In their book, *The Art of Intimacy*, they define intimacy as "the experience of connectivity." Their understanding of intimacy begins with a thorough examination of our "connectivity" with other people, but they do not, however, limit their concept of intimacy to human relationships. Their definition is so broad, in fact, that it includes our relationship with inanimate objects—trees, stars, and even *space*.

Concepts of the most ideal form of intimacy also vary throughout the world and history. The romantic notion of that "One Special Person" with whom we have a passionate intimate relationship is a product of our time and culture. But this model of intimacy is not universally accepted among all cultures. For instance, the Japanese seem to rely more on friendships to gain intimacy, whereas Americans seek it more in romantic relationships with a boyfriend, girlfriend, or spouse. In noting this, some researchers have suggested that Asians who tend to be less focused on personal feelings such as passion and are more concerned with the practical aspects of social attachments appear less vulnerable to the kind of disillusionment that leads to the crumbling of relationships.

In addition to variations among cultures, concepts of intimacy have also dramatically changed over time. In colonial America, the level of physical intimacy and proximity was generally greater than it is today, as family and even strangers shared close spaces and slept together in one room and used a common room for bathing, eating, and sleeping. Yet the customary level of communication among spouses was quite formal by today's standards—not much different from the way acquaintances or neighbors spoke to one another. Only a century later, love and marriage became highly romanticized and intimate self-disclosure was expected to be an ingredient in any loving partnership.

Ideas of what is considered to be private and intimate behavior have also changed over time. In sixteenth-century Germany, for instance, a new husband and wife were expected to consummate their marriage on a bed carried by witnesses who would validate the marriage.

How people express their emotions has also changed. In the Middle Ages it was considered normal to publicly express a wide range of feelings with great intensity and directness—joy, rage, fear, piety, and even pleasure at torturing and killing enemies. Extremes of hysterical laughter, passionate weeping, and violent rage were expressed much more than would be accepted in our society. But the commonplace expression of emotions and feelings in that society ruled out the concept of emotional intimacy; if one is to display all emotions openly and indiscriminately, then there are no private feelings left to express to a special few.

Clearly, the notions we take for granted about intimacy are not universal. They change over time and are often shaped by economic, social, and cultural conditions. And it is easy to become confused by the variety of different contemporary Western definitions of intimacy—with manifestations ranging from a haircut to our relationship with Neptune's moons. So

◆

where does this leave us in our quest to understand what intimacy is? I think that the implication is clear:

There is an incredible diversity among human lives, infinite
variations among people with respect to how they can experience a sense of closeness. This realization alone offers us a great
opportunity. It means that *at this very moment* we have vast
resources of intimacy available to us. Intimacy is all around us.

Today, so many of us are oppressed by a feeling of something
missing in our lives, intensely suffering from a lack of intimacy.
This is particularly true when we go through the inevitable periods in our life when we're not involved in a romantic relationship or when the passion wanes from a relationship. There's a
widespread notion in our culture that deep intimacy is best
achieved within the context of a passionate romantic relationship—that Special Someone who we set apart from all others.
This can be a profoundly limiting viewpoint, cutting us off from
other potential sources of intimacy, and the cause of much misery and unhappiness when that Special Someone isn't there.

But we have within our power the means to avoid this; we
need only courageously expand our concept of intimacy to
include all the other forms that surround us on a daily basis. By
broadening our definition of intimacy, we open ourselves to discovering many new and equally satisfying ways of connecting
with others. This brings us back to my initial discussion of loneliness with the Dalai Lama, a discussion triggered by a chance
perusal of the "Personals" section of a local newspaper. It makes
me wonder. At the very moment that those people were com-
posing their ads, struggling to find just the right words that
would bring romance into their lives and end the loneliness,

◆

how many of those people were *already* surrounded by friends, family, or acquaintances—relationships that could easily be cultivated into genuine and deeply satisfying intimate relationships? Many, I would guess. If what we seek in life is happiness, and intimacy is an important ingredient of a happier life, then it clearly makes sense to conduct our lives on the basis of a model of intimacy that includes as many forms of connection with others as possible. The Dalai Lama's model of intimacy is based on a willingness to open ourselves to many others, to family, friends, and even strangers, forming genuine and deep bonds based on our common humanity.

Chapter 6

DEEPENING OUR
CONNECTION TO OTHERS

O ne afternoon following his public lecture, I arrived at the
Dalai Lama's hotel suite for my daily appointment. I was
a few minutes early. An attendant discreetly glided into the hall-
way to relate that His Holiness was occupied in a private audience and would be several more minutes. I assumed my familiar
post outside his hotel suite door and used the time to review my
notes in preparation for our session, trying at the same time to
avoid the suspicious gaze of a security guard—the same look
perfected by convenience store clerks for use on junior high
school students loitering around the magazine racks.

Within a few moments, the door opened and a well-dressed

middle-aged couple were shown out. They looked familiar. I remembered that I had been briefly introduced to them several days earlier. I had been told that the wife was a well-known heiress and the husband an extremely wealthy, high-powered Manhattan attorney. At the time of introduction we had only exchanged a few words, but they had both struck me as unbelievably haughty. As they emerged from the Dalai Lama's hotel suite, I noted a startling change. Gone was the arrogant manner and smug expressions, and in their place were two faces suffused with tenderness and emotion. They were like two children. Streams of tears ran down both faces. Although the Dalai Lama's effect on others was not always so dramatic, I noticed that invariably others responded to him with some shift of emotion. I had long marveled at his ability to bond with others, whatever their walk of life, and establish a deep and meaningful emotional exchange.

ESTABLISHING EMPATHY

While we had spoken of the importance of human warmth and compassion during our conversations in Arizona, it wasn't until some months later at his home in Dharamsala that I had an opportunity to explore human relationships with him in greater detail. By that time I was very eager to see if we could discover an underlying set of principles that he uses in his interactions with others—principles that might be applied to improve any relationship, whether it be with strangers, family, friends, or lovers. Anxious to begin, I jumped right in:

◆

"Now, on the topic of human relationships . . . what would you say is the most effective method or technique of connecting with others in a meaningful way and of reducing conflicts with others?"

He glared at me for a moment. It wasn't an unkindly glare, but it made me feel as if I had just asked him to give me the precise chemical composition of moon dust.

After a brief pause, he responded, "Well, dealing with others is a very complex issue. There is no way that you can come up with one formula that could solve all problems. It's a bit like cooking. If you are cooking a very delicious meal, a special meal, then there are various stages in the cooking. You may have to first boil the vegetables separately and then you have to fry them and then you combine them in a special way, mixing in spices and so on. And finally, the end result would be this delicious product. Similarly here, in order to be skillful in dealing with others, you need many factors. You can't just say, 'This is the method' or 'This is the technique.'"

It wasn't exactly the answer I was looking for. I thought he was being evasive and felt that surely he must have something more concrete to offer. I pressed on: "Well, given that there is no single solution to improving our relationships, are there perhaps some more general guidelines that might be useful?"

The Dalai Lama thought for a moment before replying, "Yes. Earlier we spoke of the importance of approaching others with the thought of compassion in one's mind. That is crucial. Of course, just telling someone, 'Oh, it's very important to be compassionate; you must have more love' isn't enough. A simple prescription like that alone isn't going to work. But one effective means of teaching someone how to be more warm and compassionate is to begin by using reasoning to educate the individual about the value and practical benefits of compassion, and also having them reflect on how they feel when someone is kind to them and so on. In a sense this primes them, so there will be more of an effect as they proceed in their efforts to be more compassionate.

"Now in looking at the various means of developing compassion, I think that empathy is an important factor. The ability to appreciate another's suffering. In fact, traditionally, one of the Buddhist techniques for enhancing compassion involves imagining a situation where there is a sentient being suffering—for instance, like a sheep about to be slaughtered by the butcher. And then try to imagine the suffering that the sheep may be going through and so on . . ." The Dalai Lama stopped for a moment to reflect, absently running a string of prayer beads through his fingers. He commented, "It occurs to me that if we were dealing with someone who was very cold and indifferent, then this kind of technique may not be very effective. It would be as if you were to ask the butcher to do this visualization: the butcher is so hardened, so used to the whole thing, that it wouldn't have any impact. So, for example, it would be very difficult to explain and utilize that technique for some Westerners who are accustomed to hunting and fishing for fun, as a form of recreation . . ."

"In that case," I suggested, "it might not be an effective technique to ask a hunter to imagine the suffering of his prey, but you might be able to awaken feelings of compassion by beginning with having him visualize his favorite hunting dog caught in a trap and squealing with pain . . ."

◆

"Yes, exactly . . ." agreed the Dalai Lama. "I think depending on the circumstances one might modify that technique. For instance, the person may not have a strong feeling of empathy towards animals but at least may have some empathy towards a close family member or friend. In that case the person could visualize a situation where the beloved person is suffering or going through a tragic situation and then imagine how he or she would respond to that, react to that. So one can attempt to increase compassion by trying to empathize with another's feeling or experience.

"I think that empathy is important not only as a means of enhancing compassion, but I think that generally speaking, when dealing with others on any level, if you're having some difficulties, it's extremely helpful to be able to try to put yourself in the other person's place and see how you would react to the situation. Even if you have no common experience with the other person or have a very different lifestyle, you can try to do this through imagination. You may need to be slightly creative. This technique involves the capacity to temporarily suspend insisting on your own viewpoint but rather to look from the other person's perspective, to imagine what would be the situation if you were in his shoes, how you would deal with this. This helps you develop an awareness and respect for another's feelings, which is an important factor in reducing conflicts and problems with other people."

Our interview that afternoon was brief. I had been fitted into the Dalai Lama's busy schedule at the last minute, and like sev-

◆

eral of our conversations, it occurred late in the day. Outside, the sun was beginning to set, filling the room with a bittersweet dusky light, turning the pale yellow walls a deep amber, and illuminating the Buddhist icons in the room with rich golden hues. The Dalai Lama's attendant silently entered the room, signaling the end of our session. Wrapping up the discussion, I asked, "I know that we have to close, but do you have any other words of advice or methods that you use to help establish empathy with others?"

Echoing the words he had spoken in Arizona many months before, with a gentle simplicity he answered, "Whenever I meet people I always approach them from the standpoint of the most basic things we have in common. We each have a physical structure, a mind, emotions. We are all born in the same way, and we all die. All of us want happiness and do not want to suffer. Looking at others from this standpoint rather than emphasizing secondary differences such as the fact that I am Tibetan, or a different color, religion, or cultural background, allows me to have a feeling that I'm meeting someone just the same as me. I find that relating to others on that level makes it much easier to exchange and communicate with one another." With that, he rose, smiled, clasped my hand briefly, and retired for the evening.

The following morning, we continued our discussion at the Dalai Lama's home.

"In Arizona we spoke a great deal about the importance of compassion in human relationships, and yesterday we discussed the role of empathy in improving our ability to relate to one another . . ."

"Yes," the Dalai Lama nodded.

"Besides that, can you suggest any additional specific methods or techniques to help one deal more effectively with other people?"

"Well, as I mentioned yesterday, there is no way that you can come up with one or two simple techniques that can solve all problems. Having said that, however, I think there are some other factors that can help one deal with others more skillfully. First, it is helpful to understand and appreciate the background of the people you are dealing with. Also, being more open-minded and honest are useful qualities when it comes to dealing with others."

I waited, but he didn't say anything more.

"Can you suggest any other methods of improving our relationships?"

The Dalai Lama thought for a moment. "No," he laughed.

I felt that these particular bits of advice were too simplistic, commonplace really. Still, as that seemed to be all he had to say on the subject for the moment, we turned to other topics.

That evening, I was invited to dinner at the home of some Tibetan friends in Dharamsala. My friends arranged an evening that proved to be quite lively. The meal was excellent, featuring a dazzling array of special dishes and starring Tibetan *Mo Mos*, a tasty meat dumpling. As dinner wore on, the conversation became more animated. Soon, the guests were swapping off-color stories about the most embarrassing thing they ever did while drunk. Several guests had been invited to the gathering, including a well-known couple from Germany, the wife an architect and the husband a writer, author of a dozen books.

Having an interest in books, I approached the author and began a conversation. I asked about his writing. His replies were short and perfunctory, his manner blunt and standoffish. Thinking him rather unfriendly, even snobbish, I took an immediate dislike to him. Well, at least I made an attempt to connect with him, I consoled myself, and, satisfied that he was simply a disagreeable person, I turned to conversation with some of the more amiable guests.

The following day, I ran into a friend at a cafe in the village and over tea I recounted the events of the evening before.

". . . I really enjoyed everyone, except for Rolf, that writer . . . He seemed so arrogant or something . . . so unfriendly."

"I've known him for several years," my friend said, ". . . I know that he comes across that way, but it's just that he's a bit shy, a bit reserved at first. He really is a wonderful person if you get to know him . . ." I wasn't convinced. My friend continued, explaining, ". . . even though he is a successful writer, he has had more than his share of difficulties in his life. Rolf has really suffered a lot. His family suffered tremendously at the hands of the Nazis during World War II. And he's had two children, whom he has been very devoted to, born with some rare genetic disorder that left them extremely physically and mentally handicapped. And instead of becoming bitter or spending his life playing the martyr, he dealt with his problems by reaching out to others and spent many years devoting himself to working with the handicapped as a volunteer. He really is quite special if you get to know him."

◆

As it turned out, I met Rolf and his wife once again at the end of that week, at a small strip field serving as the local airport. We were scheduled on the same flight to Delhi, which turned out to be canceled. The next flight to Delhi wasn't for several days, so we decided to share a car to Delhi, a grueling ten-hour ride. The few bits of background information that my friend had shared with me had changed my feeling toward Rolf, and on the long ride down to Delhi I felt more open toward him. As a result, I made an effort to sustain a conversation with him. Initially, his manner remained the same. But with just that little bit of openness and persistence, I soon discovered that, as my friend had said, his standoffishness was more likely due to shyness than snobbery. As we rattled through the sweltering, dusty northern Indian countryside, moving ever deeper into conversation, he proved to be a warm, genuine human being and a stalwart traveling companion.

By the time we reached Delhi, I realized that the Dalai Lama's advice to "understand the background of people" was not as elementary and superficial as it first appeared. Yes, it was simple perhaps, but not simplistic. Sometimes it is the most basic and straightforward of advice, the kind that we tend to dismiss as naive, that can be the most effective means of enhancing communication.

Several days later I was still in Delhi on a two-day stopover before returning home. The change from the tranquillity of Dharamsala was jarring, and I was in a foul mood. Besides battling the stifling heat, the pollution, and the crowds, the sidewalks swarmed with a common species of urban predator dedicated to the Street Swindle. Walking the scorching Delhi streets, a Westerner, a Foreigner, a Target, approached by a half-dozen hustlers per block, it felt as if I had "CHUMP" tattooed on my forehead. It was demoralizing.

That morning, I fell for a common two-man street scam. One partner splattered a splotch of red paint on my shoes while I wasn't looking. Down the block, his confederate, an innocent looking shoeshine boy, brought the paint to my attention and offered to shine my shoes at the usual going rate. He deftly shined the shoes within minutes. When finished, he calmly demanded a huge sum—two months wages for many in Delhi. When I balked, he claimed that that was the price he had quoted me. I objected again, and the boy began to bellow, drawing a crowd, crying that I was refusing to pay him for services already rendered. Later that day I learned that this was a common scam played on unsuspecting tourists; after demanding a huge sum, the shoeshine boy deliberately raises a fuss, drawing a crowd, with the intention of extorting the money from the tourist by embarrassment and the desire to avoid a scene.

That afternoon I lunched with a colleague at my hotel. The events of the morning were quickly forgotten as she inquired about my recent series of interviews with the Dalai Lama. We became engrossed in a discussion about the Dalai Lama's ideas regarding empathy and the importance of taking the other person's perspective. After lunch we jumped into a cab and set off to visit some mutual friends. As the cab pulled away, my thoughts returned to the shoeshine scam that morning, and as dark images rustled in my mind, I happened to glance at the meter.

"Stop the taxi!" I yelled. My friend jumped at the sudden outburst. The taxi driver scowled at me in the rearview mirror but kept driving.

"Pull over!" I demanded, my voice now quivering with a trace of hysteria. My friend appeared shocked. The taxi stopped. I pointed at the meter, furiously stabbing at the air. "You didn't reset the meter! There was over twenty rupees on the meter when we started!"

"So sorry, sir," he said with a dull indifference that further infuriated me, "I forgot to reset. . . . I will restart . . ."

"You're not restarting anything!" I exploded. "I'm fed up with you people trying to pad fares, drive around in circles, or do whatever you can to rip people off . . . I'm just . . . just . . . fed up!" I sputtered and fumed with a sanctimonious intensity. My friend looked embarrassed. The taxi driver merely stared at me with the same defiant expression found most often among the sacred cows that strolled out into the middle of a busy Delhi street and stopped, with the seditious intent to hold up traffic. He looked at me as if my outburst was merely tiresome and boring. I threw a few rupees into the front seat, and without further comment opened the car door for my friend and followed her out.

Within a few minutes we hailed another taxi and were on our way again. But I couldn't let it drop. As we drove through the streets of Delhi, I continued to complain about how "everyone" in Delhi was out to cheat tourists and that we were nothing but quarry. My colleague listened silently as I ranted and raved. Finally she said, "Well, twenty rupees is only around a quarter. Why get so worked up?"

I seethed with pious indignation. "But it's the principle that counts!" I proclaimed. "I can't see how you can be so calm about this whole thing anyway when it happens all the time. Doesn't it bother you?"

"Well," she said slowly, "it did for a minute, but I started thinking about what we were talking about at lunch, about the Dalai Lama saying how important it is to see things from another's perspective. While you were getting worked up, I tried to think about what I might have in common with the cabdriver. We both want good food to eat, to sleep well, to feel good, to be loved, and so on. Then, I tried to imagine myself as the cabdriver. I sit in a stifling cab all day without air conditioning, maybe I'm angry and jealous of rich foreigners. . . . and the best way I can come up with to try to make things 'fair,' to be happy, is to derive ways to cheat people out of their money. But the thing is, even when it works and I squeeze a few extra rupees out of an unsuspecting tourist, I can't imagine that it's a very satisfying way to be happier or a very satisfying life. . . . Anyway, the more I imagined myself as the cabdriver, somehow the less angry I was at him. His life just seemed sad. . . . I mean, I still don't agree with what he did and we were right to get out of the cab, but I just couldn't get worked up enough to hate him for it. . . ."

I was silent. Startled, in fact, at how little I had actually absorbed from the Dalai Lama. By that time I was beginning to develop an appreciation of the practical value of his advice, such as "understanding another's background," and of course I found his examples of how he implemented these principles in his own life to be inspiring. But as I thought back over our series of discussions, beginning in Arizona and now continuing in India, I

◆

realized that right from the beginning our interviews had taken on a clinical tone, as if I were asking him about human anatomy, only in this case, it was the anatomy of the human mind and spirit. Until that moment, however, somehow it hadn't occurred to me to apply his ideas fully to my own life, at least not right now—I always had a vague intention of trying to implement his ideas in my life at some point in the future, perhaps when I had more time.

EXAMINING THE UNDERLYING
BASIS OF A RELATIONSHIP

My conversations with the Dalai Lama in Arizona had begun with a discussion about the sources of happiness. And despite the fact that he has chosen to live his life as a monk, studies have shown that marriage is a factor that can, in fact, bring happiness—providing the intimacy and close bonds that enhance health and overall life satisfaction. There have been many thousands of surveys of Americans and Europeans that show that generally, married people are happier and more satisfied with life than single or widowed people—or especially compared to divorced or separated people. One survey found that six in ten Americans who rate their marriage as "very happy" also rate their life as a whole as "very happy." In discussing the topic of human relationships, I thought it important to bring up the subject of that common source of happiness.

Minutes before one scheduled interview with the Dalai Lama, I sat with a friend on an outdoor patio at the hotel in Tucson enjoying a cool drink. Mentioning the topics of romance and marriage which I was intending to bring up in my interview, my friend and I soon began commiserating about being single. As we talked, a healthy-looking young couple, golfers maybe, happily vacationing on the cusp of the tourist season, sat down at a table near us. They had the look of a midrange marriage—no longer honeymooners perhaps, but still young and no doubt in love. It must be nice, I thought.

No sooner had they sat down, than they began to bicker.

". . . I told you we'd be late!" the woman accused acidly, her voice surprisingly husky, the rasp of vocal cords pickled by years of cigarette smoke and alcohol. "Now we barely have enough time to eat. I can't even enjoy my food!"

". . . if you didn't take so long to get ready . . ." the man shot back automatically, in quieter tones, but every syllable laden with annoyance and hostility.

Rebuttal. "I was ready a half-hour ago. You're the one who had to finish reading the paper . . ."

And on it went. It didn't stop. Like the Greek dramatist Euripides said, "Marry, and it may go well. But when a marriage fails, then those who marry live at home in hell."

The argument, rapidly escalating, put a quick end to our lamentations about the single life. My friend merely rolled his eyes and, quoting a line from *Seinfeld*, said, "Oh yeah! I want to get married *real* soon!"

Only moments before, I had every intention of starting our session by soliciting the Dalai Lama's opinion about the joys and virtues of romance and marriage. Instead, I entered his hotel suite and almost before sitting down, asked, "Why do you suppose that conflicts seem to arise so often in marriages?"

"When dealing with conflicts, of course it can be quite complex," the Dalai Lama explained. "There can be many factors involved. *So, when we are dealing with trying to understand relationship problems, the first stage in this process involves deliberately reflecting on the underlying nature and basis of that relationship.*

"So, first of all, one has to recognize that there are different types of relationships and understand the differences between them. For example, leaving aside the issue of marriage for a moment, even within ordinary friendships we can recognize that there are different types of friendships. Some friendships are based on wealth, power, or position. In these cases your friendship continues as long as your power, wealth, or position is sustained. Once these grounds are no longer there, then the friendship will also begin to disappear. On the other hand, there is another kind of friendship. Friendships that are based not on considerations of wealth, power, and position but rather on true human feeling, a feeling of closeness in which there is a sense of sharing and connectedness. This type of friendship is what I would call genuine friendship because it would not be affected by the status of the individual's wealth, position, or power, whether it is increasing or whether it is declining. The factor that sustains a genuine friendship is a feeling of affection. If you lack that, then you won't be able to sustain a genuine friendship. Of course, we have mentioned this before and all this is very obvious, but if you're running into relationship problems, it's often very helpful to simply stand back and reflect on the basis of that relationship.

◆

"In the same way, if someone is running into problems with his or her spouse, it can be helpful to look at the underlying basis of the relationship. For example, you often find relationships very much based on immediate sexual attraction. When a couple has just met, seen each other on just a few occasions, they may be madly in love and very happy," he laughed, "but any decision about marriage made at that instant would be very shaky. Just as one can become, in some sense, insane from the power of intense anger or hatred, it is also possible for an individual to become in some sense insane by the power of passion or lust. And sometimes you might even find situations where an individual could feel, 'Oh, my boyfriend or girlfriend is not really a good person, not a kind person, but still I feel attracted to him or her.' So a relationship that is based on that initial attraction is very unreliable, very unstable, because it is very much based on temporary phenomena. That feeling is very short lived, so after some time, that will go." He snapped his fingers. "So it shouldn't be much of a surprise if that kind of relationship runs into trouble, and a marriage based on that will eventually run into trouble . . . But what do you think?"

"Yes, I'd have to agree with you on that," I answered. "It seems that in any relationship, even the most ardent ones, the initial passion eventually cools down. Some research has shown that those who regard the initial passion and romance as essential to their relationship may end up disillusioned or divorced. One social psychologist, Ellen Berscheid, at the University of Minnesota I think, looked at that issue and concluded that the failure to appreciate the limited half-life of passionate love can doom a relationship. She and her colleagues felt that the

◆

increase in divorce rates over the past twenty years is partly linked to the increased importance people place on intense positive emotional experiences in their lives—experiences like romantic love. But one problem is that those types of experiences may be particularly difficult to sustain over time . . ."

"This seems very true," he said. "So, when dealing with relationship problems you can see the tremendous importance of examining and understanding the underlying nature of the relationship.

"Now, while some relationships are based on immediate sexual attraction, you can have other types of relationships, on the other hand, in which the person in a cool state of mind will realize that physically speaking, in terms of appearance, my boyfriend or girlfriend may not be that attractive but he or she is really a good person, a kind, gentle person. A relationship that is built on that forms a kind of a bond that is more long lasting, because there is a kind of genuine communication at a very human and personal level between the two . . ."

The Dalai Lama paused for a moment as if mulling the issue over, then added, "Of course, I should make it clear that one can have a good, healthy relationship that includes sexual attraction as one component. So it seems, then, that there can be two principal types of relationships based on sexual attraction. One type is based on pure sexual desire. In this case the motive or the impetus behind the bond really is just temporary satisfaction, immediate gratification. In that type of relationship, individuals are relating to each other not so much as people but rather as objects. That type of relationship is not very sound. If the relationship is based only on sexual desire, without a component of

mutual respect, then the relationship becomes almost like pros-
titution, in which neither side has respect for the other. A relationship built primarily on sexual desire is like a house built on
a foundation of ice; as soon as the ice melts, the building col-
lapses.

"However, there is a second type of relationship which is also
based on sexual attraction, but in which the physical attraction
is not the predominant basis of the relationship. In this second
type of relationship there is an underlying appreciation of the
value of the other person based on your feeling that the other
person is kind, nice, and gentle, and you accord respect and dignity to that other individual. Any relationship that is based on
that will be much more long lasting and reliable. It's more appropriate. And in order to establish that type of relationship, it is
crucial to spend enough time to get to know each other in a genuine sense, to know each other's basic characteristics.

"Therefore, when my friends ask me about their marriage, I
usually ask how long they've known each other. If they say a few
months, then I usually say, 'Oh, this is too short.' If they say a
few years, then it seems to be better. Now they not only know
each other's face or appearance but, I think, the deeper nature
of the other person . . ."

"That's kind of like Mark Twain's quote that 'no man or
woman really knows what perfect love is until they have been
married a quarter of a century . . .'"

The Dalai Lama nodded and continued, "Yes . . . So, I think
many problems occur simply because of insufficient time to
know each other. Anyway, *I think that if one is seeking to build a truly
satisfying relationship, the best way of bringing this about is to get to know*

♦

the deeper nature of the person and relate to her or him on that level, instead of merely on the basis of superficial characteristics. And in this type of relationship there is a role for genuine compassion.

"Now, I've heard many people claim that their marriage has a deeper meaning than just a sexual relationship, that marriage involves two people trying to bond their lives together, share life's ups and downs together, share a certain intimacy. If that claim is honest, then I believe that's the proper basis on which a relationship should be built. A sound relationship should include a sense of responsibility and commitment towards each other. Of course, the physical contact, the appropriate or normal sexual relationship between a couple, can provide a certain satisfaction that could have a calming effect on one's mind. But, after all, biologically speaking, the main purpose of a sexual relationship is reproduction. And to successfully achieve that, you need to have a sense of commitment towards the offspring, in order for them to survive and thrive. So, developing a capacity for responsibility and commitment is crucial. Without that, the relationship provides only temporary satisfaction. It's just for fun." He laughed, a laugh that seemed to be infused with wonder at the vast scope of human behavior.

RELATIONSHIPS BASED ON ROMANCE

It felt odd, speaking about sex and marriage to a man, now over sixty years old, who had been celibate all his life. He didn't seem averse to talking about these issues, but there was a certain detachment to his comments.

In thinking about our conversation later that evening, it occurred to me that there was still one important component of relationships that we hadn't covered, and I was curious to learn of his take on the subject. I brought it up the following day.

"Yesterday we were discussing relationships and the importance of basing a close relationship or marriage on more than just sex," I began. "But, in Western culture, it is not just the physical sex act but the whole idea of *romance*—the idea of falling in love, of being deeply in love with one's partner—that is seen as a highly desirable thing. In movies, literature, and popular culture there's a kind of exaltation of this kind of romantic love. What's your view of this?"

Without hesitation, the Dalai Lama said, "I think that, leaving aside how the endless pursuit of romantic love may affect our deeper spiritual growth, even from the perspective of a conventional way of life, the idealization of this romantic love can be seen as an extreme. Unlike those relationships based on caring and genuine affection, this is another matter. It cannot be seen as a positive thing," he said decisively. "It's something that is based on fantasy, unattainable, and therefore may be a source of frustration. So, on that basis it cannot be seen as a positive thing."

There was a finality to the Dalai Lama's tone which conveyed that he had nothing more to say on the subject. In view of the tremendous emphasis our society places on romance, I felt that he was dismissing the lure of romantic love too lightly. Given the Dalai Lama's monastic upbringing, I supposed that he didn't fully appreciate the joys of romance, and questioning him further about issues related to romance would be as helpful as asking him to come out to the parking lot to take a look at a problem I was having with my car's transmission. Mildly disappointed, I fumbled with my notes for several moments and passed on to other topics.

What is it that makes romance so appealing? In looking at this question, one finds that Eros—romantic, sexual, passionate love—the ultimate ecstasy, is a potent cocktail of cultural, biological, and psychological ingredients. In Western culture, the idea of romantic love has flourished over the past two hundred years under the influence of Romanticism, a movement which has done much to shape our perception of the world. Romanticism grew up as a rejection of the previous Age of Enlightenment, with its emphasis on human reason. The new movement exalted intuition, emotion, feeling, and passion. It emphasized the importance of the sensory world, the subjective experience of the individual, and tended toward the world of imagination, of fantasy, the search for a world that is not—an idealized past or utopian future. This idea has had profound impact not only in art and literature but also in politics and all aspects of the development of modern Western culture.

The most compelling element of our pursuit of romance is the feeling of falling in love. Powerful forces are at work driving us to seek this feeling, much more than simply the glorification of romantic love which we pick up from our culture. Many researchers feel that these forces are programmed into our genes from birth. The feeling of falling in love, invariably mixed with a sense of sexual attraction, may be a genetically determined

instinctual component of mating behavior. From an evolutionary perspective, the number-one job of the organism is to survive, reproduce, and assure continued survival of the species. It
is in the best interest of the species, therefore, if we are programmed to fall in love; it certainly increases the odds that we
will mate and reproduce. Thus, we have built-in mechanisms to
help make that happen; in response to certain stimuli, our brains
manufacture and pump out chemicals that create a euphoric
feeling, the "high" associated with falling in love. And while our
brains are marinading in those chemicals, that feeling so overwhelms us at times that everything else seems to be blocked out.

The psychological forces driving us to seek the feeling of
being in love are as compelling as the biological forces. In Plato's
Symposium, Socrates tells the story of the myth of Aristophanes,
concerning the origin of sexual love. According to this myth,
the original inhabitants of Earth were round creatures with four
hands and four feet and with their back and sides forming a circle. These self-sufficient sexless beings were very arrogant and
repeatedly attacked the gods. To punish them, Zeus hurled
thunderbolts at them and split them apart. Each creature was
now two, each half longing to merge with its other half.

Eros, the drive toward passionate, romantic love, can be seen
as this ancient desire for fusion with the other half. It seems to
be a universal, unconscious human need. The feeling involves a
sensation of merging with the other, of boundaries breaking
down, of becoming one with the loved one. Psychologists call
this the collapse of ego boundaries. Some feel that this process
is rooted in our earliest experience, an unconscious attempt to
re-create the experience we had as infants, a primal state in

which the child is completely merged with the parent or primary caregiver.

Evidence suggests that newborn infants do not distinguish between themselves and the rest of the universe. They have no sense of personal identity, or at least their identity includes the mother, others, and all objects in their environment. They don't know where they end and the "other" begins. They lack what is known as object permanence: objects have no independent existence; if they are not interacting with an object, it doesn't exist. For example, if an infant is holding a rattle, the baby recognizes the rattle as part of herself or himself, and if the rattle is taken away and hidden from view, it ceases to exist.

At birth, the brain is not yet fully "hard wired," but as the baby grows and the brain matures, the baby's interaction with the world becomes more sophisticated and the baby gradually gains a sense of personal identity, of "me" as opposed to "other." Along with this, a sense of isolation develops, and gradually the child develops an awareness of his or her own limitations. The formation of identity, of course, continues to develop throughout childhood and adolescence as the child comes in contact with the world. People's sense of who they are comes about as the result of developing internal representations, formed in large part by reflections of their early interactions with the important people in their lives, and reflections of their role in society in general. Gradually, the personal identity and intrapsychic structure become more complex.

But some part of us may still seek to regress to an earlier state of existence, a state of bliss in which there is no feeling of isolation, no feeling of separation. Many contemporary psycholo-

◆

gists feel that the early "oneness" experience is incorporated into our subconscious mind, and as an adult it permeates our unconscious and private fantasies. They believe that the merging with the loved one when one is "in love" echoes the experience of being merged with the mother in infancy. It re-creates that magic feeling, a feeling of omnipotence, as if all things are possible. A feeling like that is hard to beat.

It is no wonder then that the pursuit of romantic love is so powerful. So what's the problem, and why does the Dalai Lama so easily assert that the pursuit of romance is a negative thing?

I considered the problem of basing a relationship on romantic love, of taking refuge in romance as a source of happiness. A former patient, David, came to mind. David, a thirty-four-year-old landscape architect, initially presented to my office with classic symptoms of a severe clinical depression. He explained that his depression may have been triggered by some minor work-related stresses, but "mostly it just kinda came on." We discussed the option of an antidepressant medication, which he was in favor of, and we instituted a trial of a standard antidepressant. The medication proved to be very effective, and within three weeks his acute symptoms improved and he was back to his normal routine. In exploring his history, however, it didn't take long to realize that in addition to his acute depression, he also suffered from dysthymia, a more insidious form of chronic low-grade depression that had been present for many years. After he recovered from his acute depression, we began to explore his personal history, laying a foundation that would help us understand the internal psychological dynamics that may have contributed to his many-year history of dysthymia.

After only a few sessions, David entered the office one day in a jubilant mood. "I feel great!" he declared. "I haven't felt this good in years!"

My reaction to this wonderful news was to immediately assess him for the possibility of a shift into a manic phase of a mood disorder. That wasn't the case, however.

"I'm in love!" he told me. "I met her last week at a site that I'm bidding on. She's the most beautiful girl that I've ever seen . . . We've gone out almost every night this week, and, I dunno, it's like we're soul mates—perfect for each other. I just can't believe it! I haven't dated for the past two or three years, and I was getting to the point that I thought I'd never meet anyone; then all of a sudden there she was."

David spent most of that session cataloging all the remarkable virtues of his new girlfriend. "I think we're perfect for each other in every way. It's not just a sexual thing either; we're interested in the same things, and it's frightening how much we think alike. Of course, I'm being realistic, and I realize that no one is perfect . . . Like the other night it bothered me a bit because I thought she was flirting a little with some guys at a club we were at . . . but we both had been drinking a lot and she was just having fun. We discussed it afterward and worked it out."

David returned the following week to inform me that he had decided to quit therapy. "Everything is going so great in my life, I just can't see what there is to talk about in therapy," he explained. "My depression is gone, I'm sleeping like a baby, I'm back at work doing really well, and I'm in a great relationship that just seems to be getting better and better. I think I've gotten something from our sessions, but right now I just can't see spending money for therapy when there's nothin' to work on."

I told him I was happy he was doing so well but reminded him about some of the family issues that we had begun to identify that may have led to his history of chronic dysthymia. All the while, common psychiatric terms like "resistance" and "defenses" began to surface in my mind.

He wasn't convinced. "Well, those may be things that I might want to look at someday," he said, "but I really think that it just had a lot to do with loneliness, a feeling that there was someone missing, a special person that I could share things with, and now I've found her."

He was adamant in his desire to end therapy that day. We made arrangements for his family physician to follow up on his medication regimen, spent the session in review and closure, and I ended by assuring him that my door was open at any time.

Several months later, David returned to my office:

"I've been miserable," he said with a dejected tone. "Last time I saw you, things were going so great. I really thought that I had found my ideal mate. I even brought up the subject of marriage. But it seemed that the closer I wanted to become, the more she pulled away. She finally broke up with me. I got really depressed again for a couple of weeks after that. I even started calling her and hanging up just to hear her voice, and driving by her work just to see if her car was there. After about a month I got sick of doing that—it was just so ridiculous—and at least my symptoms of depression got better. I mean I'm eating and sleeping fine, still doing well at work, and I have plenty of energy and all, but it still feels as if part of me is missing. It's like I'm back at square one, feeling just the same as I have for years . . ."

We resumed therapy.

It seems clear that as a source of happiness, romance leaves a lot to be desired. And perhaps the Dalai Lama was not far off the mark in rejecting the notion of romance as a basis for a relationship and in describing romance as merely "a fantasy . . . unattainable," something not worthy of our efforts. On closer examination, perhaps he was objectively describing the nature of romance rather than providing a negative value judgment colored by his years of training as a monk. Even an objective reference source such as the dictionary, which contains well over a dozen definitions of "romance" and "romantic," is liberally peppered with phrases such as "a fictitious tale," "an exaggeration," "a falsehood," "fanciful or imaginative," "not practical," "without a basis in fact," "characteristic of or preoccupied with idealized lovemaking or courting," and so on. It is apparent that somewhere along the road of Western civilization a change has taken place. The ancient concept of *Eros*, with the underlying sense of becoming one, of fusion with another, has taken on new meaning. Romance has acquired an artificial quality, with flavors of fraudulence and deception, the quality that had led Oscar Wilde to bleakly observe, "When one is in love, one always begins by deceiving oneself, and one always ends up by deceiving others. That is what the world calls a romance."

Earlier, we explored the role of closeness and intimacy as an important component of human happiness. There's no doubt of this. But if one is looking for lasting satisfaction in a relationship, the foundation of that relationship must be solid. It is for this reason that the Dalai Lama encourages us to examine the underlying basis of a relationship, should we find ourselves in a relationship that is going sour. Sexual attraction, or even the intense feeling of falling in love, may play a role in forming an initial bond between two people, to draw them together, but like a good epoxy glue, that initial bonding agent needs to be mixed with other ingredients before it will harden into a lasting bond. In identifying these other ingredients, we turn once again to the Dalai Lama's approach to building a strong relationship—basing our relationship on the qualities of affection, compassion, and mutual respect as human beings. Basing a relationship on these qualities enables us to achieve a deep and meaningful bond not only with our lover or spouse but also with friends, acquaintances, or strangers—virtually any human being. It opens up unlimited possibilities and opportunities for connection.

Chapter 7

THE VALUE AND BENEFITS
OF COMPASSION

DEFINING COMPASSION

As our conversations progressed, I discovered that the development of compassion plays a far greater role in the Dalai Lama's life than simply a means to cultivating a feeling of warmth and affection, a means of improving our relationship with others. It became clear, in fact, that as a practicing Buddhist, the development of compassion was an integral part of his spiritual path.

"Given the importance that Buddhism places on compassion as an essential part of one's spiritual development," I asked, "can you more clearly define what you mean by 'compassion'?"

The Dalai Lama replied, "Compassion can be roughly defined in terms of a state of mind that is nonviolent, nonharming, and nonaggressive. It is a mental attitude based on the wish for others to be free of their suffering and is associated with a sense of commitment, responsibility, and respect towards the other.

"In discussing the definition of compassion, the Tibetan word *Tse-wa*, there is also a sense to the word of its being a state of mind that can include a wish for good things for oneself. In developing compassion, perhaps one could begin with the wish that oneself be free of suffering, and then take that natural feeling towards oneself and cultivate it, enhance it, and extend it out to include and embrace others.

"Now, when people speak of compassion, I think that there is often a danger of confusing compassion with attachment. So when we discuss compassion, we must first make a distinction between two types of love or compassion. One kind of compassion is tinged with attachment—the feeling of controlling someone, or loving someone so that person will love you back. This ordinary type of love or compassion is quite partial and biased. And a relationship based on that alone is unstable. That kind of partial relationship, based on perceiving and identifying the person as a friend, may lead to a certain emotional attachment and feeling of closeness. But if there is a slight change in the situation, a disagreement perhaps, or if your friend does something to make you angry, then all of a sudden your mental projection changes; the concept of 'my friend' is no longer there. Then you'll find the emotional attachment evaporating, and instead of that feeling of love and concern, you may have a feeling of hatred. So, that kind of love, based on attachment, can be closely linked with hatred.

◆

"But there is a second type of compassion that is free from such attachment. That is genuine compassion. That kind of compassion isn't so much based on the fact that this person or that person is dear to me. Rather, genuine compassion is based on the rationale that all human beings have an innate desire to be happy and overcome suffering, just like myself. And, just like myself, they have the natural right to fulfill this fundamental aspiration. On the basis of the recognition of this equality and commonality, you develop a sense of affinity and closeness with others. With this as a foundation, you can feel compassion regardless of whether you view the other person as a friend or an enemy. It is based on the other's fundamental rights rather than your own mental projection. Upon this basis, then, you will generate love and compassion. That's genuine compassion.

"So, one can see how making the distinction between these two kinds of compassion and cultivating genuine compassion can be quite important in our day-to-day life. For instance, in marriage there is generally a component of emotional attachment. But I think that if there is a component of genuine compassion as well, based on mutual respect as two human beings, the marriage tends to last a long time. In the case of emotional attachment without compassion, the marriage is more unstable and tends to end more quickly."

The idea of developing a different kind of compassion, a more universal compassion, a kind of generic compassion divorced from personal feeling, seemed like a tall order. Turning it over in my mind, as if thinking aloud, I asked, "But love or compassion is a subjective feeling. It seems that the emotional tone or *feeling* of love or compassion would be the same whether it was 'tinged with attachment' or 'genuine.' So if the person would experience the same emotion or feeling in both types, why is it important to distinguish between the two?"

With a decisive tone, the Dalai Lama answered, "First, I think that there is a different quality between the feeling of genuine love, or compassion, and love based on attachment. It's not the same feeling. The feeling of genuine compassion is much stronger, much wider; it has a very profound quality. Also, genuine love and compassion are much more stable, more reliable. For example, if you see an animal intensely suffering, like a fish writhing with a hook in its mouth, you might spontaneously experience a feeling of not being able to bear its pain. That feeling isn't based on a special connection with that particular animal, a feeling of 'Oh, that animal is my friend.' In that case you're basing your compassion simply on the fact that that being also has feeling, can experience pain, and has a right not to experience such pain. So, that type of compassion, not mixed with desire or attachment, is much more sound, and more durable in the long run."

Moving deeper into the subject of compassion, I continued, "Now in your example of seeing a fish intensely suffering with a hook in its mouth, you bring up a vital point—that it is associated with a feeling of not being able to bear its pain."

"Yes," said the Dalai Lama. "In fact, in one sense one could define compassion as the feeling of unbearableness at the sight of other people's suffering, other sentient being's suffering. And in order to generate that feeling one must first have an appreciation of the seriousness or intensity of another's suffering. So, I think that the more fully one understands suffering, and the various kinds of suffering that we are subject to, the deeper will be one's level of compassion."

I raised the question, "Well, I appreciate the fact that greater awareness of other's suffering can enhance our capacity for compassion. In fact, by definition, compassion involves opening oneself to another's suffering. Sharing another's suffering. But there's a more basic question: Why would we want to take on another's suffering when we don't even want our own? I mean, most of us go to great lengths to avoid our own pain and suffering, even to the point of taking drugs and so on. Why would we then deliberately take on someone else's suffering?"

Without hesitation the Dalai Lama responded, "I feel that there is a significant difference between your own suffering and the suffering you might experience in a compassionate state in which you take upon yourself and share other people's suffering—a qualitative difference." He paused, and then as if effortlessly targeting my own feelings at the moment, he continued, "When you think about your own suffering, there is a feeling of being totally overwhelmed. There is a sense of being burdened, of being pressed under something—a feeling of helplessness. There's a dullness, almost as if your faculties have become numb.

"Now, in generating compassion, when you are taking on another's suffering, you may also initially experience a certain degree of discomfort, a sense of uncomfortableness or unbearableness. But in the case of compassion, the feeling is much different; underlying the uncomfortable feeling is a very high level of alertness and determination because you are voluntarily and deliberately accepting another's suffering for a higher purpose. There is a feeling of connectedness and commitment, a willing-

◆

ness to reach out to others, a feeling of freshness rather than dullness. This is similar to the case of an athlete. While undergoing rigorous training, an athlete may suffer a lot—working out, sweating, straining. I think it can be quite a painful and exhausting experience. But the athlete doesn't see it as a painful experience. The athlete would take it as a great accomplishment, an experience associated with a sense of joy. But if the same person were subject to some other physical work that was not part of his athletic training, then the athlete would think, 'Oh, why have I been subjected to this terrible ordeal?' So the mental attitude makes a tremendous difference."

These few words, spoken with such conviction, lifted me from an oppressed feeling to one of a feeling of the possibility of the resolution of suffering, of transcending suffering.

"You mention that the first step in generating that kind of compassion is an appreciation of suffering. But are there any other specific Buddhist techniques used to enhance one's compassion?"

"Yes. For example in the Mahayana tradition of Buddhism we find two principal techniques for cultivating compassion. These are known as the 'seven-point cause-and-effect' method and the 'exchange and equality of oneself with others.' The 'exchange-and-equality' method is the technique that you'll find in the eighth chapter of Shantideva's *Guide to the Bodhisattva's Way of Life*. But," he said, glancing at his watch and realizing that our time was running out, "I think that we will practice some exercises or meditations on compassion during the public talks later this week."

With this, he smiled warmly and rose to end our session.

THE REAL VALUE OF HUMAN LIFE

Continuing our discussion of compassion in our next conversation, I began, "Now, we've been speaking about the importance of compassion, about your belief that human affection,
warmth, friendship, and so on are conditions absolutely necessary for happiness. But I'm just wondering—suppose, let's say, a
wealthy businessman came to you and said, 'Your Holiness, you
say that warmth and compassion are crucial for one to be happy.
But by nature I'm just not a very warm or affectionate person. To
be honest I really don't feel particularly compassionate or altruistic. I tend to be a rather rational, practical, and perhaps intellectual person, and I just don't feel those kinds of emotions. Yet,
I feel good about my life, I feel happy with my life the way it is.
I have a very successful business, friends, and I provide for my
wife and children and seem to have a good relationship with
them. I just don't feel that anything is missing. Developing compassion, altruism, warmth, and so on sounds nice, but for me,
what's the point? It just seems so sentimental . . .'"

"First of all," the Dalai Lama replied, "if a person said that, I
would still have doubts whether that person was really happy
deep down. I truly believe that compassion provides the basis of
human survival, the real value of human life, and without that
there is a basic piece missing. A deep sensitivity to other's feelings is an element of love and compassion, and without that, for
example, I think there would be problems in the man's ability to
relate with his wife. If the person really had that attitude of indif-

◆

ference to other's suffering and feelings, then even if he was a billionaire, had a good education, had no problems with his family or children, and was surrounded with friends, other rich businesspeople, politicians, and leaders of nations, I think that in spite of all these things that the effect of all these positive things would just remain on the surface.

"But if he continued to maintain that he didn't feel compassion, yet he didn't feel anything missing . . . then it might be a little bit difficult to help him understand the importance of compassion . . ."

The Dalai Lama stopped speaking for a moment to reflect. His intermittent pauses, which occurred throughout our conversations, did not seem to create an awkward silence; rather, they were like a gravitational force, gathering greater weight and meaning to his words when the conversation resumed.

Finally, he continued, "Still, even if that was the case, there are several things that I could point out. First, I might suggest that he reflect on his own experience. He can see that if someone treats him with compassion and affection, then it makes him feel happy. So, on the basis of that experience, it would help him realize that other people also feel good when they are shown warmth and compassion. Therefore, recognizing this fact might make him more respectful of other people's emotional sensitivity and make him more inclined to give them compassion and warmth. At the same time he would discover that the more you give others warmth, the more warmth you receive. I don't think that it would take him very long to realize that. And as a result, this becomes the basis of mutual trust and friendship.

"Now suppose this man had all these material facilities, was

◆

successful in life, surrounded by friends, financially secure, and so on. I think it is even possible that his family and children might relate to him and experience a kind of contentment because the man is successful and they have plenty of money and a comfortable life. I think that it is conceivable that up to a certain point, even without feeling human warmth and affection, he may not experience a feeling of lacking something. But if he felt that everything was OK, that there was no real requirement for developing compassion, I would suggest that this view is due to ignorance and shortsightedness. Even if it appeared that others were relating to him quite fully, in reality what is happening is that much of the people's relationship or interaction with him is based on their perception of him as a successful, wealthy resource. They may be influenced by his wealth and power and relate to that rather than to the person himself. So in some sense, although they may not receive human warmth and affection from him, they may be contented; they may not expect more. But what happens is if his fortune declined, then that basis of the relationship would weaken. Then he would begin to see the effect of not having warmth and immediately begin to suffer.

"However, if people have compassion, naturally that's something they can count on; even if they have economic problems and their fortune declines, they still have something to share with fellow human beings. World economies are always so tenuous and we are subject to so many losses in life, but a compassionate attitude is something that we can always carry with us."

A maroon-robed attendant entered the room and silently poured tea, as the Dalai Lama continued, "Of course, in attempting to explain to someone the importance of compassion, in some cases, you might be dealing with a very hard-ened, individualistic, and selfish person, someone concerned only with her or his own interests. And it is even possible that there are people who may not have the capacity to empathize with even someone whom they love or who may be close to them. But even to such people, it is still possible to present the importance of compassion and love on the grounds that it's the best way to fulfill their self-interests. They wish to have good health, live a longer life, and have peace of mind, happiness, and joy. And if these are things that they desire, I've heard that there is even scientific evidence that these things can be enhanced by feelings of love and compassion . . . But as a doc-tor, a psychiatrist, perhaps you would know better about these scientific claims?"

"Yes," I agreed. "I think there is definitely supporting scien-tific evidence to back up the claims about the physical and emo-tional benefits of compassionate states of mind."

"So I think that educating someone about these facts and sci-entific studies could certainly encourage some people to cultivate a more compassionate state of mind . . . ," the Dalai Lama com-mented. "But I think that even aside from these scientific studies, there are other arguments that people could understand and appreciate from their own practical or direct everyday experi-ence. For example, you could point out that lack of compassion leads to a certain ruthlessness. There are many examples indicat-ing that at some level deep down, ruthless people generally suf-fer from a kind of unhappiness and discontent, people like Stalin and Hitler. Such people suffer from a kind of nagging sense of insecurity and fear. Even when they are sleeping I think that sense

◆

of fear remains . . . All that might be very difficult for some people to understand, but one thing you could say is that these people lack something that you can find in a more compassionate person—a sense of freedom, a sense of abandonment, so when you sleep you can relax and let go. Ruthless people never have that experience. Something is always gripping them; there is some kind of hold on them, and they aren't able to experience that feeling of letting go, that sense of freedom."

He paused for a moment, absently scratching his head, then continued, "Although I'm just speculating, I would guess that if you asked some of these ruthless people, 'When were you happier, during your childhood, when you were being cared for by your mother and had more of a closeness with your family, or now, when you have more power, influence and position?' I think they would say that their youth was more pleasant. I think even Stalin was loved by his mother in childhood."

"In bringing up Stalin," I observed, "I think you've hit on a perfect example of what you're saying, of the consequences of living without compassion. It's well known that the two main features that characterized his personality were his ruthlessness and his suspiciousness. He viewed ruthlessness as a virtue, in fact, and changed his name from Djugashvili to Stalin, meaning 'man of steel.' And as his life progressed, the more ruthless he became, the more suspicious he became. His suspiciousness was legendary. His fearfulness and suspiciousness of others eventually led to massive purges and campaigns against various groups of people in his country, resulting in the imprisonment and execution of millions. But he still continued to see enemies everywhere. Not long before his death he told Nikita Khrushchev, 'I trust no one, not even myself.' In the end he even turned on his most faithful staff. And clearly the more ruthless and powerful he became, the more unhappy he was. One friend said that finally the only human trait he had left was his unhappiness. And his daughter Svetlana described how he was plagued by loneliness and an emptiness inside and got to the point that he no longer believed that people were capable of being genuinely sincere or warmhearted.

"Anyway, I know it would be very difficult to understand people like Stalin and why they did the horrible things that they did. But one of the points that we're talking about is that even these extreme examples of ruthless people might look back with nostalgia on some of the more pleasant aspects of their childhood, such as the love they received from their mothers. But where does that leave the many people who didn't have pleasant childhoods or loving mothers? People who were abused and so on? Now, we are discussing the topic of compassion. In order for people to develop the capacity for compassion, don't you think that it's necessary for them to be raised by parents or caretakers who showed them warmth and affection?"

"Yes, I think that's important." He paused, deftly and automatically rotating his rosary between his fingers as he reflected. "There are some people who, right from the beginning, have suffered much and have lacked other's affection—so that later in life it seems almost as if they have no human feeling, no capacity for compassion and affection, those who are hardened and brutal...." The Dalai Lama paused again, and for several moments seemed to ponder the question earnestly. As he bent over his tea, even the contour of his shoulders suggested that he was deep in thought. He showed no inclination to continue immediately, however, and we drank our tea in silence. Finally he shrugged his shoulders, as if acknowledging that he had no solution.

"So do you think that techniques to enhance empathy and develop compassion would not be helpful to people with that sort of difficult background?"

"There are always different degrees of benefit that one might receive from practicing various methods and techniques, depending on one's particular circumstances," he explained. "It's also possible that in some cases these techniques may not be effective at all . . ."

Trying to clarify, I interrupted, "And the specific techniques to enhance compassion that you're referring to are . . . ?"

"Just what we have been talking about. First, through learning, thoroughly understanding the value of compassion—this gives you a feeling of conviction and determination. Then, employing methods to enhance empathy, such as using your imagination, your creativity, to visualize yourself in another's situation. And later this week in the public talks we'll discuss certain exercises or practices that you can undertake, such as the practice of Tong-Len, that serves to strengthen your compassion. But I think it's important to remember that these techniques, such as the practice of Tong-Len, were developed to help as many as possible, at least some portion of the human population. But it was never expected that these techniques could help 100 percent of people, the entire human population.

"But the main point really . . . if we are talking about various methods to develop compassion—the important thing is that people make a sincere effort to develop their capacity for compassion. The degree to which they will actually be able to cultivate compassion depends on so many variables, who can tell? But if they make their best efforts to be kinder, to cultivate compassion and make the world a better place, then at the end of the day they can say, 'At least I've done my best!'"

THE BENEFITS OF COMPASSION

In recent years there have been many studies that support the idea that developing compassion and altruism has a positive impact on our physical and emotional health. In one well-known experiment, for example, David McClelland, a psychologist at Harvard University, showed a group of students a film of Mother Teresa working among Calcutta's sick and poor. The students reported that the film stimulated feelings of compassion. Afterward, he analyzed the students' saliva and found an increase in immunoglobulin-A, an antibody that can help fight respiratory infections. In another study done by James House at the University of Michigan Research Center, investigators found that doing regular volunteer work, interacting with others in a warm and compassionate way, dramatically increased life expectancy, and probably overall vitality as well. Many other researchers in the new field of mind-body medicine have demonstrated similar findings, documenting that positive states of mind can improve our physical health.

In addition to the beneficial effects on one's physical health, there is evidence that compassion and caring behavior contribute to good emotional health. Studies have shown that reaching out to help others can induce a feeling of happiness, a calmer mind, and less depression. In a thirty-year study of a group of Harvard graduates, researcher George Vaillant concluded, in fact, that adopting an altruistic lifestyle is a critical component of good mental health. Another survey by Allan Luks, conducted with several thousand people who were regularly involved in volunteer activities that helped others, revealed that over 90 percent of these volunteers reported a kind of "high" associated with the activity, characterized by a feeling of warmth, more energy, and a kind of euphoria. They also had a distinct feeling of calmness and enhanced self-worth following the activity. Not only did these caring behaviors provide an interaction that was emotionally nourishing, but it was also found that this "helper's calm" was linked to relief from a variety of stress-related physical disorders as well.

While the scientific evidence clearly backs up the Dalai Lama's position on the very real and practical value of compassion, one needn't rely solely on experiments and surveys to confirm the truth of this view. We can discover the close links between caring, compassion, and personal happiness in our own lives and in the lives of those around us. Joseph, a sixty-year-old building contractor whom I first met some years ago, serves as a good illustration of this. For thirty years Joseph rode the gravy train, capitalizing on a seemingly limitless construction boom in Arizona to become a multimillionaire. In the late 1980s, however, came the biggest real estate crash in Arizona's history. Joseph was heavily leveraged and lost everything. He ended up declaring bankruptcy. His financial problems created a strain on his marriage, which finally resulted in a divorce after twenty-five

◆

years of marriage. Not surprisingly, Joseph didn't take all this very well. He started drinking heavily. Fortunately, he was able to eventually quit drinking with the help of AA. As part of his AA program he became a sponsor and helped other alcoholics stay sober. He discovered that he enjoyed his role as a sponsor, reaching out to help others, and started volunteering in other organizations as well. He put his business knowledge to use in helping the economically underprivileged. In talking about his current life, Joseph said, "I own a very small remodeling business now. It brings a modest income, but I realize that I'll never be as rich as I once was. The funny thing is, though, that I don't really want that kind of money again. I much prefer spending my time volunteering for different groups, working directly with people, helping them out the best I can. These days, I get more pure enjoyment out of one day than I did in a month when I was makin' the big money. I'm happier than I've ever been in my life!"

MEDITATION ON COMPASSION

As promised during the course of our conversations, true to his word, the Dalai Lama concluded one public talk in Arizona with a meditation on compassion. It was a simple exercise. Yet in a powerful and elegant way, he seemed to summarize and crystallize his previous discussion of compassion, turning it into a formal five-minute exercise that was direct and to the point.

"In generating compassion, you start by recognizing that you do not want suffering and that you have a right to have happiness. This can be verified or validated by your own experience. You then recognize that other people, just like yourself, also do not want to suffer and that they have a right to have happiness. So this becomes the basis of your beginning to generate compassion.

"So . . . let us meditate on compassion today. Begin by visualizing a person who is acutely suffering, someone who is in pain or is in a very unfortunate situation. For the first three minutes of the meditation, reflect on that individual's suffering in a more analytic way—think about their intense suffering and the unfortunate state of that person's existence. After thinking about that person's suffering for a few minutes, next, try to relate that to yourself, thinking, 'that individual has the same capacity for experiencing pain, joy, happiness, and suffering that I do.' Then, try to allow your natural response to arise—a natural feeling of compassion towards that person. Try to arrive at a conclusion: thinking how strongly you wish for that person to be free from that suffering. And resolve that you will help that person to be relieved from their suffering. Finally, place your mind single-pointedly on that kind of conclusion or resolution, and for the last few minutes of the meditation try to simply generate your mind in a compassionate or loving state."

With that, the Dalai Lama assumed a cross-legged meditation posture, remaining completely immobile as he practiced the meditation along with the audience. Stark silence. But there was something quite stirring about sitting among the assembly that morning. I imagine that even the most-hardened individual

◆

could not help being moved when surrounded by fifteen hundred people, every one of them holding the thought of compassion in their minds. After a few minutes, the Dalai Lama broke into a low Tibetan chant, his voice deep, melodic, gently breaking and falling in tones that soothed, comforted.

Part III

TRANSFORMING
SUFFERING

Chapter 8

FACING SUFFERING

In the time of the Buddha, a woman named Kisagotami suffered the death of her only child. Unable to accept it, she ran from person to person, seeking a medicine to restore her child to life. The Buddha was said to have such a medicine.

Kisagotami went to the Buddha, paid homage, and asked, "Can you make a medicine that will restore my child?"

"I know of such a medicine," the Buddha replied. "But in order to make it, I must have certain ingredients."

Relieved, the woman asked, "What ingredients do you require?"

"Bring me a handful of mustard seed," said the Buddha.

The woman promised to procure it for him, but as she was leaving, he added, "I require the mustard seed be taken from a household where no child, spouse, parent, or servant has died."

The woman agreed and began going from house to house in search of the mustard seed. At each house the people agreed to give her the seed, but when she asked them if anyone had died in that household, she could find no home where death had not visited—in one house a daughter, in another a servant, in others a husband or parent had died. Kisagotami was not able to find a home free from the suffering of death. Seeing she was not alone in her grief, the mother let go of her child's lifeless body and returned to the Buddha, who said with great compassion, "You thought that you alone had lost a son; the law of death is that among all living creatures there is no permanence."

Kisagotami's search taught her that no one lives free from suffering and loss. She hadn't been singled out for this terrible misfortune. This insight didn't eliminate the inevitable suffering that comes from loss, but it did reduce the suffering that came from struggling against this sad fact of life.

Although pain and suffering are universal human phenomena, that doesn't mean we have an easy time accepting them. Human beings have devised a vast repertoire of strategies for avoiding having to experience suffering. Sometimes we use external means, such as chemicals—deadening and medicating our emotional pain with drugs or alcohol. We have an array of internal mechanisms as well—psychological defenses, often unconscious, that buffer us from feeling too much emotional pain and anguish when we are confronted with problems. Sometimes these defense mechanisms can be quite primitive, such as simply refusing to recognize that a problem exists. At other times, we may vaguely recognize that we have a problem but immerse ourselves in a million distractions or entertainments to avoid thinking about it. Or we might use projection—unable to accept that we have a problem, we unconsciously project it onto others and blame them for our suffering: "Yeah, I'm miserable. But it's not *me* that has the problem; it's someone else who has the problem. If it wasn't for that damn boss constantly giving me a hard time [or "my partner ignoring me" or . . .], I'd be fine."

Suffering can only be avoided temporarily. But like a disease that's left untreated (or perhaps superficially treated with medication that just masks the symptoms but doesn't cure the underlying condition), the disease invariably festers and worsens. The high from drugs or alcohol certainly eases our pain for a while, but with continued use, the physical damage to our bodies and the social damage to our lives can cause far more suffering than the diffuse dissatisfaction or the acute emotional pain that led us to these substances in the first place. The internal psychological defenses like denial or repression may shield and protect us from feeling the pain a bit longer, but it still doesn't make the suffering disappear.

Randall lost his father to cancer a little over a year ago. He was quite close to his father, and at the time everyone was surprised by how well he was taking the death. "Of course I'm sad," he explained in a stoic tone. "But really I'm fine. I'll miss him, but life goes on. And anyway, I can't focus on missing him right now; I have to arrange the funeral and take care of his estate for my mom . . . But I'll be fine," he reassured everyone. One year later, however, shortly after the anniversary of his father's death, Randall began to spiral into a severe depression. He came to see me and explained, "I just can't understand what is causing this depression. Everything seems to be going well right now. It can't be the death of my father; he died over a year ago, and I've already come to terms with his death." With very little therapy it became clear, however, that in struggling to keep a tight reign on his emotions, in order to "be strong," he had never fully dealt with his feelings of loss and grief. These feelings continued to grow until finally manifesting as an overpowering depression that he was forced to deal with.

In Randall's case, his depression lifted rather quickly as we focused on his pain and feelings of loss, and he was able to fully confront and experience his grief. Sometimes, however, our unconscious strategies to avoid facing our problems are more deep-seated—deeply ingrained coping mechanisms that can become embedded in our personality and are hard to extract. Most of us know a friend, acquaintance, or family member, for example, who avoids problems by projecting onto others and blaming them—accusing others of having faults that, in fact, are his or her own. This certainly isn't an effective method of eliminating problems, however, and many of these individuals are condemned to a lifetime of unhappiness as long as they continue in that pattern.

The Dalai Lama detailed his approach to human suffering—an approach that ultimately includes a belief in the possibility of freedom from suffering but starts with accepting suffering as a natural fact of human existence, and courageously facing our problems head-on.

In our daily lives problems are bound to arise. The biggest problems in our lives are the ones that we inevitably have to face, like old age, illness, and death. Trying to avoid our problems or simply not thinking about them may provide temporary relief, but I think that there is a better approach. If you directly confront your suffering, you will be in a better position to appreciate the depth and nature of the problem. If you are in a battle, as long as you remain ignorant of the status and combat capability of your enemy, you will be totally unprepared and paralyzed by fear. However, if you know the fighting capability of your opponents, what sort of weapons they have and so on, then you're in a much better position when you engage in the war. In the same way, if you confront your problems rather than avoid them, you will be in a better position to deal with them."

This approach to one's problems was clearly reasonable, but pressing the issue a bit further, I asked, "Yes, but what if you directly confront a problem, and find out that there's no solution? That's pretty tough to face."

"But I think it's still better to face it," he replied with a martial spirit. "For example, you might consider things like old age and death as negative, unwanted, and simply try to forget about them. But eventually these things will come anyway. And if you've avoided thinking about these things, when the day comes that any of these events occur, it will come as a shock causing an unbearable mental uneasiness. However, if you spend some time thinking about old age, death, and these other unfortunate things, your mind will be much more stable when these things happen as you have already become acquainted with these problems and kinds of suffering and have anticipated that they will occur.

"That's why I believe it can be useful to prepare yourself ahead of time by familiarizing yourself with the kinds of suffering you might encounter. To use the battle analogy again, reflecting on suffering could be seen as a military exercise. People who never heard of war, guns, bombing, and so on might faint if they had to go into battle. But through military drills you could familiarize your mind with what might occur, so if a war erupted, it would not be so hard on you."

"Well, I can see how familiarizing ourselves with the kinds of suffering we might encounter would have some value in reducing fear and apprehension, but it still seems that sometimes certain dilemmas present no option but the possibility of suffering. How can we avoid worry in those circumstances?"

"A dilemma such as?"

I stopped to consider. "Well, let's say, for example, that a woman is pregnant and they do an amniocentesis or sonogram and find out that the child will have a significant birth defect. They discover that the child will have some extreme mental or physical handicap. So, obviously the woman is filled with anxiety because she doesn't know what to do. She can choose to do something about the situation and get an abortion, to save the baby from a life of suffering, but then she will experience a feeling of great loss and pain and perhaps she will also experience other feelings such as guilt. Or, she can choose to let nature take its course and have the baby. But then, she may be faced with a lifetime of hardship and suffering for herself and the child."

The Dalai Lama listened intently as I spoke. With a somewhat wistful tone, he replied, "Whether one approaches these problems from the Western or the Buddhist perspective, these kinds of dilemmas are very difficult, very difficult. Now your example regarding the decision to abort the fetus with a birth defect—nobody really knows what would be better in the long run. Even if a child is born with a defect, maybe in the long run it would be better for the mother or the family or the child itself. But also there's the possibility that taking into account the long-term con-

sequences, it is better to abort; maybe that could be more positive in the long run. But then who decides? It's very difficult. Even
from the Buddhist viewpoint, that sort of judgment is beyond our
rational ability." He paused, then added, "I think, though, that
their background and beliefs would play a role in how particular
individuals might respond to this kind of difficult situation . . ."

We sat in silence.

Shaking his head, he finally said, "By reflecting on the types of
suffering that we are subject to, you can mentally prepare for these
things ahead of time to some degree, by reminding yourself about
the fact that you may come across these kinds of dilemmatic situations in your life. So you can prepare yourself mentally. But you
should not forget the fact that this does not alleviate the situation. It may help you *mentally* cope with it, reduce the fear and so
on, but it does not alleviate the problem itself. For instance, if a
child with a birth defect is going to be born, no matter how
strongly you thought about it ahead of time, you still have to find
a way to handle it. So this is still difficult."

As he said this there was a note of sadness in his voice—more
than a note, perhaps a chord. But the underlying melody was not
one of hopelessness. For a full minute, the Dalai Lama stopped
speaking once again, gazing out the window as if looking out
onto the world at large, then continued, "There's really no avoiding the fact that suffering is part of life. And of course we have
a natural tendency to dislike our suffering and problems. But I
think that ordinarily people don't view the very nature of our
existence to be characterized by suffering . . ." The Dalai Lama
suddenly began to laugh, "I mean on your birthday people usually say, 'Happy Birthday!,' when actually the day of your birth

◆

was the birth of your suffering. But nobody says, 'Happy Birth-of-Sufferingday!" he joked.

"In accepting that suffering is part of your daily existence, you could begin by examining the factors that normally give rise to feelings of discontent and mental unhappiness. Generally speaking, for instance, you feel happy if you or people close to you receive praise, fame, fortune, and other pleasant things. And you feel unhappy and discontent if you don't achieve these things or if your rival is receiving them. If you look at your normal day-to-day life, however, you often find that there are so many factors and conditions that cause pain, suffering, and feelings of dissatisfaction, whereas the conditions that give rise to joy and happiness are comparatively rare. This is something that we have to undergo, whether we like it or not. And since this is the reality of our existence, our attitude towards suffering may need to be modified. *Our attitude towards suffering becomes very important because it can affect how we cope with suffering when it arises.* Now, our usual attitude consists of an intense aversion and intolerance of our pain and suffering. *However, if we can transform our attitude towards suffering, adopt an attitude that allows us greater tolerance of it, then this can do much to help counteract feelings of mental unhappiness, dissatisfaction, and discontent.*

"For me personally, the strongest and most effective practice to help tolerate suffering is to see and understand that suffering is the underlying nature of *Samsara*,* of unenlightened exis-

---

Samsara (Skt.) is a state of existence characterized by endless cycles of life, death, and rebirth. This term also refers to our ordinary state of day-to-day existence, which is characterized by suffering. All beings remain in this state, propelled by karmic imprints from past actions and negative "delusory" states of mind, until one removes all negative tendencies of mind and achieves a state of Liberation.

ence. Now when you experience some physical pain or other problem, of course at that moment there is a feeling of 'Oh! This suffering is so bad!' There's a feeling of rejection associated with the suffering, a kind of feeling of 'Oh, I shouldn't be experiencing this.' But at that moment if you can look at the situation from another angle and realize that this very body . . .," he slapped an arm in demonstration, "is the very basis of suffering, then this reduces that feeling of rejection—that feeling that somehow you don't deserve to suffer, that you are a victim. So, once you understand and accept this reality, then you experience suffering as something that is quite natural.

"So, for example, when dealing with the suffering the Tibetan people have undergone, in one way you could look at the situation and feel overwhelmed, wondering, 'How in the world has this happened?' But from another angle you could reflect on the fact that Tibet also is in the middle of Samsara," he laughed, "as is this planet and the whole galaxy." He laughed again.

"So, anyway, I think that how you perceive life as a whole plays a role in your attitude about suffering. For instance, if your basic outlook is that suffering is negative and must be avoided at all costs and in some sense is a sign of failure, this will add a distinct psychological component of anxiety and intolerance when you encounter difficult circumstances, a feeling of being overwhelmed. On the other hand, if your basic outlook accepts that suffering is a natural part of your existence, this will undoubtedly make you more tolerant towards the adversities of life. And without a certain degree of tolerance towards your suffering, your life becomes miserable; then it's like having a very bad night. That night seems eternal; it never seems to end."

"It seems to me that when you speak about the underlying nature of existence as being characterized by suffering, as basically unsatisfactory, that sounds like a pretty pessimistic view, really discouraging in fact," I noted.

The Dalai Lama quickly clarified, "When I speak of the unsatisfactory nature of existence, one needs to understand that this is in the context of the overall Buddhist path. These reflections have to be understood in their proper context, which is within the framework of the Buddhist path. Unless this view of suffering is seen in its proper context, I agree that there is a danger, or even a likelihood, of misunderstanding this type of approach as being rather pessimistic and negative. Consequently, it's important to understand the basic Buddhist stance towards the whole issue of suffering. We find that in Buddha's own public teachings, the first thing he taught was the principle of the Four Noble Truths, the first of which is the Truth of Suffering. And here, a lot of emphasis is placed on the realization of the suffering nature of one's existence.

"The point that has to be borne in mind is that the reason why reflection on suffering is so important is because there is a possibility of a way out; there is an alternative. There is a possibility of freedom from suffering. By removing the causes of suffering, it is possible to attain a state of Liberation, a state free from suffering. According to Buddhist thought, the root causes of suffering are ignorance, craving, and hatred. These are called the 'three poisons of the mind.' These terms have specific connotations when used within a Buddhist context. For example, 'ignorance' doesn't refer to a lack of information as it is used in an everyday sense but rather refers to a fundamental misperception of the true nature of the self and all phenomena. By generating insight into the true nature of reality and eliminating afflictive states of mind such as craving and hatred, one can achieve a completely purified state of mind, free from suffering. Within a Buddhist context, when one reflects on the fact that one's ordinary day-to-day existence is characterized by suffering, this serves to encourage one to engage in the practices that will eliminate the root causes of one's suffering. Otherwise, if there was no hope, or no possibility of freedom from suffering, mere reflection on suffering just becomes morbid thinking, and would be quite negative."

As he spoke, I began to sense how reflecting on our "suffering nature" could play a role in accepting life's inevitable sorrows and could even be a valuable method of putting our daily problems in proper perspective. And I began to perceive how suffering might even be seen in a wider context, as part of a greater spiritual path, particularly in view of the Buddhist paradigm, which recognizes the possibility of purifying the mind and ultimately achieving a state in which there is no more suffering. But, turning away from these grand philosophical speculations, I was curious to learn how the Dalai Lama dealt with suffering on a more personal level, how he handled the loss of a loved one, for instance.

When I first visited Dharamsala many years ago, I had gotten to know the Dalai Lama's older brother, Lobsang Samden. I became quite fond of him and was saddened to hear of his sudden death a few years back. Knowing that he and the Dalai Lama were particularly close, I said, "I imagine that the death of your brother Lobsang was very hard on you . . ."

"Yes."

"I was just wondering how you handled that."

"Of course, I was very, very sad when I learned of his death," he said quietly.

"And how did you deal with that feeling of sadness? I mean was there something in particular that helped you get over it?"

"I don't know," he said pensively. "I felt that feeling of sadness for some weeks, but that feeling gradually lifted. Still, there was a feeling of regret . . ."

"Regret?"

"Yes. I was gone at the time he died, and I think if I had been there, maybe there was something I could have done to help. So I have this feeling of regret."

A lifetime of contemplating the inevitability of human suffering may have played a role in helping the Dalai Lama accept his loss, but it did not create a cold emotionless individual with grim resignation in the face of suffering—the sadness in his voice revealed a man with deep human feeling. At the same time, his candor and frankness of manner, completely devoid of self-pity or self-recrimination, created the unmistakable impression of a man who had fully accepted his loss.

On that day, our conversation had lasted well into the late afternoon. Daggers of golden light, cutting through wooden shutters, were slowly advancing across the darkening room. I sensed a melancholy atmosphere pervading the room and knew that our discussion was coming to the end. Yet I hoped to question him in greater detail about the issue of loss, to see if he had additional advice about how to survive the death of a loved one, other than simply accepting the inevitability of human suffering.

As I was about to expand on the subject, however, he appeared somewhat distracted, and I noticed a cast of weariness around his eyes. Shortly, his secretary quietly entered the room and gave me The Look: honed by years of practice, it indicated that it was time to leave.

"Yes . . . ," the Dalai Lama said apologetically, "perhaps we should close . . . I'm a bit tired."

The next day, before I had an opportunity to return to the subject in our private conversations, the issue was raised in his public talk. An audience member, clearly in pain, asked the Dalai Lama, "Do you have any suggestions about how to handle a great personal loss, such as the loss of a child?"

With a gentle tone of compassion, he answered, "To some degree, that depends on people's personal beliefs. If people believe in rebirth, then accordingly, I think there is some way to reduce sorrow or worry. They can take consolation in the fact that their loved one will be reborn.

"For those people who do not believe in rebirth, then I think there are still some simple ways to help deal with the loss. First, they could reflect that if they worried too much, allowing themselves to be too overwhelmed by the sense of loss and sorrow, and if they carried on with that feeling of being overwhelmed, not only would it be very destructive and harmful to themselves, ruining their health, but also it would not have any benefit to the person who has passed away.

"For example, in my own case, I have lost my most respected

tutor, my mother, and also one of my brothers. When they passed away, of course, I felt very, very sad. Then I constantly kept thinking that it's no use to worry too much, and if I really loved these people, then I must fulfill their wishes with a calm mind. So I try my best to do that. So I think if you've lost someone who is very dear to you, that's the proper way to approach it. You see, the best way to keep a memory of that person, the best remembrance, is to see if you can carry on the wishes of that person.

"Initially, of course, feelings of grief and anxiety are a natural human response to a loss. But if you allow these feelings of loss and worry to persist, there's a danger; if these feelings are left unchecked, they can lead to a kind of self-absorption. A situation where the focus becomes your own self. And when that happens you become overwhelmed by the sense of loss, and you get a feeling that it's only you who is going through this. Depression sets in. But in reality, there are others who will be going through the same kind of experience. So, if you find yourself worrying too much, it may help to think of the other people who have similar or even worse tragedies. Once you realize that, then you no longer feel isolated, as if you have been single-pointedly picked out. That can offer you some kind of condolence."

Although pain and suffering are experienced by all human beings, I have often felt that those brought up in some Eastern cultures appear to have a greater acceptance and tolerance for suffering. Part of this may be due to their beliefs, but perhaps it is because suffering is more visible in poorer nations such as

India than it is in wealthier countries. Hunger, poverty, illness, and death are in plain view. When a person becomes old or sick, they aren't marginalized, shipped off to nursing homes to be cared for by health professionals—they remain in the community, to be cared for by the family. Those living in daily contact with the realities of life cannot easily deny that life is characterized by suffering, that it is a natural part of existence.

As Western society gained the ability to limit the suffering caused by harsh living conditions, it seems to have lost the ability to cope with the suffering that remains. Studies by social scientists have emphasized that most people in modern Western society tend to go through life believing that the world is basically a nice place in which to live, that life is mostly fair, and that they are good people who deserve to have good things happen to them. These beliefs can play an important role in leading a happier and healthier life. But the inevitable arising of suffering undermines these beliefs and can make it difficult to go on living happily and effectively. In this context, a relatively minor trauma can have a massive psychological impact as one loses faith in one's basic beliefs about the world as fair and benevolent. As a result, suffering is intensified.

There's no doubt that with growing technology, the general level of physical comfort has improved for many in Western society. It is at this point that a critical shift in perception takes place; as suffering becomes less visible, it is no longer seen as part of the fundamental nature of human beings—but rather as an anomaly, a sign that something has gone terribly wrong, a sign of "failure" of some system, an infringement on our guaranteed right to happiness!

This kind of thinking poses hidden dangers. If we think of suffering as something unnatural, something that we shouldn't be experiencing, then it's not much of a leap to begin to look for someone to blame for our suffering. If I'm unhappy, then I must be the "victim" of someone or something—an idea that's all to common in the West. The victimizer may be the government, the educational system, abusive parents, a "dysfunctional family," the other gender, or our uncaring mate. Or we may turn blame inward: there's something wrong with me, I'm the victim of disease, of defective genes perhaps. But the risk of continuing to focus on assigning blame and maintaining a victim stance, is the perpetuation of our suffering—with persistent feelings of anger, frustration, and resentment.

Of course, the wish to get free of suffering is the legitimate goal of every human being. It is the corollary of our wish to be happy. Thus it is entirely appropriate that we seek out the causes of our unhappiness and do whatever we can to alleviate our problems, searching for solutions on all levels—global, societal, familial, and individual. But as long as we view suffering as an unnatural state, an abnormal condition that we fear, avoid, and reject, we will never uproot the causes of suffering and begin to live a happier life.

Chapter 9

SELF-CREATED SUFFERING

O n his initial visit, the well-groomed middle-aged gentle-man, elegantly dressed in an austere black Armani suit, sat down in a polite yet reserved manner and began to relate what had brought him into the office. He spoke rather softly, in a controlled, measured voice. I ran through the list of standard questions: presenting complaint, age, background, marital status, ...

"That bitch!" he cried suddenly, his voice seething with rage. "My damn wife! EX-wife, now. She was having an affair behind my back! And after everything I did for her. That little . . . that little . . . SLUT!" His voice became louder, more angry, and more

venomous, as for the next twenty minutes he recounted grievance after grievance against his ex-wife.

Our time was coming to a close. Realizing that he was just
getting warmed up and could easily continue in this vein for
hours, I redirected him. "Well, most people have difficulty
adjusting to a recent divorce, and that is certainly something
that we can address in future sessions," I said soothingly. "By the
way, how long have you been divorced?"

"Seventeen years, last May."

In the last chapter we discussed the importance of accepting suffering as a natural fact of human existence. While some kinds of
suffering are inevitable, other kinds are self-created. We explored, for instance, how the refusal to accept suffering as a natural part of life can lead to viewing oneself as a perpetual victim
and blaming others for our problems—a surefire recipe for a
miserable life.

But we also add to our own suffering in other ways. All too
often we perpetuate our pain, keep it alive, by replaying our
hurts over and over again in our minds, magnifying our injustices in the process. We repeat our painful memories with the
unconscious wish perhaps that somehow it will change the situation—but it never does. Of course, sometimes this endless
recounting of our woes can serve a limited purpose; it can add
drama and a certain excitement to our lives or elicit attention
and sympathy from others. But this seems like a poor trade-off
for the unhappiness we continue to endure.

In speaking about how we add to our own suffering, the Dalai

Lama explained, "We can see that there are many ways in which we actively contribute to our own experience of mental unrest and suffering. Although, in general, mental and emotional afflictions themselves can come naturally, often it is our own reinforcement of those negative emotions that makes them so much worse. For instance when we have anger or hatred towards a person, there is less likelihood of its developing to a very intense degree if we leave it unattended. However, if we think about the projected injustices done to us, the ways in which we have been unfairly treated, and we keep on thinking about them over and over, then that feeds the hatred. It makes the hatred very powerful and intense. Of course, the same can apply to when we have an attachment towards a particular person; we can feed that by thinking about how beautiful he or she is, and as we keep thinking about the projected qualities that we see in the person, the attachment becomes more and more intense. But this shows how through constant familiarity and thinking, we ourselves can make our emotions more intense and powerful.

"We also often add to our pain and suffering by being overly sensitive, overreacting to minor things, and sometimes taking things too personally. We tend to take small things too seriously and blow them up out of proportion, while at the same time we often remain indifferent to the really important things, those things which have profound effects on our lives and long-term consequences and implications.

"So I think that to a large extent, whether you suffer depends on how you *respond* to a given situation. For example, say that you find out that someone is speaking badly of you behind your back. If you react to this knowledge that someone is speaking badly of you, this negativity, with a feeling of hurt or anger, then *you yourself* destroy your own peace of mind. Your pain is your own personal creation. On the other hand, if you refrain from reacting in a negative way, let the slander pass by you as if it were a silent wind passing behind your ears, you protect yourself from that feeling of hurt, that feeling of agony. So, although you may not always be able to avoid difficult situations, you can modify the extent to which you suffer by how you choose to respond to the situation."

We also often add to our pain and suffering by being overly sensitive, over-reacting to minor things, and sometimes taking things too personally . . ." With these words, the Dalai Lama recognizes the origin of many of the day-to-day aggravations that can add up to be a major source of suffering. Therapists sometimes call this process *personalizing* our pain—the tendency to narrow our psychological field of vision by interpreting or misinterpreting everything that occurs in terms of its impact on us.

One night I had dinner with a colleague at a restaurant. The service at the restaurant turned out to be very slow, and from the time we sat down, my colleague began to complain: "Look at that! That waiter is so damn slow! Where is he? I think he's purposely ignoring us!"

Although neither of us had pressing engagements, my colleague's complaints about the slow service continued to escalate throughout the meal and expanded into a litany of complaints about the food, tableware, and anything else that was not to his liking. At the end of the meal, the waiter presented us with two free desserts, explaining, "I apologize for the slow service this evening," he said sincerely, "but we're a little understaffed. One of the cooks had a death in the family and is off tonight, and one of the servers called in sick at the last minute. I hope it didn't inconvenience you . . ."

"I'm still never coming here again," my colleague muttered bitterly under his breath as the waiter walked off.

This is only a minor illustration of how we contribute to our own suffering by personalizing every annoying situation, as if it were being intentionally perpetrated on us. In this case, the net result was only a ruined meal, an hour of aggravation. But when this kind of thinking becomes a pervasive pattern of relating to the world and extends to every comment made by our family or friends, or even events in society at large, it can become a significant source of our misery.

In describing the wider implications of this kind of narrow thinking, Jacques Lusseyran once made an insightful observation. Lusseyran, blind from the age of eight, was a founder of a resistance group in World War II. Eventually, he was captured by the Germans and imprisoned in Buchenwald concentration camp. In later recounting his experiences in the camps, Lusseyran stated, " . . . Unhappiness, I saw then, comes to each of us because we think ourselves at the center of the world, because we have the miserable conviction that we alone suffer to the point of unbearable intensity. Unhappiness is always to feel oneself imprisoned in one's own skin, in one's own brain."

"BUT IT'S NOT FAIR!"

In our daily life, problems invariably arise. But problems themselves do not automatically cause suffering. If we can directly address our problem and focus our energies on finding a solution, for instance, the problem can be transformed into a challenge. If we throw into the mix, however, a feeling that our problem is "unfair," we add an additional ingredient that can become a powerful fuel in creating mental unrest and emotional suffering. And now we not only have two problems instead of one, but that feeling of "unfairness" distracts us, consumes us, and robs us of the energy needed to solve the original problem.

Raising this issue with the Dalai Lama one morning, I asked, "How can we deal with the feeling of unfairness that so often seems to torture us when problems arise?"

The Dalai Lama replied, "There may be a variety of ways that one might deal with the feeling that one's suffering is unfair. I've already spoken of the importance of accepting suffering as a natural fact of human existence. And I think that in some ways Tibetans might be in a better position to accept the reality of these difficult situations, because they will say, 'Maybe it is because of my Karma in the past.' They will attribute it to negative actions committed in either this or a previous life, and so there is a greater degree of acceptance. I have seen some families in our settlements in India, with very difficult situations—living under very poor conditions, and on top of that having children with both eyes blind or sometimes retarded. And somehow these poor ladies still manage to look after them, simply saying, 'This is due to their Karma; it is their fate.'

"In mentioning Karma, here I think that it is important to point out and understand that sometimes due to one's misunderstanding of the doctrine of Karma, there is a tendency to blame everything on Karma and try to exonerate oneself from the responsibility or from the need to take personal initiative. One could quite easily say, 'This is due to my past Karma, my negative past Karma, and what can I do? I am helpless.' This is a totally wrong understanding of Karma, because although one's experiences are a consequence of one's past deeds, that does not mean that the individual has no choice or that there is no room for initiative to change, to bring about positive change. And this is the same in all areas of life. One should not become passive and try to excuse oneself from having to take personal initiative on the grounds that everything is a result of Karma, because if one understands the concept of Karma properly, one will understand that Karma means 'action.' Karma is a very active process. And when we talk of Karma, or action, it is the very action committed by an agent, in this case, ourselves, in the past. So what type of future will come about, to a large extent, lies within our own hands in the present. It will be determined by the kind of initiatives that we take now.

"So, Karma should not be understood in terms of a passive, static kind of force but rather should be understood in terms of an active process. This indicates that there is an important role for the individual agent to play in determining the course of the Karmic process. For instance, even a simple act or a simple purpose, like fulfilling our needs for food . . . In order to achieve

◆

that simple goal, we need an action on the part of ourselves. We need to look for food, and then we need to eat it; this shows that even for the simplest act, even a simple goal is achieved through action . . ."

"Well, reducing the feeling of unfairness by accepting that it is a result of one's Karma may be effective for Buddhists," I interjected. "But what about those who don't believe in the doctrine of Karma? Many in the West for instance . . ."

"People who believe in the idea of a Creator, of God, may accept these difficult circumstances more easily by viewing them as part of God's creation or plan. They may feel that even though the situation appears to be very negative, God is all powerful and very merciful, so there may be some meaning, some significance, behind the situation that they may not be aware of. I think that kind of faith can sustain and help them during their times of suffering."

"And what about those who don't believe in either the doctrine of Karma or the idea of a Creator God?"

"For a nonbeliever . . . ," the Dalai Lama pondered for several moments before responding, " . . . perhaps a practical, scientific approach could help. I think that scientists usually consider it very important to look at a problem objectively, to study it without much emotional involvement. With this kind of approach, you can look at the problem with the attitude 'If there's a way to fight the problem, then fight, even if you have to go to court!'" He laughed. "Then, if you find that there's no way to win, you can simply forget about it.

"An objective analysis of difficult or problematic situations can be quite important, because with this approach you'll often discover that behind the scenes there may be other factors at play. For instance, if you feel that you're being treated unfairly by your boss at work, there may be other factors at play; he may be annoyed by something else, an argument with his wife that morning or something, and his behavior may have nothing to do with you personally, may not be specifically directed at you. Of course, you must still face whatever the situation may be, but at least with this approach you may not have the additional anxiety that would come along with it."

"Could this kind of 'scientific' approach, in which one objectively analyzes a situation, also possibly help one to discover ways in which oneself may be contributing to the problem? And could that help reduce the feeling of unfairness associated with the difficult situation?"

"Yes!" he responded enthusiastically. "That would definitely make a difference. In general, if we carefully examine any given situation in a very unbiased and honest way, we will realize that to a large extent we are also responsible for the unfolding of events.

"For instance, many people blamed the Gulf War on Ṣaddam Hussein. Afterwards, on various occasions I expressed, 'That's not fair!' Under such circumstances, I really feel kind of sorry for Saddam Hussein. Of course, he is a dictator, and of course, there are many other bad things about him. If you look at the situation roughly, it's easy to place all the blame on him—he's a dictator, totalitarian, and even his eyes look a little bit frightening!" he laughed. "But without his army his capacity to harm is limited, and without military equipment that powerful army cannot function. All this military equipment is not produced by itself from thin air! So, when we look at it like that, many nations are involved.

"So," the Dalai Lama continued, "often our normal tendency is to try to blame our problems on others, on external factors. Furthermore, we tend to look for one single cause, and then try to exonerate ourselves from the responsibility. It seems that whenever there are intense emotions involved, there tends to be a disparity between how things appear and how they really are. In this case if you go further and analyze the situation very carefully, you'll see that Saddam Hussein is part of the source of the problem, one of the factors, but there are other contributing conditions as well. Once you realize this, your earlier attitude that he is the *only* cause automatically falls away and the reality of the situation emerges.

"This practice involves looking at things in a holistic way— realizing that there are many events contributing to a situation. For example, our problem with the Chinese—again, there is much contribution made by ourselves. I think perhaps our generation may have contributed to the situation, but definitely our previous generations I think were very negligent, at least a few generations back. So I think we, as Tibetans, contributed to this tragic situation. It's not fair to blame everything on China. But there are so many levels. Of course, although we might be a contributing factor to a situation, that doesn't mean we are solely to blame. For example, Tibetans have never completely bowed down to Chinese oppression; there has been continued resistance. Because of this the Chinese developed a new policy— transferring large masses of Chinese to Tibet so that the Tibetan population becomes insignificant, the Tibetans displaced, and the movement for freedom cannot be effective. In this case we cannot say that the Tibetan resistance is to blame or is responsible for the Chinese policy."

"When you are looking for your own contribution to a situation, what about those situations that clearly aren't your own fault, that you have nothing to do with, even relatively insignificant everyday situations, such as when someone intentionally lies to you?" I asked.

"Of course, I may initially feel a sense of disappointment when somebody isn't truthful, but even here, if I examine the situation, I might discover that in fact their motive for hiding something from me may not be the result of a bad motive. It may be that they simply have a certain lack of confidence in me. So sometimes when I feel disappointed by these kinds of incidents, I try to look at them from another angle; I'll think that maybe the person did not want to fully confide in me because I won't be able to keep it secret. My nature usually tends to be quite straightforward, so, because of this, the person might have decided that I'm not the right person who can keep the secrets, that I may not be able to keep secrets as many people would expect. In other words, I am not worthy of the person's full trust because of my personal nature. So, looking at it in that way, I would consider the cause to be due to my own fault."

Even coming from the Dalai Lama, this rationale seemed like a bit of a stretch—finding "your own contribution" to another's dishonesty. But there was a genuine sincerity in his voice as he spoke, which suggested that in fact this was a technique he had used to practical advantage in his personal life to help deal with adversity. In applying this technique to our own lives, of course, we might not always be so successful in finding our own contribution to a problematic situation. But whether we are successful or not, even the honest *attempt* to search for our own contribution to a problem allows a certain shift of focus that helps to break through the narrow patterns of thinking that lead to the destructive feeling of unfairness that is the source of so much discontent in ourselves and in the world.

GUILT

As products of an imperfect world, all of us are imperfect. Every one of us has done some wrong. There are things we regret— things we have done or things we should have done. Acknowledging our wrongdoings with a genuine sense of remorse can serve to keep us on the right track in life and encourage us to rectify our mistakes when possible and take action to correct things in the future. But if we allow our regret to degenerate into excessive guilt, holding on to the memory of our past transgressions with continued self-blame and self-hatred, this serves no purpose other than to be a relentless source of self-punishment and self-induced suffering.

During an earlier conversation in which we had briefly discussed the death of his brother, I recalled that the Dalai Lama had spoken of some regrets related to his brother's death. Curious about how he dealt with feelings of regret, and possibly guilt feelings, I returned to the subject in a later conversa-

◆

tion, asking, "When we were talking about Lobsang's death, you mentioned some regrets. Have there been other situations in your life that you've regretted?"

"Oh, yes. Now for instance there was one older monk who lived as a hermit. He used to come to see me to receive teachings, although I think he was actually more accomplished than I and came to me as a sort of formality. Anyway, he came to me one day and asked me about doing a certain high-level esoteric practice. I remarked in a casual way that this would be a difficult practice and perhaps would be better undertaken by someone who was younger, that traditionally it was a practice that should be started in one's midteens. I later found out that the monk had killed himself in order to be reborn in a younger body to more effectively undertake the practice . . ."

Surprised by this story, I remarked, "Oh, that's terrible! That must have been hard on you when you heard . . ."

The Dalai Lama nodded sadly.

"How did you deal with that feeling of regret? How did you eventually get rid of it?"

The Dalai Lama silently considered for quite a while before replying, "I didn't get rid of it. It's still there." He stopped again, before adding, "But even though that feeling of regret is still there, it isn't associated with a feeling of heaviness or a quality of pulling me back. It would not be helpful to anyone if I let that feeling of regret weigh me down, be simply a source of discouragement and depression with no purpose, or interfere with going on with my life to the best of my ability."

At that moment, in a very visceral way, I was struck once again by the very real possibility of a human being's fully facing life's tragedies and responding emotionally, even with deep regret, but without indulging in excessive guilt or self-contempt. The possibility of a human being's wholly accepting herself or himself, complete with limitations, foibles, and lapses of judgment. The possibility of recognizing a bad situation for what it is and responding emotionally, but without overresponding. The Dalai Lama sincerely felt regret over the incident he described but carried his regret with dignity and grace. And while carrying this regret, he has not allowed it to weigh him down, choosing instead to move ahead and focus on helping others to the best of his ability.

Sometimes I wonder if the ability to live without indulging in self-destructive guilt is partly cultural. In recounting my conversation with the Dalai Lama about regret to a friend who is a Tibetan scholar, I was told that, in fact, the Tibetan language doesn't even have an equivalent for the English word "guilt," although it does have words meaning "remorse" or "repentance" or "regret," with a sense of "rectifying things in the future." Whatever the cultural component may be, however, I believe that by challenging our customary ways of thinking and by cultivating a different mental outlook based on the principles described by the Dalai Lama, any of us can learn to live without the brand of guilt that does nothing but cause ourselves needless suffering.

RESISTING CHANGE

Guilt arises when we convince ourselves that we've made an irreparable mistake. The torture of guilt is in thinking that any problem is permanent. Since there is nothing that doesn't change, however, so too pain subsides—a problem doesn't persist. This is the positive side of change. The negative side is that we resist change in nearly every arena of life. The beginning of being released from suffering is to investigate one of the primary causes: resistance to change.

In describing the ever-changing nature of life, the Dalai Lama explained, "It's extremely important to investigate the causes or origins of suffering, how it arises. One must begin that process by appreciating the impermanent, transient nature of our existence. All things, events, and phenomena are dynamic, changing every moment; nothing remains static. Meditating on one's blood circulation could serve to reinforce this idea: the blood is constantly flowing, moving; it never stands still. This momentarily changing nature of phenomena is like a built-in mechanism. And since it is the nature of all phenomena to change every moment, this indicates to us that all things lack the ability to endure, lack the ability to remain the same. And since all things are subject to change, nothing exists in a permanent condition, nothing is able to remain the same under its own independent power. Thus, all things are under the power or influence of other factors. So, at any given moment, no matter how pleasant or pleasurable your experience may be, it will not last. This becomes the basis of a category of suffering known in Buddhism as the 'suffering of change.' "

The concept of impermanence plays a central role in Buddhist thought, and the contemplation of impermanence is a key practice. Contemplation of impermanence serves two main vital functions within the Buddhist path. On a conventional level, or in an everyday sense, the Buddhist practitioner contemplates his or her own impermanence—the fact that life is tenuous and we never know when we'll die. When this reflection is combined with a belief in the rarity of human existence and the possibility of attaining a state of spiritual Liberation, of release from suffering and endless rounds of rebirth, then this contemplation serves to increase the practitioner's resolve to use her or his time to best advantage, by engaging in the spiritual practices that will bring about this Liberation. On a deeper level, the contemplation of the more subtle aspects of impermanence, the impermanent nature of all phenomena, begins the practitioner's quest to understand the true nature of reality and, through this understanding, dispel the ignorance that is the ultimate source of our suffering.

So, while the contemplation of impermanence has tremendous significance within a Buddhist context, the question arises: does the contemplation and understanding of impermanence have any practical application in the everyday lives of non-Buddhists as well? If we view the concept of "impermanence" from the standpoint of "change," then the answer is a definite yes. After all, whether one looks at life from a Buddhist perspective or a Western perspective, the fact remains that *life is change*. And to the degree that we refuse to accept this fact and resist the natural life changes, we will continue to perpetuate our own suffering.

The acceptance of change can be an important factor in reducing a large measure of our self-created suffering. So often, for instance, we cause our own suffering by refusing to relinquish the past. If we define our self-image in terms of what we used to look like or in terms of what we used to be able to do and can't do now, it is a pretty safe bet that we won't grow happier as we grow older. Sometimes, the more we try to hold on, the more grotesque and distorted life becomes.

While the acceptance of the inevitability of change, as a general principle, can help us cope with many problems, taking a more active role by specifically learning about normal life changes can prevent an even greater amount of the day-to-day anxiety that is the cause of many of our troubles.

Revealing the value of recognizing normal life changes, a new mother told me about a visit to the emergency room she had made at two o'clock in the morning.

"What seems to be the problem?" the pediatrician asked her.

"MY BABY! SOMETHING'S WRONG!" she cried frantically, "I think he's choking or something! His tongue keeps protruding; he just keeps sticking it out . . . over and over again . . . like he's trying to get something out, but there's nothing in his mouth . . ."

After a few questions and a brief examination, the doctor assured her, "There's nothing to worry about. As a baby grows, he develops an increasing awareness of his own body and what it can do. Your baby has just discovered his tongue."

Margaret, a thirty-one-year-old journalist, illustrates the critical importance of understanding and accepting change in the context of a personal relationship. She came to me complaining of mild anxiety which she attributed to difficulty adjusting to a recent divorce.

◆

"I thought that it might be a good idea to have a few sessions just to talk to someone," she explained, "to help me really put the past to rest and make the transition back to the single life. To be honest, I'm a little nervous about it . . ."

I asked her to describe the circumstances of her divorce.

"I guess I'd have to describe it as amiable. There were no big fights or anything like that. My ex and I both have good jobs, so there weren't any problems with a financial settlement. We have one boy, but he seems to have adjusted to the divorce well, and my ex and I have a joint custody agreement that is working well . . ."

"I mean, can you tell me what led to the divorce?"

"Umm . . . I suppose we just fell out of love," she sighed. "It seemed that gradually the romance was gone; we just didn't have the same intimacy that we had when we were first married. We both got busy with our jobs and our son and just seemed to drift apart. We tried some sessions of marital counseling, but they didn't do any good. We still got along, but it was like we were brother and sister. It didn't feel like love, like a real marriage. Anyway, we mutually agreed that it would be best to get a divorce; something just wasn't there anymore."

After spending two sessions delineating her problem, we decided on a course of short-term psychotherapy, focusing specifically on helping her reduce her anxiety and adjust to her recent life changes. Overall, she was an intelligent and emotionally well-adjusted person. She responded very well to a brief course of therapy and easily made the transition back to single life.

Despite obviously caring for each other, it was clear that

◆

Margaret and her husband had interpreted the change in their level of passion as a sign that the marriage should end. All too often we interpret a diminution of passion as a signal that there is a fatal problem in the relationship. And more often than not, the first whisper of change in our relationship may create a sense of panic, a feeling that something is drastically wrong. Perhaps we did not pick the right partner after all. Our mate just doesn't seem like the person we fell in love with. Disagreements come up—we may be in the mood for sex and our partner is tired, we may want to see a special movie but our partner has no interest in it or is always busy. We may discover differences that we never noticed before. So, we conclude, it must be over; after all, there's no getting around the fact that we are growing apart. Things just aren't *the same* anymore; maybe we should get a divorce.

So what do we do? Relationship experts churn out books by the dozen, cookbooks telling us exactly what to do when the passion and flame of romance grow dim. They offer a myriad of suggestions designed to help rekindle the romance—restructure your schedule to make romantic time a priority, plan romantic dinners or weekend getaways, compliment your mate, learn how to have a meaningful conversation. Sometimes these things help. Sometimes they don't.

But before pronouncing the relationship dead, one of the most beneficial things we can do when we notice a change is to simply stand back, assess the situation, and arm ourselves with as much knowledge as possible about the normal patterns of change in relationships.

As our lives play out, we develop from infancy to childhood, to adulthood, to old age. We accept these changes in individual development as a natural progression. But a relationship is also a dynamic living system, composed of two organisms interacting in a living environment. And as a living system, it is equally natural and right that the relationship go through stages. In any relationship, there are different dimensions of closeness—physical, emotional, and intellectual. Bodily contact, sharing emotions, thoughts, and exchanging ideas are all legitimate ways of connecting with those we love. It is normal for the balance to wax and wane: sometimes physical closeness decreases but emotional closeness can increase; at other times we don't feel like sharing words but just want to be held. If we are sensitive to this issue, we can rejoice in the initial bloom of passion in a relationship, but if it cools, instead of feeling worry or anger, we can open ourselves to new forms of intimacy that can be equally— or perhaps more—satisfying. We can delight in our partner as a companion, enjoy a steadier love, a deeper bond.

In his book *Intimate Behavior,* Desmond Morris describes the normal changes that occur in a human being's need for closeness. He suggests that each of us repeatedly goes through three stages: "Hold me tight," "Put me down," and "Leave me alone." The cycle first becomes apparent in the first years of life when children move from the "hold me tight" phase characteristic of infancy to the "put me down" stage when the child first begins to explore the world, crawl, walk, and achieve some independence and autonomy from the mother. This is part of normal development and growth. These phases do not just move in one direction, however; at various stages a child may experience some anxiety when the feeling of separateness becomes too great, and then the child

◆

will return to the mother for soothing and closeness. In adolescence, "leave me alone" becomes the predominant phase as the child struggles to form an individual identity. Although this may be difficult or painful for the parents, most experts recognize it as a normal and necessary phase in the transition from childhood to adulthood. Even within this phase, there is still a mixture of phases. While the adolescent is crying "Leave me alone!" to his parents at home, the "hold me tight" needs may be met by strong identification with the peer group.

In adult relationships as well, the same flux occurs. Levels of intimacy change, with periods of greater intimacy alternating with periods of greater distance. This is also part of the normal cycle of growth and development. To reach our full potential as human beings, we need to be able to balance our needs for closeness and union with times when we must turn inward, with a sense of autonomy, to grow and develop as individuals.

As we come to understand this, we will no longer react with horror or panic when we first notice ourselves "growing apart" from our partner, any more than we would panic while watching the tide go out at the seashore. Of course, sometimes a growing emotional distance can signal serious problems in a relationship (an unspoken undercurrent of anger for instance), and even breakups can occur. In those cases, measures such as therapy can be very helpful. But the main point to keep in mind is that a growing distance doesn't *automatically* spell disaster. It can also be part of a cycle that returns to redefine the relationship in a new form that can recapture or even surpass the intimacy that existed in the past.

So, the act of acceptance, of acknowledging that change is a natural part of our interactions with others, can play a vital role in our relationships. We may discover that it is at the very time when we may feel most disappointed, as if something has gone out of the relationship, that a profound transformation can occur. These transitional periods can become pivotal points when true love can begin to mature and flower. Our relationship may no longer be based on intense passion, the view of the other as the embodiment of perfection, or the feeling that we are merged with the other. But in exchange for that, we are now in a position to truly begin to know the other—to see the other as he or she is, a separate individual, with faults and weaknesses perhaps, but a human being like ourselves. It is only at this point that we can make a genuine commitment, a commitment to the growth of another human being—an act of true love.

Perhaps Margaret's marriage could have been salvaged by accepting the natural change in the relationship and forming a new relationship based on factors other than passion and romance.

Fortunately, however, the story didn't end there. Two years after my last session with Margaret, I ran into her at a shopping mall (the situation of running into an ex-patient in a social setting is one that invariably makes me, like most therapists, feel a bit awkward).

"How have you been?" I asked.

"Things couldn't be better!" she exclaimed. "Last month, my ex-husband and I remarried."

"Really?"

"Yeah, and it's going great. We continued to see each other, of course, because of the joint custody. Anyway, it was difficult at first . . . but after the divorce, somehow the pressure was off. We didn't have any expectations anymore. And we found out that we really did like each other and love each other. Things still aren't the same as when we were first married, but it doesn't seem to matter; we're really happy together. It just feels right."

Chapter 10

SHIFTING PERSPECTIVE

Once there was a disciple of a Greek philosopher who was commanded by his Master for three years to give money to everyone who insulted him. When this period of trial was over the Master said to him, "Now you can go to Athens and learn Wisdom." When the disciple was entering Athens, he met a certain wise man who sat at the gate insulting everybody who came and went. He also insulted the disciple, who burst out laughing. "Why do you laugh when I insult you?" said the wise man. "Because," said the disciple, "for three years I have been paying for this kind of thing and now you give it to me for nothing." "Enter the city," said the wise man, "it is all yours . . ."

The fourth-century Desert Fathers, an assortment of eccentric characters who retired to the deserts around Scete for a life of sacrifice and prayer, taught this story to illustrate the value of suffering and hardship. It wasn't hardship alone, however, that opened the "city of wisdom" to the disciple. The prime factor that allowed him to deal so effectively with a difficult situation was his capacity to *shift perspective*, to view his situation from a different vantage point.

The ability to shift perspective can be one of the most powerful and effective tools we have to help us cope with life's daily problems. The Dalai Lama explained:

"The ability to look at events from different perspectives can be very helpful. Then, practicing this, one can use certain experiences, certain tragedies to develop a calmness of mind. One must realize that every phenomena, every event, has different aspects. Everything is of a relative nature. For example, in my own case, I lost my country. From that viewpoint, it is very tragic—and there are even worse things. There's a lot of destruction happening in our country. That's a very negative thing. But if I look at the same event from another angle, I realize that as a refugee, I have another perspective. As a refugee there is no need for formalities, ceremony, protocol. If everything were status quo, if things were okay, then on a lot of occasions you merely go through the motions; you pretend. But when you are passing through desperate situations, there's no time to pretend. So from that angle, this tragic experience has been very useful to me. Also, being a refugee creates a lot of new opportunities for meeting with many people. People from different religious traditions, from different walks of life, those who I may not have met had I remained in my country. So in that sense it's been very, very useful.

"It seems that often when problems arise, our outlook becomes narrow. All of our attention may be focused on worrying about the problem, and we may have a sense that we're the only one that is going through such difficulties. This can lead to a kind of self-absorption that can make the problem seem very intense. When this happens, I think that seeing things from a wider perspective can definitely help—realizing, for instance, that there are many other people who have gone through similar experiences, and even worse experiences. This practice of shifting perspective can even be helpful in certain illnesses or when in pain. At the time the pain arises it is of course often very difficult, at that moment, to do formal meditation practices to calm the mind. But if you can make comparisons, view your situation from a different perspective, somehow something happens. If you only look at that one event, then it appears bigger and bigger. If you focus too closely, too intensely, on a problem when it occurs, it appears uncontrollable. But if you compare that event with some other greater event, look at the same problem from a distance, then it appears smaller and less overwhelming."

Shortly before one session with the Dalai Lama, I happened to run into an administrator of a facility where I used to work. During my tenure at his facility we had a number of run-ins because I believed that he was compromising patient care in favor of financial considerations. I hadn't seen him in quite a while, but as soon as I spotted him, all of our arguments came flooding back and I could feel the anger and hatred welling up inside me. By the time I was ushered into the Dalai Lama's hotel suite for our session later that day, I was considerably calmer, but still feeling a bit unsettled.

"Let's say that someone makes you angry," I began. "Your natural response to being hurt, your immediate response, is to get angry. But in a lot of cases, it's not just a matter of getting angry at the time you're being hurt. You might think about the event later, even much later, and every time you think about it you become angry all over again. How would you suggest dealing with that kind of situation?"

The Dalai Lama nodded thoughtfully, and looked at me. I wondered if he sensed that I wasn't bringing up the topic for purely academic reasons.

"If you look from a different angle," he said, "then surely the person who caused this anger in you will have a lot of other positive aspects, positive qualities. If you look carefully, you will also find that the act which has made you angry has also given you certain opportunities, something which otherwise would not have been possible, even from your point of view. So with effort you'll be able to see many different angles to a single event. This will help."

"But what about if you look for the positive angles of a person or event and can't find any?"

"Here, I think, we would be dealing with a situation where you might need to make some effort. Spend some time seriously searching for a different perspective on the situation. Not just in a superficial way. But in a very pointed and direct way. You need to use all your powers of reasoning and look at the situation as objectively as possible. For instance, you might reflect on the fact that when you are really angry at someone you tend to perceive them as having 100 percent negative qualities. Just as when you are strongly attracted to someone the tendency is to see them as having 100 percent positive qualities. But this perception does not correspond with reality. If your friend, who you view as so wonderful, were to purposely harm you in some way, suddenly you would become acutely aware that they aren't composed of 100 percent good qualities. Similarly, if your enemy, the one you hate, were to sincerely beg your forgiveness and continue to show you kindness, it's unlikely that you would continue to perceive them as 100 percent bad. So, even though when you are angry at someone you might feel that the person has no positive qualities, the reality is that nobody is 100 percent bad. They must have some good qualities if you search hard enough. So, the tendency to see someone as completely negative is due to your own perception based on your own mental projection, rather than the true nature of that individual.

"In the same way, a situation that you initially perceive as 100 percent negative may have some positive aspects to it. But I think that even if you have discovered a positive angle to a bad situation, that alone is often not enough. You still need to reinforce that idea. So you may need to remind yourself of that positive angle many times, until gradually your feeling changes. *Generally speaking, once you're already in a difficult situation, it isn't possible to change your attitude simply by adopting a particular thought once or twice. Rather it's through a process of learning, training, and getting used to new viewpoints that enables you to deal with the difficulty.*"

The Dalai Lama reflected for a moment, and, adhering to his usual pragmatic stance, he added, "If, however, in spite of your efforts, you do not find any such positive angles or perspectives to a person's act, then for the time being the best course of action may be to simply try to forget about it."

I

Inspired by the Dalai Lama's words, later that evening I tried to discover some "positive angles" to the administrator, ways in which he was not "100 percent bad." It wasn't hard. I knew him to be a loving father, for instance, trying to raise his children the best he could. And I had to admit that my run-ins with him had ultimately benefited me—they had been instrumental in my decision to quit working at that facility, which ultimately led to more satisfying work. While these reflections didn't immediately result in an overwhelming liking for this man, they unquestionably took the bite out of my feelings of hatred with surprisingly little effort. Soon, the Dalai Lama would offer an even more profound lesson: how to completely transform one's attitude toward one's enemies and learn to cherish them.

A NEW PERSPECTIVE ON THE ENEMY

The Dalai Lama's primary method of transforming our attitude about our enemies involves a systematic and rational analysis of our customary response to those who harm us. He explained:

"Let's begin by examining our characteristic attitude toward our rivals. Generally speaking, of course, we do not wish good things for our enemies. But even if your enemy is made unhappy through your actions, what is there for you to be so joyful about? If you think about it carefully, how can there be anything more wretched than that? Carrying around the burden of such feelings of hostility and ill will. And do you really want to be that mean?

"If we take revenge upon one's enemy, then it creates a kind of vicious cycle. If you retaliate, the other person is not going to accept that—he or she is going to retaliate against you, and then you will do the same, so it will go on. And especially when this happens at the community level, it can go on from generation to generation. The result is that both sides suffer. Then, the whole purpose of life becomes spoiled. You can see this in the refugee camps, where hatred is cultivated towards another group. This happens from childhood on. It is very sad. So, anger or hatred is like a fisherman's hook. It's very important for us to ensure that we are not caught by this hook.

"Now, some people consider that strong hatred is good for national interest. I think this is very negative. It is very short-sighted. Counteracting this way of thinking is the basis of the spirit of nonviolence and understanding."

Having challenged our characteristic attitude toward one's enemy, the Dalai Lama went on to offer an alternative way of viewing one's enemy, a new perspective that could have a revolutionary impact on one's life. He explained:

"In Buddhism in general, a lot of attention is paid to our attitudes towards our rivals or enemies. This is because hatred can be the greatest stumbling block to the development of compassion and happiness. If you can learn to develop patience and tolerance towards your enemies, then everything else becomes much easier—your compassion towards all others begins to flow naturally.

"So, for a spiritual practitioner, one's enemies play a crucial role. As I see it, compassion is the essence of a spiritual life. And in order for you to become fully successful in practicing love and compassion, the practice of patience and tolerance is indispensable. There is no fortitude similar to patience, just as there is no affliction worse than hatred. Therefore, one must exert one's best efforts not to harbor hatred towards the enemy, but rather use the encounter as an opportunity to enhance one's practice of patience and tolerance.

"*In fact, the enemy is the necessary condition for practicing patience.* Without an enemy's action, there is no possibility for patience or tolerance to arise. Our friends do not ordinarily test us and provide the opportunity to cultivate patience; only our enemies do this. So, from this standpoint we can consider our enemy as a great teacher, and revere them for giving us this precious opportunity to practice patience.

"Now there are many, many people in the world, but relatively few with whom we interact, and even fewer who cause us problems. So when you come across such a chance for practicing patience and tolerance, you should treat it with gratitude. It is rare. Just as having unexpectedly found a treasure in your own house, you should be happy and grateful towards your enemy for providing that precious opportunity. Because if you are ever to be successful in your practice of patience and tolerance, which are critical factors in counteracting negative emotions, it is due to the combination of your own efforts and also the opportunity provided by your enemy.

"Of course, one might still feel, 'Why should I venerate my enemy, or acknowledge his or her contribution, because the enemy had no intention to give me this precious opportunity for practicing patience, no intention of helping me? And not only do they have no wish or intention to help me, but they have a deliberate malicious intention to harm me! Therefore, it's appropriate to hate them—they are definitely not worthy of respect.' Actually, it is in fact the presence of this hateful state of mind in

◆

the enemy, the intention to hurt us, that makes the enemy's action unique. Otherwise, if it is just the actual act of hurting us, then we would hate doctors and consider them as enemies because sometimes they adopt methods that can be painful, such as surgery. But still, we do not consider these acts as harmful or the acts of an enemy because the intention on the part of the doctor was to help us. So, therefore, it is exactly this willful intention to harm us that makes the enemy unique and gives us this precious opportunity to practice patience."

The Dalai Lama's suggestion to venerate one's enemies because of the opportunities for growth they provide might be a bit hard to swallow at first. But the situation is analogous to a person seeking to tone and strengthen one's body through weight training. Of course, the activity of lifting is uncomfortable at first— the weights are heavy. One strains, sweats, struggles. Yet it is the very act of struggling against the resistance that ultimately results in our strength. One appreciates good weight equipment not for any immediate pleasure it provides, but for the ultimate benefit one receives.

Perhaps even the Dalai Lama's claims about the "rarity" and "preciousness" of The Enemy are more than just fanciful rationalizations. As I listen to my patients describe their difficulties with others, this becomes quite clear—when it comes down to it, most people don't have legions of enemies and antagonists they're struggling with, at least on a personal level. Usually the conflict is just confined to a few people. A boss perhaps, or a coworker, an ex-spouse, a sibling. From that standpoint, The

Enemy is truly "rare"—our supply is limited. And it's the struggle, the process of resolving the conflict with The Enemy— through learning, examining, finding alternative ways of dealing with them—that ultimately results in true growth, insight, and a successful psychotherapeutic outcome.

Imagine what it would be like if we went through life never encountering an enemy or any other obstacles for that matter, if from the cradle to the grave everyone we met pampered us, held us, hand-fed us (soft bland food, easy to digest), amused us with funny faces and the occasional "goo-goo" noise. If from infancy we were carried around in a basket (later on, perhaps on a litter), never encountering any challenge, never tested—in short, if everyone continued to treat us like a baby. That might sound good at first. For the first few months of life it might be appropriate. But if it persisted it could only result in one becoming a sort of gelatinous mass, a monstrosity really—with the mental and emotional development of veal. It's the very struggle of life that makes us who we are. And it is our enemies that test us, provide us with the resistance necessary for growth.

IS THIS ATTITUDE PRACTICAL?

The practice of approaching our problems rationally and learning to view our troubles or our enemies from alternative perspectives certainly seemed like a worthwhile pursuit, but I wondered to what degree this could really bring about a fundamental transformation of attitude. I remembered once reading in an interview that one of the Dalai Lama's daily spiritual practices was the recitation of a prayer, *The Eight Verses on the Training of the Mind*, written in the eleventh century by the Tibetan saint, Langri Thangpa. It reads, in part:

> *Whenever I associate with someone, may I think myself the lowest among all and hold the other supreme in the depth of my heart!* . . .
> *When I see beings of wicked nature, pressed by violent sin and affliction, may I hold these rare ones dear as if I had found a precious treasure!* . . .
> *When others, out of envy, treat me badly with abuse, slander and the like, may I suffer the defeat and offer the victory to others!* . . .
> *When the one, whom I have benefited with great hope, hurts me very badly, may I behold him as my supreme Guru!*
> *In short may I, directly and indirectly, offer benefit and happiness to all beings; may I secretly take upon myself the harm and suffering of all beings!* . . .

After I read about this, I asked the Dalai Lama, "I know that you've contemplated this prayer a great deal, but do you really think it is applicable these days? I mean, it was written by a monk living in a monastery—a setting where the worst thing that might happen is someone gossiping about you or telling lies about you or perhaps the occasional punch or slap. In that case it might be easy to 'offer the victory' to them—but in today's society the 'hurt' or bad treatment one receives from others might include rape, torture, murder, etc. From that standpoint, the attitude in the prayer really doesn't seem applicable." I felt a bit smug, having made an observation that I thought was rather apt, the ol' *bon mot*.

The Dalai Lama was silent for several moments, his brow furrowed deep in thought, then said, "There may be something in what you are saying." He then went on to discuss instances where there may need to be some modification to that attitude, where one may need to take strong countermeasures to other's aggression to prevent harm to oneself or others.

Later that evening I thought over our conversation. Two points vividly emerged. First, I was struck by his extraordinary readiness to take a fresh look at his own beliefs and practices—in this case, demonstrating a willingness to reevaluate a cherished prayer that had no doubt fused with his very being through years of repetition. The second point was less inspiring. I was overcome with a sense of my own arrogance! It occurred to me that I had suggested to him that the prayer might not be appropriate because it wasn't in keeping with the harsh realities of today's world. But it wasn't until later that I reflected on who I had been speaking to—a man who had lost an entire country as a result of one of the most brutal invasions in history. A man who has lived in exile for almost four decades while an entire nation placed their hopes and dreams of freedom on him. A man with a deep sense of personal responsibility, who has listened with compassion to a continuous stream of refugees pouring out their stories of the murder, rape, torture, and degradation of the Tibetan people by the Chinese. More than once I've seen the look of infinite caring and sadness on his face as he listened to these accounts, often told by people who crossed the Himalayas on foot (a two-year journey) just to catch a glimpse of him.

◆

And these stories aren't of physical violence only. Often they involved the attempt to destroy the spirit of the Tibetan people. A Tibetan refugee once told me about the Chinese "school" he was required to attend as a youngster growing up in Tibet. The mornings were devoted to indoctrination and study of Chairman Mao's "little red book." The afternoons were devoted to reporting on various homework assignments. The "homework" was generally devised to eradicate the deeply ingrained spirit of Buddhism among the Tibetan people. For example, knowing about the Buddhist prohibition against killing and the belief that every living creature is equally a precious "sentient being," one schoolteacher assigned his students the task of killing something and bringing it to school the following day. The students were graded. Each dead animal was given a certain point value—a fly was worth one point, a worm—two, a mouse— five, a cat—ten, and so on. (When I recounted this story to a friend recently, he shook his head with a look of disgust, and mused, "I wonder how many points the student would get for killin' the damn teacher?")

Through his spiritual practices, such as recitation of *The Eight Verses on the Training of the Mind*, the Dalai Lama has been able to come to terms with the reality of this situation yet continue to campaign actively for freedom and human rights in Tibet for forty years. At the same time he has maintained an attitude of humility and compassion toward the Chinese, which has inspired millions worldwide. And here was I, suggesting that this prayer might not be relevant to the "realities" of today's world. I still flush with embarrassment whenever I think of that conversation.

◆

DISCOVERING NEW PERSPECTIVES

In trying to apply the Dalai Lama's method of shifting perspective on "the enemy," I happened to stumble upon another technique one afternoon. During the course of preparing for this book I attended some teachings by the Dalai Lama on the East Coast. On my return home I took a nonstop flight back to Phoenix. As usual, I had booked an aisle seat. Despite having just attended spiritual teachings, I was in a rather cranky mood as I boarded the packed plane. Then I discovered I had been mistakenly assigned a center seat—sandwiched between a man of generous proportions who had the annoying habit of draping his thick forearm over *my* side of the armrest and a middle-aged woman whom I took an immediate dislike to because, I decided, she had usurped *my* aisle seat. There was something about this woman that really bothered me—her voice a bit too shrill, her manner a bit too imperial, I'm not sure. Right after takeoff she began talking continuously to the man sitting directly in front of her. The man turned out to be her husband, and I "gallantly" offered to exchange seats with him. But they wouldn't have it— they both wanted aisle seats. I grew more annoyed. The prospect of five solid hours seated next to this woman seemed unbearable.

Realizing that I was reacting so strongly to a woman whom I didn't even know, I decided that it must be "transference"—she must subconsciously remind me of someone from my childhood—the ol' unresolved-feelings-of-hate-toward-my-mother or something. I racked my brain but couldn't come up with a likely candidate—she just didn't remind me of anyone from my past.

It then occurred to me that this was the perfect opportunity to practice developing patience. So, I started in on the technique of visualizing my enemy in my aisle seat as a cherished bene-factor, placed next to me to teach me patience and tolerance. I figured this should be a snap—after all, as "enemies" go you couldn't get any milder than this—I had just met this woman, and she hadn't actually done anything to harm me. After about twenty minutes, I gave it up—she still bugged me! I resigned myself to remaining irritable for the rest of the flight. Sulking, I glared at one of her hands that was furtively encroaching on my armrest. I hated everything about this woman. I was staring absently at her thumbnail when it occurred to me: Do I hate that thumbnail? Not really. It was just an ordinary thumbnail. Unremarkable. Next, I glanced at her eye and asked myself: Do I really hate that eye? Yes, I did. (Of course, for no good rea-son—which is the purest form of hate). I focused in closer. Do I hate that pupil? No. Do I hate that cornea, that iris, or that sclera? No. So, do I really hate that eye? I had to admit that I didn't. I felt that I was on to something. I moved on to a knuckle, a finger, a jaw, an elbow. With some surprise I realized that there were parts of this woman that I didn't hate. Focusing on details, on particulars, instead of overgeneralizations, allowed a subtle internal change, a softening. This shift of perspective tore an opening in my prejudice, just wide enough to look at her as sim-ply another human being. As I was feeling this, she suddenly turned to me and started a conversation. I don't remember what we talked about—it was small talk mostly—but by the end of the flight my anger and annoyance had been diffused. Granted, she wasn't my New Best Friend but also she was no longer The Evil Usurper of My Aisle Seat—just another human being, like me, moving through life as best she could.

A SUPPLE MIND

The ability to shift perspective, the capacity to view one's problems "from different angles," is nurtured by *a supple quality of mind*. The ultimate benefit of a supple mind is that it allows us to embrace all of life—to be fully alive and human. Following a long day of public talks in Tucson one afternoon, the Dalai Lama walked back to his hotel suite. As he slowly walked back to his room, a bank of magenta rain clouds spanned the sky, absorbing the late afternoon light and sending the Catalina Mountains into deep relief, the entire landscape a vast palette of purple hues. The effect was spectacular. The warm air, laden with the fragrance of desert plants, of sage, a dampness, a restless breeze, holding the promise of an unbridled Sonoran storm. The Dalai Lama stopped. For several moments he quietly surveyed the horizon, taking in the entire panorama, finally commenting on the beauty of the setting. He walked on, but after a few steps he paused again, bending down to examine a tiny lavender bud on a small plant. He touched it gently, noting its delicate form, and wondered aloud about the name of the plant. I was struck by the facility with which his mind functioned. His awareness seemed to move so easily from taking in the complete landscape to focusing on a single bud, a simultaneous appreciation of the totality of the environment as well as the smallest detail. A capacity to encompass all facets and the full spectrum of life.

Every one of us can develop this same suppleness of mind. It comes about, at least in part, directly through our efforts to stretch our perspective and deliberately try on new viewpoints. The end result is a simultaneous awareness of the big picture as well as our individual circumstances. This dual outlook, a concurrent view of the "Big World" and our own "Little World," can act as a kind of triage, helping us separate what is important in life from what isn't.

In my own case, it took a bit of gentle prodding by the Dalai Lama, during the course of our conversations, before I began to break out of my own limited perspective. By nature and training, I've always tended to address problems from the standpoint of individual dynamics—psychological processes occurring purely within the domain of the mind. Sociological or political perspectives have never held much interest for me. In one discussion with the Dalai Lama I started questioning him about the importance of achieving a wider perspective. Having had several cups of coffee earlier, my conversation started to become quite animated and I began to speak about the ability to shift perspective as an internal process, a solitary pursuit, based solely on an individual's conscious decision to adopt a different view.

In the midst of my spirited discourse, the Dalai Lama finally interrupted to remind me, "When you speak of adopting a wider perspective this includes working cooperatively with other people. When you have crises which are global by nature for instance, such as the environment or problems of modern economic structure, this calls for a coordinated and concerted effort among many people, with a sense of responsibility and commitment. This is more encompassing than an individual or personal issue."

I was annoyed that he was dragging in the subject of *the world* while I was trying to concentrate on the subject of *the individual* (and this attitude, I'm embarrassed to admit, on the very topic of widening one's viewpoint!).

"But this week," I insisted, "in our conversations and in your public talks, you've spoken a lot about the importance of effecting personal change from within, through internal transformation. For instance, you've spoken about the importance of developing compassion, a warm heart, of overcoming anger and hatred, cultivating patience and tolerance . . ."

"Yes. Of course, change must come from within the individual. But when you are seeking solutions to global problems, you need to be able to approach these problems from the standpoint of the individual as well as from the level of society at large. So, when you're talking about being flexible, about having a wider perspective and so on, this requires the ability to address problems from various levels: the individual level, the community level, and the global level.

"Now, for instance, at the talk at the university the other evening, I spoke about the need to reduce anger and hatred through the cultivation of patience and tolerance. Minimizing hatred is like internal disarmament. But, as I also mentioned in that talk, that internal disarmament must go with external disarmament. That I think is very, very important. Fortunately, after the Soviet empire collapsed, at least for the time being, there is no more threat of nuclear holocaust. So, I think this is a very good time, a very good start—we should not miss this opportunity! Now I think we must strengthen the genuine force of peace. Real peace—not just mere absence of violence or absence of war. Mere absence of war can be produced by weapons—like the nuclear deterrent. But a mere absence of war is not genuine, lasting world peace. Peace must develop on mutual trust. And since weapons are the greatest obstacle for development of mutual trust, I think the time has now come to figure out how to get rid of these weapons. That is very important. Of course, we cannot achieve this overnight. I think the realistic way is step by step. But anyway, I think we must make our ultimate goal very clear: The whole world should be demilitarized. So, on one level we should be working toward developing inner peace, but at the same time it's very important to work towards external disarmament and peace as well, making a small contribution in whatever way we can. That's our responsibility."

THE IMPORTANCE OF FLEXIBLE THINKING

There is a reciprocal relationship between a supple mind and the ability to shift perspective: A supple, flexible mind helps us address our problems from a variety of perspectives, and, conversely, deliberately trying to objectively examine our problems from a variety of perspectives can be seen as a kind of flexibility training for the mind. In today's world, the attempt to develop a flexible mode of thinking isn't simply a self-indulgent exercise for idle intellectuals—it can be a matter of survival. Even on an evolutionary scale, the species that have been most flexible, most adaptable to environmental changes, have survived and thrived. Life today is characterized by sudden, unexpected, and sometimes violent change. A supple mind can help us reconcile the external changes going on all around us. It can also help us integrate all of our internal conflicts, inconsistencies, and ambivalence. Without cultivating a pliant mind, our outlook becomes brittle and our relationship to the world becomes characterized by fear. But by adopting a flexible, malleable approach to life, we can maintain our composure even in the most restless and turbulent conditions. It is through our efforts to achieve a flexible mind that we can nurture the resiliency of the human spirit.

As I got to know the Dalai Lama, I became amazed at the extent of his flexibility, his capacity to entertain a variety of viewpoints. One would expect that his unique role as probably the world's most recognized Buddhist might put him in the position of being a sort of Defender of The Faith.

With this in mind, I asked him, "Do you ever find yourself being too rigid in your viewpoint, too narrow in your thinking?"

"Hmm . . ." he pondered for a moment before replying decisively. "No, I don't think so. In fact, it's just the opposite. Sometimes I'm so flexible that I'm accused of having no consistent policy." He broke into a robust laugh. "Someone will come to me and present a certain idea, and I'll see the reason in what they're saying and agree, telling them, 'Oh, that's great!' . . . But then the next person comes along with the opposite viewpoint, and I'll see the reason in what they are saying as well and agree with them also. Sometimes I'm criticized for this and have to be reminded, 'We're committed to this course of action, so for the time being let's just keep to this side.' "

From this statement alone one might get the impression that the Dalai Lama is indecisive, with no guiding principles. In fact, that couldn't be further from the truth. The Dalai Lama clearly has a set of basic beliefs that act as a substrate for all his actions: A belief in the underlying goodness of all human beings. A belief in the value of compassion. A policy of kindness. A sense of his commonality with all living creatures.

In speaking of the importance of being flexible, malleable, and adaptable, I don't mean to suggest that we become like chameleons—soaking up any new belief system that we happen to be around at the time, changing our identity, passively absorbing every idea that we're exposed to. Higher stages of growth and development depend on an underlying set of values that can guide us. A value system that can provide continuity and coherence to our lives, by which we can measure our experiences. A value system that can help us decide which goals are truly worthwhile and which pursuits are meaningless.

The question is, how can we consistently and steadfastly maintain this set of underlying values and yet remain flexible? The Dalai Lama has seemed to achieve this by first reducing his belief system to a few fundamental facts: 1) I am a human being. 2) I want to be happy and I don't want to suffer. 3) Other human beings, like myself, also want to be happy and don't want to suffer. Emphasizing the common ground he shares with others, rather than the differences, results in a feeling of connection with all human beings and leads to his basic belief in the value of compassion and altruism. Using the same approach, it can be tremendously rewarding simply to take some time to reflect on our own value system and reduce it to its fundamental principles. It is the ability to reduce our value system to its most basic elements, and live from that vantage point, that allows us the greatest freedom and flexibility to deal with the vast array of problems that confront us on a daily basis.

FINDING BALANCE

Developing a flexible approach to living is not only instrumental in helping us cope with everyday problems—it also becomes the cornerstone for a key element of a happy life: *balance.*

Settling comfortably into his chair one morning, the Dalai Lama explained the value of leading a balanced life.

"A balanced and skillful approach to life, taking care to avoid extremes, becomes a very important factor in conducting one's everyday existence. It is important in all aspects of life. For instance, in planting a sapling of a plant or a tree, at its very early stage you have to be very skillful and gentle. Too much moisture will destroy it, too much sunlight will destroy it. Too little will also destroy it. So what you need is a very balanced environment where the sapling can have a healthy growth. Or, for a person's physical health, too much or too little of any one thing can have destructive effects. For example, too much protein I think is bad, and too little is bad.

"This gentle and skillful approach, taking care to avoid extremes, applies to healthy mental and emotional growth as well. For instance, if we find ourselves becoming arrogant, being puffed up by self-importance based on one's supposed or actual achievements or qualities, then the antidote is to think more about one's own problems and suffering, contemplating the unsatisfactory aspects of existence. This will assist you in bringing down the level of your heightened state of mind, bringing you more down to earth. And on the contrary, if you find that reflecting on the unsatisfactory nature of existence, suffering and pain and so forth, makes you feel quite overwhelmed by the whole thing, then, again, there's a danger of going to the other extreme. In that case you might become totally discouraged, helpless, and depressed, thinking that 'Oh, I can't do anything, I'm worthless.' So under such circumstances, it's important to be able to uplift your mind by reflecting on your achievements, the progress that you have made so far, and your other positive qualities so that you can uplift your mind and get out of that discouraged or demoralized state of mind. So what is required here is a kind of very balanced and skillful approach.

"Not only is this approach helpful for one's physical and emotional health, but it applies to one's spiritual growth as well. Now, for instance, the Buddhist tradition includes many different techniques and practices. But it is very important to be very skillful in one's application of the various techniques, and not to be too extreme. One needs a balanced and skillful approach here too. When undertaking Buddhist practice it is important to have a coordinated approach, combining studying and learning with the practices of contemplation and meditation. This is important so that there won't be any imbalances between academic or intellectual learning and practical implementation. Otherwise, there is a danger that too much intellectualization will kill the more contemplative practices. But then, too much emphasis on practical implementation without study will kill the understanding. So there has got to be a balance. . . ."

After a moment's reflection, he added, "So, in other words, the practice of *Dharma*, real spiritual practice, is in some sense like a voltage stabilizer. The function of the stabilizer is to prevent irregular power surges and instead give you a stable and constant source of power."

"You stress the importance of avoiding extremes," I inserted, "but isn't going to extremes what provides the excitement and zest in life? By avoiding all extremes in life, always choosing the 'middle way,' doesn't that just lead to a bland, colorless existence?"

Shaking his head no, he answered, "I think you need to understand the source or basis of extreme behavior. Take for example the pursuit of material goods—shelter, furniture, clothing, and so on. On one hand, poverty can be seen as a sort of extreme and we have every right to strive to overcome this and assure our physical comfort. On the other hand, too much luxury, pursuing excessive wealth is another extreme. Our ultimate aim in seeking more wealth is a sense of satisfaction, of happiness. But the very basis of seeking *more* is a feeling of not having enough, a feeling of discontentment. That feeling of discontentment, of wanting more and more and more, doesn't arise from the inherent desirability of the objects we are seeking but rather from our own mental state.

"So I think that our tendency to go to extremes is often fueled by an underlying feeling of discontentment. And of course there may be other factors which lead to extremes. But I think it is important to recognize that while going to extremes may seem appealing or 'exciting' on the surface, it can in fact be harmful. There are many examples of the dangers of going to extremes, of extreme behavior. I think that by examining these situations you'll be able to see that the consequence of going to extremes is that you, yourself, will eventually suffer. For example, on a planetary scale if we engage in excessive fishing, without proper regard for long-term consequences, without a sense of responsibility, then it results in depletion of the fish population. . . Or sexual behavior. Of course there is the biological sexual drive for reproduction and so on, and the satisfaction one gets from sexual activity. But if sexual behavior becomes extreme, without proper responsibility, it leads to so many problems, abuses . . . like sexual abuse and incest."

"You mentioned that in addition to a feeling of discontentment, there may be other factors that lead to extremes. . . ."

"Yes, certainly." He nodded.

"Can you give an example?"

"I think narrow-mindedness could be another factor that leads to extremes."

"Narrow-mindedness in the sense of. . .?"

"The example of excessive fishing leading to depletion of the fish population would be an instance of narrow thinking, in the sense that one is looking *only* at the short term, and ignoring the wider picture. Here, one could use education and knowledge to widen one's perspective and become less narrow in one's viewpoint."

The Dalai Lama picked up his rosary from a side table, rubbing it between his hands as he silently mulled over the issue under discussion. Glancing at his rosary, he suddenly continued, "I think in many ways narrow-minded attitudes lead to extreme thinking. And this creates problems. For instance, Tibet was a Buddhist nation for many centuries. Naturally that resulted in Tibetans feeling that Buddhism was the best religion, and a tendency to feel that it would be a good thing if *all* of humanity became Buddhist. The idea that *everyone* should be Buddhist is quite extreme. And that kind of extreme thinking just causes problems. But now that we've left Tibet, we've had a chance to come into contact with other religious traditions and learn about them. This has resulted in coming closer to reality—realizing that among humanity there are so many different mental dispositions. Even if we tried to make the whole world Buddhist it would be impractical. Through closer contact with other traditions you realize the positive things about them. Now, when confronted with another religion, initially a positive feeling, a comfortable feeling, will arise. We'll feel if that person finds a different tradition more suitable, more effective, then that's good! Then it's like going to a restaurant—we can all sit down at one table and order different dishes according to one's own taste. We might eat different dishes, but nobody argues about it!

"So, I think that by deliberately broadening our outlook we can often overcome the kind of extreme thinking that leads to such negative consequences."

With this thought, the Dalai Lama slipped his rosary around his wrist, patted my hand amiably, and rose to end the discussion.

Chapter 11

FINDING MEANING IN PAIN
AND SUFFERING

Victor Frankl, a Jewish psychiatrist imprisoned by the Nazis in World War II, once said, "Man is ready and willing to shoulder any suffering as soon and as long as he can see a meaning in it." Frankl used his brutal and inhumane experience in the concentration camps to gain insight into how people survived the atrocities. Closely observing who survived and who didn't, he determined that survival wasn't based on youth or physical strength but rather on the strength derived from purpose, and the discovery of meaning in one's life and experience.

Finding meaning in suffering is a powerful method of helping us cope even during the most trying times in our lives. But finding meaning in our suffering is not an easy task. Suffering often seems to occur at random, senselessly and indiscriminately, with no meaning at all, let alone a purposeful or positive meaning. And while we are in the midst of our pain and suffering, all our energy is focused on getting away from it. During periods of acute crisis and tragedy it seems impossible to reflect on any possible meaning behind our suffering. At those times, there is often little we can do but endure. And it's natural to view our suffering as senseless and unfair, and wonder, "Why me?" Fortunately, however, during times of comparative ease, periods before or after acute experiences of suffering, we can reflect on suffering, seeking to develop an understanding of its meaning. And the time and effort we spend searching for meaning in suffering will pay great rewards when bad things begin to strike. But in order to reap those rewards, we must begin our search for meaning when things are going well. A tree with strong roots can withstand the most violent storm, but the tree can't grow roots just as the storm appears on the horizon.

So where do we begin in our search for meaning in suffering? For many people, the search begins with their religious tradition. Although different religions may have different ways of understanding the meaning and purpose of human suffering, every world religion offers strategies for responding to suffering based on its underlying beliefs. In the Buddhist and Hindu models, for example, suffering is a result of our own negative past actions and is seen as a catalyst for seeking spiritual liberation.

In the Judeo-Christian tradition, the universe was created by a good and just God, and even though His master plan may be mysterious and indecipherable at times, our faith and trust in His plan allow us to tolerate our suffering more easily, trusting, as the Talmud says, that "Everything God does, He does for the best." Life may still be painful, but like the pain a woman experiences in childbirth, we trust that the pain will be outweighed by the ultimate good it produces. The challenge in these traditions lies in the fact that, unlike in childbirth, the ultimate good is often not revealed to us. Still, those with a strong faith in God are sustained by a belief in God's ultimate purpose for our suffering, as a Hasidic sage advises, "When a man suffers, he ought not to say, 'That's bad! That's bad!' Nothing God imposes on man is bad. But it is all right to say, 'That's bitter! That's bitter!' For among medicines there are some that are made with bitter herbs." So, from the Judeo-Christian perspective, suffering can serve many purposes: it can test and potentially strengthen our faith, it can bring us closer to God in a very fundamental and intimate way, or it can loosen the bonds to the material world and make us cleave to God as our refuge.

While a person's religious tradition may offer valuable assistance in finding meaning, even those who do not subscribe to a religious worldview may upon careful reflection find meaning and value behind their suffering. Despite the universal unpleasantness, there is little doubt that our suffering can test, strengthen, and deepen the experience of life. Dr. Martin Luther King, Jr., once said, "What does not destroy me, makes me stronger." And while it is natural to recoil from suffering, suffering can also challenge us and at times even bring out the best in us. In *The Third Man*, author Graham Green observes, "In Italy for thirty years under the Borgias, they had warfare, terror, murder, and bloodshed—but they produced Michelangelo, Leonardo da Vinci, and the Renaissance. In Switzerland, they have brotherly love, five hundred years of democracy and peace, and what did they produce? The cuckoo clock."

While at times suffering can serve to toughen us, to strengthen us, at other times it can have value by functioning in the opposite manner—to soften us, to make us more sensitive and gentle. The vulnerability we experience in the midst of our suffering can open us and deepen our connection with others. The poet William Wordsworth once claimed, "A deep distress hath humanized my soul." In illustrating this humanizing effect of suffering, an acquaintance, Robert, comes to mind. Robert was the CEO of a very successful corporation. Several years ago, he suffered a serious financial setback that triggered a severe immobilizing depression. We met one day during the depths of his depression. I had always known Robert to be the model of confidence and enthusiasm, and I was alarmed to see him looking so despondent. With intense anguish in his voice, Robert reported, "This is the worst I've ever felt in my life. I just can't seem to shake it. I didn't know that it was even possible to feel so overwhelmed and hopeless and out of control." After discussing his difficulties for a while, I referred him to a colleague for treatment of his depression.

Several weeks later, I ran into Robert's wife Karen and asked her how he was doing. "He's doing much better thanks. The psychiatrist you recommended prescribed an antidepressant medication which is helping a lot. Of course, it's still going to take a while for us to work through the problems with the business, but he's feeling much better now and we're going to be all right . . ."

"I'm really glad to hear that."

Karen hesitated a moment, then confided, "You know, I hated to see him go through that depression. But in a way, I think it has been a blessing. One night during a fit of depression he began crying uncontrollably. He couldn't stop. I ended up just holding him in my arms for hours while he wept, until he finally fell asleep. In twenty-three years of marriage, that's the first time something like that has happened . . . and to be honest I've never felt so close to him in my life. And even though his depression is better now, things are different somehow. Something seemed to just break open . . . and that feeling of closeness is still there. The fact that he shared his problem and we went through it together somehow changed our relationship, made us much closer."

In searching for ways that one's personal suffering can take on meaning, we turn once again to the Dalai Lama, who illustrated how suffering can be put to practical use within the context of the Buddhist path.

"In Buddhist practice, you can use your personal suffering in a formal way to enhance your compassion—by using it as an opportunity for the practice of *Tong-Len*. This is a Mahayana visualization practice in which one mentally visualizes taking on another's pain and suffering, and in turn giving them all of your resources, good health, fortune, and so on. I will give instruction on this practice in greater detail later on. So, in doing this practice, when you undergo illness, pain, or suffering, you can use that as an opportunity by thinking, 'May my suffering be a substitute for the suffering of all other sentient beings. By experiencing this, may I be able to save all other sentient beings who may have to undergo similar suffering.' So you use your suffering as an opportunity for the practice of taking others' suffering upon yourself.

"Here, I should point out one thing. If, for instance, you become ill and practice this technique, thinking, 'May my illness act as a substitute for others who are suffering from similar illnesses,' and you visualize taking on their illness and suffering and giving them your good health, I'm not suggesting that you ignore your own health. When dealing with illnesses, first of all it's important to take preventative measures so you don't suffer from these illnesses, like taking all the precautionary measures such as adopting the right diet or whatever it may be. And then when you become ill, it is important not to overlook the necessity of taking the appropriate medications and all the other methods that are conventional.

"However, once you do become ill, practices such as *Tong-Len* can make a significant difference in *how you respond* to the situation of illness in terms of your mental attitude. Instead of moaning about your situation, feeling sorry for yourself, and being overwhelmed by anxiety and worry, you can, in fact, save yourself from additional mental pain and suffering by adopting the right attitude. Practicing *Tong-Len* meditation, or 'giving and receiving,' may not necessarily succeed in alleviating the real physical pain or lead to a cure in physical terms, but what it can do is protect you from unnecessary additional psychological pain, suffering, and anguish. You can think, 'May I, by experiencing this pain and suffering, be able to help other people and save others who may have to go through the same experience.' *Then your suffering takes on new meaning as it is used as the basis for a religious or spiritual practice.* And on top of that, it is also possible in the cases of some individuals practicing this technique, that instead of being sorry and saddened by the experience, the person can see it as a kind of privilege. The person can perceive it as a kind of opportunity and, in fact, be joyful because this particular experience has made him or her richer."

"You mention that suffering can be used in the practice of *Tong-Len.* And earlier you discussed the fact that intentional contemplation of our suffering nature ahead of time can be helpful in preventing us from becoming overwhelmed when difficult situations arise . . . in the sense of developing greater acceptance of suffering as a natural part of life. . ."

"That's very true . . .," the Dalai Lama nodded.

"Are there other ways that our suffering can be seen as having some meaning, or at least the contemplation of our suffering as having some practical value?"

"Yes," he replied, "definitely. I think earlier we mentioned that within the framework of the Buddhist path, reflecting on suffering has tremendous importance because by realizing the nature of suffering, you will develop greater resolve to put an end to the causes of suffering and the unwholesome deeds that lead to suffering. And it will increase your enthusiasm for engaging in the wholesome actions and deeds that lead to happiness and joy."

"And do you see any benefits of reflecting on suffering for non-Buddhists?"

"Yes, I think it can have some practical value in some situations. For example, reflecting on your suffering can reduce your arrogance, your feeling of conceit. Of course," he laughed heartily, "this may not be seen as a practical benefit or be a convincing reason for someone who doesn't consider arrogance or pride to be a fault."

Becoming more serious, the Dalai Lama added, "But anyway, I think that there is one aspect to our experience of suffering that is of vital importance. When you are aware of your pain and suffering, it helps you to develop your capacity for empathy, the capacity that allows you to relate to other people's feelings and suffering. This enhances your capacity for compassion towards others. So as an aid in helping us connect with others, it can be seen as having value.

"So," the Dalai Lama concluded, "looking at suffering in these ways, our attitude may begin to change; our suffering may not be as worthless and bad as we think."

DEALING WITH PHYSICAL PAIN

By reflecting on suffering during the quieter moments of our lives, when things are relatively stable and going well, we may often discover a deeper value and meaning in our suffering. Sometimes, however, we may be confronted with kinds of suffering that seem to have no purpose, with no redeeming qualities whatsoever. Physical pain and suffering often seem to belong to that category. But there is a difference between physical pain, which is a physiological process, and suffering, which is our mental and emotional response to the pain. So, the questions arises: Can finding an underlying purpose and meaning behind our pain modify our attitude about it? And can a change in attitude lessen the degree to which we suffer when we are physically injured?

In his book, *Pain: The Gift Nobody Wants*, Dr. Paul Brand explores the purpose and value of physical pain. Dr. Brand, a world-renowned hand surgeon and leprosy specialist, spent his early years in India where, as the son of missionaries, he was surrounded by people living under conditions of extreme hardship and suffering. Noticing that physical pain seemed to be expected and tolerated much more than in the West, Dr. Brand became interested in the pain system in the human body Eventually, he began working with leprosy patients in India and made a remarkable discovery. He found that the ravages of leprosy and the horrible disfigurements were not due to the disease organism directly causing the rotting of the flesh, but rather it was because the disease caused loss of pain sensation in the limbs. Without the protection of pain, the leprosy patients lacked the system to warn them of tissue damage. Thus, Dr. Brand observed patients walking or running on limbs with broken skin or even exposed bones; this caused continuous deterioration. Without pain, sometimes they would even stick their hands in a fire to retrieve something. He noticed an utter nonchalance toward self-destruction. In his book, Dr. Brand recounted story after story of the devastating effects of living without pain sensation—of the repetitive injuries, of cases of rats gnawing off fingers and toes while the patient slept peacefully.

After a lifetime of working with patients suffering from pain and those suffering from lack of pain, Dr. Brand gradually came to view pain not as the universal enemy as seen in the West but as a remarkable, elegant, and sophisticated biological system that warns us of damage to our body and thus protects us. But why must the experience of pain be so unpleasant? He concluded that the very unpleasantness of pain, the part that we hate, is what makes it so effective in protecting us and warning us of danger and injury. The unpleasant quality of pain forces the entire human organism to attend to the problem. Although the body has automatic reflexive movements that form an outer layer of protection and move us quickly away from the pain, it is the feeling of unpleasantness that galvanizes and compels the entire organism to attend and act. It also sears the experience into the memory and serves to protect us in the future.

In the same way that finding meaning in our suffering can help us cope with life's problems, Dr. Brand feels that an understanding of the purpose of physical pain can lessen our suffering when pain arises. In view of this theory, he offers the concept of "pain insurance." He feels that we can prepare for pain ahead of time, while healthy, by gaining insight into the reason we have it and taking the time to reflect on what life would be without pain. However, since acute pain can demolish objectivity, we must reflect on these things before pain strikes. But if we can begin to think of pain as a "speech your body is delivering about a subject that is of vital importance to you, in the most effective way of getting your attention," then our attitude about pain will begin to change. And as our attitude about pain changes, our suffering will diminish. As Dr. Brand states, "I am convinced that the attitude we cultivate in advance may well determine how suffering will affect us when it does strike." He believes that we can even develop gratitude in the face of pain. We may not be grateful for the *experience* of pain, but we can be grateful for the *system* of pain perception.

There is no doubt that our attitude and mental outlook can strongly affect the degree to which we suffer when we are in physical pain. Let's say, for instance, that two individuals, a construction worker and a concert pianist, suffer the same finger injury. While the amount of physical pain might be the same for both individuals, the construction worker might suffer very little and in fact rejoice if the injury resulted in a month of paid vacation which he or she was in need of, whereas the same injury could result in intense suffering to the pianist who viewed playing as his or her primary source of joy in life.

The idea that our mental attitude influences our ability to perceive and endure pain isn't limited to theoretical situations such as this; it has been demonstrated by many scientific studies and experiments. Researchers looking into this issue began by tracing the pathways of how pain is perceived and experienced. Pain begins with a sensory signal—an alarm that goes off when nerve endings are stimulated by something that is sensed as dangerous. Millions of signals are sent through the spinal cord to the base of the brain. These signals are then sorted out and a message is sent to higher areas of the brain telling of pain. The brain then sorts through the prescreened messages and decides on a response. It is at this stage that the mind can assign value and meaning to the pain and intensify or modify our perception of pain; *we convert pain into suffering in the mind*. To lessen the suffering of pain, we need to make a crucial distinction between the pain of pain and the pain we create by our thoughts about the pain. Fear, anger, guilt, loneliness, and helplessness are all mental and emotional responses that can intensify pain. So, in developing an approach to dealing with pain, we can of course work at the lower levels of pain perception, using the tools of modern medicine such as medications and other procedures, but we can also work at the higher levels by modifying our outlook and attitude.

Many researchers have examined the role of the mind in the perception of pain. Pavlov even trained dogs to overcome the pain instinct by associating an electrical shock with a food reward. Researcher Ronald Melzak took Pavlov's experiments a step further. He raised Scottish terrier pups in a padded environment in which they wouldn't encounter the normal knocks and scrapes of growing up. These dogs failed to learn basic responses to pain; they failed to react, for instance, when their paws were pricked with a pin, as opposed to their littermates who squealed with pain when pricked. On the basis of experiments such as these, he concluded that much of what we call pain, including the unpleasant emotional response, was learned rather than instinctive. Other experiments with human beings, involving hypnosis and placebos, have also demonstrated that in many cases the higher brain functions can overrule the pain signals from the lower stages on the pain pathway. This indicates how the mind can often determine how we perceive pain and helps explain the interesting findings of investigators such as Dr. Richard Sternback and Bernard Tursky at Harvard Medical School (and later reaffirmed in a study by Dr. Maryann Bates et al.) who noted that there were significant differences among different ethnic groups in their ability to perceive and withstand pain.

So it seems that the assertion that our attitude about pain can influence the degree to which we suffer is not simply based on philosophical speculation but is backed up by scientific evidence. And if our investigation into the meaning and value of pain results in a change of attitude about pain, our efforts will not be wasted. In seeking to discover an underlying purpose of our pain, Dr. Brand makes one additional fascinating and critical observation. He describes many reports of leprosy patients' claiming, "Of course, I can see my hands and my feet, but somehow they don't feel like part of *me*. It feels as if they are just tools." Thus, pain not only warns us and protects us, but *it unifies us*. Without pain sensation in our hands or feet, those parts no longer seem to belong to our body.

In the same way that physical pain unifies our sense of having a body, we can conceive of the general experience of suffering acting as a unifying force that connects us with others. Perhaps that is the ultimate meaning behind our suffering. *It is our suffering that is the most basic element that we share with others, the factor that unifies us with all living creatures.*

We conclude our discussion of human suffering with the Dalai Lama's instruction on the practice of *Tong-Len*, which he referred to in our earlier conversation. As he will explain, the purpose of this visualization meditation is to strengthen one's compassion. But it can also be seen as a powerful tool in helping transmute one's personal suffering. When undergoing any form of suffer-

◆

ing or hardship, one can use this practice to enhance one's compassion by visualizing relieving others who are going through similar suffering, by absorbing and dissolving their suffering into your own—a kind of suffering by proxy.

The Dalai Lama presented this instruction before a large audience on a particularly hot September afternoon in Tucson. The hall's air conditioning units, struggling against the soaring desert temperatures outside, were ultimately overcome by the additional heat generated by sixteen hundred bodies. Temperatures in the room began to climb, creating a general level of discomfort that was particularly appropriate for the practice of a meditation on suffering.

The Practice of Tong-Len

"This afternoon, let us meditate on the practice of *Tong-Len*, 'Giving and Receiving.' This practice is meant to help train the mind, to strengthen the natural power and force of compassion. This is achieved because *Tong-Len* meditation helps counteract our selfishness. It increases the power and strength of our mind by enhancing our courage to open ourselves to others' suffering.

"To begin this exercise, first visualize on one side of you a group of people who are in desperate need of help, those who are in an unfortunate state of suffering, those living under conditions of poverty, hardship, and pain. Visualize this group of people on one side of you clearly in your mind. Then, on the other side, visualize yourself as the embodiment of a self-centered person, with a customary selfish attitude, indifferent to the well-being and needs of others. And then in between this suffering group of people and this selfish representation of you see yourself in the middle, as a neutral observer.

"Next, notice which side you are naturally inclined towards. Are you more inclined towards that single individual, the embodiment of selfishness? Or do your natural feelings of empathy reach out to the group of weaker people who are in need? If you look objectively, you can see that the well-being of a group or large number of individuals is more important than that of one single individual.

"After that, focus your attention on the needy and desperate people. Direct all your positive energy to them. Mentally give them your successes, your resources, your collection of virtues. And after you have done that, visualize taking upon yourself their suffering, their problems, and all their negativities.

"For example, you can visualize an innocent starving child from Somalia and feel how you would respond naturally towards that sight. In this instance, when you experience a deep feeling of empathy towards the suffering of that individual, it isn't based on considerations like 'He's my relative' or 'She's my friend.' You don't even know that person. But the fact that the other person is a human being and you, yourself, are a human being allows your natural capacity for empathy to emerge and enable you to reach out. So you can visualize something like that and think, 'This child has no capacity of his or her own to be able to relieve himself or herself from his or her present state of difficulty or hardship.' Then, mentally take upon yourself all the suffering of poverty, starvation, and the feeling of deprivation, and mentally

◆

give your facilities, wealth, and success to this child. So, through practicing this kind of 'giving-and-receiving' visualization, you can train your mind.

"When engaging in this practice it is sometimes helpful to begin by first imagining your own future suffering and, with an attitude of compassion, take your own future suffering upon yourself right now, with the sincere wish of freeing yourself from all future suffering. After you gain some practice in generating a compassionate state of mind towards yourself, you can then expand the process to include taking on the suffering of others.

"When you do the visualization of 'taking upon yourself,' it is useful to visualize these sufferings, problems, and difficulties in the form of poisonous substances, dangerous weapons, or terrifying animals—things the very sight of which normally makes you shudder. So, visualize the suffering in these forms, and then absorb them directly into your heart.

"The purpose of visualizing these negative and frightening forms being dissolved into our hearts is to destroy our habitual selfish attitudes that reside there. However, for those individuals who may have problems with self-image, self-hatred, anger towards themselves, or low self-esteem, then it is important to judge for themselves whether this particular practice is appropriate or not. It may not be.

"This *Tong-Len* practice can become quite powerful if you combine the 'giving and receiving' with the breath; that is, imagine 'receiving' when inhaling and 'giving' when exhaling. When you do this visualization effectively, it will make you feel some slight discomfort. That is an indication that it is hitting its tar-

◆

get—the self-centered, egocentric attitude that we normally have. Now, let us meditate."

At the conclusion of his instruction on *Tong-Len*, the Dalai Lama made an important point. No particular exercise will appeal to or be appropriate for everyone. In our spiritual journey it's important for each of us to decide whether a particular practice is appropriate for us. Sometimes a practice will not appeal to us initially, and before it can be effective, we need to understand it better. This certainly was the case for me when I followed the Dalai Lama's instruction on *Tong-Len* that afternoon. I found that I had some difficulty with it—a certain feeling of resistance—although I couldn't put my finger on it at the moment. Later that evening, however, I thought about the Dalai Lama's instruction and realized that my feeling of resistance developed early in his instruction at the point where he concluded that the group of individuals was more important than the single individual. It was a concept I had heard before, namely, the Vulcan axiom propounded by Mr. Spock in *Star Trek: The needs of the many outweigh the needs of the one.* But there was one sticking point to that argument. Before bringing it up to the Dalai Lama, perhaps not wanting to come across as being just "out for number one," I sounded out a friend who was a longtime student of Buddhism.

"One thing bothers me . . .," I said. "Saying that the needs of a large group of people outweigh those of just one single person makes sense in theory, but in everyday life we don't interact with people *en masse*. We interact with one person at a time, with a series of individuals. Now, on that one-to-one level, why

◆

215

should that individual's needs outweigh my own? I'm also a single individual . . . We're equal . . ."

My friend thought for a moment. "Well, that's true. But I think that if you could try to consider each individual as *truly* equal to yourself—no more important *but no less either*—I think that would be enough to start with."

I never brought up the issue with the Dalai Lama.

Part IV

OVERCOMING
OBSTACLES

Chapter 12

BRINGING ABOUT
CHANGE

THE PROCESS OF CHANGE

W e've discussed the possibility of achieving happiness by working toward eliminating our negative behaviors and states of mind. In general, what would be your approach to actually accomplishing this, to overcoming negative behaviors and making positive changes in one's life?" I asked.

"The first step involves learning," the Dalai Lama replied, "education. Earlier, I think I mentioned the importance of learning . . ."

"You mean when we talked about the importance of learning about how the negative emotions and behaviors are harmful to our pursuit of happiness, and the positive emotions are helpful?"

"Yes. But in discussing an approach to bringing about positive changes within oneself, learning is only the first step. There are other factors as well: conviction, determination, action, and effort. *So the next step is developing conviction.* Learning and education are important because they help one develop conviction of the need to change and help increase one's commitment. *This conviction to change then develops into determination. Next, one transforms determination into action*—the strong determination to change enables one to make a sustained effort to implement the actual changes. *This final factor of effort is critical.*

"So, for example, if you are trying to stop smoking, first you have to be aware that smoking is harmful to the body. You have to be educated. I think, for instance, that information and public education about the harmful effects of smoking have modified people's behavior; I think that now many fewer people smoke in Western countries than in a communist country like China because of the availability of information. But that *learning* alone is often not sufficient. You have to increase that awareness until it leads to a firm *conviction* about the harmful effects of smoking. This strengthens your *determination* to change. Finally, you must exert the *effort* to establish new habit patterns. This is the way that inner change and transformation take place in all things, no matter what you are trying to accomplish.

"Now, no matter what behavior you are seeking to change, no matter what particular goal or action you are directing your efforts towards, you need to start by developing a strong willingness or wish to do it. You need to generate great enthusiasm.

◆

And, here, a sense of urgency is a key factor. This sense of urgency is a powerful factor in helping you overcome problems. For example, knowledge about the serious effects of AIDS has created a sense of urgency that has put a check on a lot of people's sexual behavior. I think that often, once you obtain the proper information, that sense of seriousness and commitment will come.

"So, this sense of urgency can be a vital factor in effecting change. It can give us tremendous energy. For instance, in a political movement, if there is a sense of desperation, there can be a tremendous sense of urgency—so much that the people may even forget that they are hungry, and there is no feeling of tiredness or exhaustion in pursuit of their objectives.

"The importance of urgency not only applies to overcoming problems on a personal level, but on a community and global level as well. When I was in St. Louis, for instance, I met the governor. There, they had recently had severe flooding. The governor told me that when the flood first happened, he was quite concerned that given the individualistic nature of society, people might not be so cooperative, that they might not commit themselves to this concerted and cooperative effort. But when the crisis happened, he was amazed by the response of the people. They were so cooperative and so committed to the concerted effort in dealing with the flood problems that he was very impressed. So to my mind, this shows that in order to accomplish important goals, we need an appreciation of the sense of urgency, like in this case; the crisis was so urgent that people instinctively joined forces and responded to the crisis. Unfortunately," he said sadly, "often we don't have that sense of urgency."

◆

I was surprised to hear him stress the importance of the sense of urgency given the Western stereotype of the Asian "Let it be" attitude engendered by a belief in many lifetimes; if it doesn't happen now, there's always next time . . .

"But then the question is, how do you develop that strong sense of enthusiasm to change or urgency in everyday life? Is there a particular Buddhist approach?" I asked.

"For a Buddhist practitioner, there are various techniques used to generate enthusiasm," the Dalai Lama answered. "In order to generate a sense of confidence and enthusiasm, we find in the Buddha's text a discussion of the preciousness of human existence. We talk about how much potential lies within our body, how meaningful it can be, the good purposes it can be used for, the benefits and advantages of having a human form, and so on. And these discussions are there to instill a sense of confidence and courage and to induce a sense of commitment to use our human body in a positive way.

"Then, in order to generate a sense of urgency to engage in spiritual practices, the practitioner is reminded of our impermanence, of death. When we talk about impermanence in this context, we are talking in very conventional terms, not about the more subtle aspects of the concept of impermanence. In other words, we are reminded that one day, we may no longer be here. That sort of understanding. That awareness of impermanence is encouraged, so that when it is coupled with our appreciation of the enormous potential of our human existence, it will give us a sense of urgency that *we must use every precious moment.*"

"That contemplation of our impermanence and death seems to be a powerful technique," I remarked, "to help motivate one, develop a sense of urgency to effect positive changes. Couldn't that be used as a technique for non-Buddhists as well?"

"I think one might take care in the application of the various techniques to non-Buddhists," he said thoughtfully. "Perhaps this might apply more to Buddhist practices. After all," he laughed, "one could use the same contemplation for exactly the opposite purpose—'Oh, there is no guarantee that I am going to be alive tomorrow, so I might as well just have lots of fun today!'"

"Do you have any suggestions for how non-Buddhists might develop that sense of urgency?"

He replied, "Well, as I pointed out, that's where information and education come in. For example, before I met certain experts or specialists, I was unaware of the crisis about the environment. But once I met them and they explained the problems that we are facing, then I became aware of the seriousness of the situation. This can apply to other problems that we face as well."

"But sometimes, even having information, we still might not have the energy to change. How can we overcome that?" I asked.

The Dalai Lama paused to think, then said, "I think that there might be different categories here. One kind may arise out of some biological factors that may be contributing to the apathy or lack of energy. When the cause of one's apathy or lack of energy is due to biological factors, one may need to work on one's lifestyle. So, if one tries to get sufficient sleep, eat a healthy diet, abstain from alcohol, and so on, these kinds of things will help make one's mind more alert. And in some cases one may even need to resort to medication or other physical remedies if the cause is due to illness. But then there's another kind of apathy or laziness—the kind that arises purely out of a certain weakness of mind . . ."

"Yes, that's the kind I was referring to . . ."

"To overcome that kind of apathy and to generate commitment and enthusiasm to overcome negative behaviors or states of mind, once again I think the most effective method, and perhaps the only solution, is to be constantly aware of the destructive effects of the negative behavior. One may need to repeatedly remind oneself of those destructive effects."

The Dalai Lama's words rang true, yet as a psychiatrist, I was acutely aware of how strongly entrenched some negative behaviors and ways of thinking could become, how difficult it was for some people to change. Assuming that there were complex psychodynamic factors at play, I had spent countless hours examining and dissecting patients' resistance to change. Turning this over in my mind, I asked:

"People often want to make positive changes in their lives, engage in healthier behaviors, and so on. But sometimes there just seems to be a sort of inertia or resistance . . . How would you explain how that occurs?"

"That's quite easy . . . ," he began casually.

EASY?

"It's because we simply become habituated or accustomed to doing things in certain ways. And then, we become sort of spoiled, doing only the things that we like to do, that we are used to doing."

"But how can we overcome that?"

"By using habituation to our advantage. *Through constant famil-*

iarity, we can definitely establish new behavior patterns. Here's an example: In Dharamsala I usually wake up and start the day at 3:30, although here in Arizona these days I wake up at 4:30; I get one more hour's sleep," he laughed. "At the beginning you need a little bit of effort to get used to this, but after a few months, it becomes sort of a set routine and you don't need to make any special effort. So even if you were to go to bed late, you might have a tendency to want a few more minutes' sleep, but you still get up at 3:30 without having to give special thought to it, and you can get up and do your daily practices. This is due to the force of habituation.

"So, by making a steady effort, I think we can overcome any form of negative conditioning and make positive changes in our lives. But you still need to realize that genuine change doesn't happen overnight. Now, for example, in my own case, I think if I compare my normal state of mind today to, say, twenty or thirty years ago, there's a big difference. But this difference, I came to step by step. I started to learn Buddhism around the age of five or six, but at that time I had no interest in Buddhist teachings," he laughed, "although I was called the highest reincarnation. I think it wasn't until I was around sixteen years old that I really began to have some serious feeling about Buddhism. And I tried to start serious practice. Then, over the course of many years, I began to develop a deep appreciation of Buddhist principles, and practices, which initially seemed so impossible and almost unnatural, became much more natural and easy to relate to. This occurred through gradual familiarization. Of course, this process took more than forty years.

"So, you see, deep down, mental development takes time. If

someone says, 'Oh, through many years of hardship things have changed,' I can take that seriously. There's a greater likelihood of the changes being genuine and longlasting. If someone says, 'Oh, within a short period, say two years, there has been a big change,' I think that is unrealistic."

While the Dalai Lama's approach to change was unarguably reasonable, there was one matter that seemed to need to be reconciled:

"Well, you've mentioned the need for a high level of enthusiasm and determination to transform one's mind, to make positive changes. Yet at the same time we acknowledge that genuine change occurs slowly and can take a long time," I noted. "When change takes place so slowly, it's easy to become discouraged. Haven't you ever felt discouraged by the slow rate of progress in relation to your spiritual practice or discouragement in other areas of your life?"

"Yes, certainly," he said.

"How do you deal with that?" I asked.

"As far as my own spiritual practice goes, *if I encounter some obstacles or problems, I find it helpful to stand back and take the long-term view rather than the short-term view.* In this regard, I find that thinking about one particular verse gives me courage and helps me sustain my determination. It says:

> *As long as space endures*
> *As long as sentient beings remain*
> *May I too live*
> *To dispel the miseries of the world.*

"However, as far as the struggle for the freedom of Tibet is concerned, if I utilize that kind of belief, those verses—being prepared to wait 'eons and eons . . . as long as space endures,' and so on—then I think I would be foolish. Here, one needs to take more immediate or active involvement. Of course, in that situation, the struggle for freedom, when I reflect on the fourteen or fifteen years of effort at negotiation with no results, when I think about the almost fifteen years of failure, I develop a certain feeling of impatience or frustration. But this feeling of frustration doesn't discourage me to the point of losing hope."

Pressing the issue a bit further, I asked, "But what exactly prevents you from losing hope?"

"Even in the situation with Tibet, I think that viewing the situation from a wider perspective can definitely help. So, for instance, if I look at the situation inside Tibet from a narrow perspective, focusing *only* on that, then the situation appears almost hopeless. However, if I look from a wider perspective, look from a world perspective, then I see the international situation in which whole communist and totalitarian systems are collapsing, where even in China there's a democracy movement, and the spirit of Tibetans remains high. So, I don't give up."

Given his extensive background and training in Buddhist philosophy and meditation, it is interesting that the Dalai Lama identifies learning and education as the first step in bringing about internal transformation, rather than more transcendental or mystical spiritual practices. Although education is commonly acknowledged as important in learning new skills or securing a good job, its role as a vital factor in achieving happiness is widely overlooked. Yet studies have shown that even purely academic education is directly linked to a happier life. Numerous surveys have conclusively found that higher levels of education have a positive correlation with better health and a longer life, and even protect an individual from depression. In trying to determine the reasons for these beneficial effects of education, scientists have reasoned that better-educated individuals are more aware of health risk factors, are better able to implement healthier lifestyle choices, feel a greater sense of empowerment and self-esteem, have greater problem-solving skills and more effective coping strategies—all factors that can contribute to a happier, healthier life. So, if merely academic education is associated with a happier life, how much more powerful can be the kind of learning and education spoken of by the Dalai Lama—education that focuses specifically on understanding and implementing the full spectrum of factors that lead to lasting happiness?

The next step in the Dalai Lama's path to change involves generating "determination and enthusiasm." This step is also widely accepted by contemporary Western science as an important factor in achieving one's goals. In one study, for instance, educational psychologist Benjamin Bloom examined the lives of some of America's most accomplished artists, athletes, and scientists. He discovered that drive and determination, not great natural talent, led to their success in their respective fields. As in any other field, one could assume that this principle would equally apply to the art of achieving happiness.

Behavioral scientists have extensively researched the mechanisms that initiate, sustain, and direct our activities, referring to this field as the study of "human motivation." Psychologists have identified three principle types of motives. The first type, *primary motives*, are drives based on biological needs that must be met for survival. This would include, for example, needs for food, water, and air. Another category of motives involves a human being's *need for stimulation and information*. Investigators hypothesize that this is an innate need, required for proper maturation, development, and functioning of the nervous system. The final category, called *secondary motives*, are motives based on learned needs and drives. Many secondary motives are related to acquired needs for success, power, status, or achievement. At this level of motivation, one's behavior and drives can be influenced by social forces and shaped by learning. It is at this stage that the theories of modern psychology meet with the Dalai Lama's conception of developing "determination and enthusiasm." In the Dalai Lama's system, however, the drive and determination generated are not used only in the pursuit of worldly success but develop as one gains a clearer understanding of the factors that lead to true happiness and are used in the pursuit of higher goals, such as kindness, compassion, and spiritual development.

"Effort" is the final factor in bringing about change. The Dalai Lama identifies effort as a necessary factor in establishing new conditioning. The idea that we can change our negative behaviors and thoughts through new conditioning is not only shared by Western psychologists, but it is in fact the cornerstone of contemporary behavior therapy. This kind of therapy is based on the basic theory that people have largely *learned* to be the way they are, and, by offering strategies to create new conditioning, behavior therapy has proven to be effective for a broad range of problems.

ˈ While science has recently revealed that one's genetic predisposition clearly plays a role in an individual's characteristic way of responding to the world, most social scientists and psychologists feel that a large measure of the way we behave, think, and feel is determined by learning and conditioning, which comes about as a result of our upbringing and the social and cultural forces around us. And since it is believed that behaviors are largely established by conditioning, and reinforced and amplified by "habituation," this opens up the possibility, as the Dalai Lama contends, of extinguishing harmful or negative conditioning and replacing it with helpful, life-enhancing conditioning.

Making a sustained effort to change external behavior is not only helpful in overcoming bad habits but also can change our underlying attitudes and feelings. Experiments have shown that not only do our attitudes and psychological traits determine our behavior, an idea that is commonly accepted, but our behavior can also change our attitudes. Investigators found that even an artificially induced frown or smile tends to induce the corresponding emotions of anger or happiness; this suggests that just "going through the motions" and repeatedly engaging in a positive behavior can eventually bring about genuine internal change. This could have important implications in the Dalai Lama's approach to building a happier life. If we begin with the simple act of regularly helping others, for instance, even if we don't *feel* particularly kind or caring, we may discover an inner transformation is taking place, as we very gradually develop genuine feelings of compassion.

REALISTIC EXPECTATIONS

In bringing about genuine inner transformation and change, the Dalai Lama emphasizes the importance of making a sustained effort. It is a gradual process. This is in sharp contrast to the proliferation of "quick fix" self help techniques and therapies that have become so popular in Western culture in recent decades— techniques ranging from "positive affirmations" to "discovering your inner child."

The Dalai Lama's approach points toward slow growth and maturity. He believes in the tremendous, perhaps even unlimited, power of the mind—but a mind that has been systematically trained, focused, concentrated, a mind tempered by years of experience and sound reasoning. It takes a long time to develop the behavior and habits of mind that contribute to our problems. It takes an equally long time to establish the new habits that bring happiness. There is no getting around these essential ingredients: determination, effort, and time. These are the real secrets to happiness.

When embarking on the path to change, it is important to set reasonable expectations. If our expectations are too high, we're setting ourselves up for disappointment. If they are too low, it extinguishes our willingness to challenge our limitations and achieve our true potential. Following our conversation about the process of change, the Dalai Lama explained:

"You should never lose sight of the importance of having a realistic attitude—of being very sensitive and respectful to the concrete reality of your situation as you proceed on the path towards your ultimate goal. Recognize the difficulties inherent in your path, and the fact that it may take time and a consistent effort. It's important to make a clear distinction in your mind between your *ideals* and the *standards* by which you judge your progress. As a Buddhist, for instance, you set your ideals very high: full Enlightenment is your ultimate expectation. Holding full Enlightenment as your ideal of achievement is not an extreme. But expecting to achieve it quickly, here and now, becomes an extreme. Using that as a *standard* instead of your *ideal* causes you to become discouraged and completely lose hope when you don't quickly achieve Enlightenment. So you need a realistic approach. On the other hand, if you say, 'I'm just going to focus on the here and now; that's the practical thing, and I don't care about the future or the ultimate attainment of Buddha-hood,' then again, that is another extreme. So we need to find an approach that is somewhere in between. We need to find a balance.

"Dealing with expectations is really a tricky issue. If you have excessive expectations without a proper foundation, then that usually leads to problems. On the other hand, without expectation and hope, without aspiration, there can be no progress. Some hope is essential. So finding the proper balance is not easy. One needs to judge each situation on the spot."

◆ ◆ ◆

◆

I still had nagging doubts; although we may certainly modify some of our negative behaviors and attitudes given enough time and effort, to what extent is it truly possible to eradicate the negative emotions? Addressing the Dalai Lama, I began, "We've spoken about the fact that ultimate happiness depends on eliminating our negative behaviors and mental states — things like anger, hatred, greed, and so on. . ."

The Dalai Lama nodded.

"But these kinds of emotions seem to be a natural part of our psychological makeup. All human beings seem to experience these darker emotions to one degree or another. And if that's the case, is it reasonable to hate, deny, and combat part of ourselves? I mean, it seems impractical, and even unnatural, to try to completely eradicate something that is an integral part of our natural makeup."

Shaking his head, the Dalai Lama replied, "Yes, some people suggest that anger, hatred, and other negative emotions are a natural part of our mind. They feel that since these are a natural part of our makeup, there is no way to really change these mental states. But that is wrong. Now, for example, all of us are born in an ignorant state. In this sense, ignorance is also quite natural. Anyway, when we are young, we are quite ignorant. But as we grow, day by day through education and learning we can acquire knowledge and dispel ignorance. However, if we leave ourselves in an ignorant state without consciously developing our learning, we won't be able to dispel ignorance. So, if we leave ourselves in a 'natural state' without making an effort to dispel it, then the opposing factors or forces of education and learning do not come naturally. And in the same way, through proper training we can gradually reduce our negative emotions and increase positive states of mind such as love, compassion, and forgiveness."

"But if these things are a part of our psyche, ultimately how can we be successful in fighting against something which is part of ourselves?"

"In considering how to fight against the negative emotions, it is useful to know how the human mind works," answered the Dalai Lama. "Now the human mind is of course very complex. But it is also very skillful. It can find many ways in which it can deal with a variety of situations and conditions. For one thing, the mind has the ability to adopt different perspectives through which it can address various problems.

"Within Buddhist practice, this ability to adopt different perspectives is utilized in a number of meditations in which you mentally isolate different aspects of yourself, then engage in a dialogue between them. For instance, there is a meditation practice designed to enhance altruism, whereby you engage in a dialogue between your own 'self-centered attitude,' a self that is the embodiment of self-centeredness, and yourself as a spiritual practitioner. There is a kind of a dialogical relationship. So similarly here, although negative traits such as hatred and anger are part of your mind, you can engage in an endeavor in which you take your anger and hatred as an object and do combat with it.

"In addition, from your own daily experience, you often find yourself in situations in which you blame or criticize yourself. You say, 'Oh, on such and such day, I let myself down.' Then you criticize yourself. Or, you blame yourself for doing something wrong or for not doing something, and you feel angry towards yourself. So here also, you engage in a kind of dialogue with yourself. In reality, there are not two distinct selves; it's just the one continuum of the same individual. But still, it makes sense to criticize yourself, to feel angry towards yourself. This is something that you all know from your own experience.

"So although, in reality, there is only one single individual continuum, you can adopt two different perspectives. What takes place when you are criticizing yourself? The 'self' that is criticizing is done from a perspective of yourself as a totality, your entire being, and the 'self' that is being criticized is a self from a perspective of a particular experience or a particular event. So you can see the possibility of having this 'self-to-self relationship.'

"To expand on this point, it may be quite helpful to reflect upon the various aspects of one's own personal identity. Let us take the example of a Tibetan Buddhist monk. That individual can have a sense of personalized identity from the perspective of his being a monk, 'myself as a monk.' And then he can also have a level of personal identity that is not so much based upon his consideration of monkhood but rather of his ethnic origin, like Tibetan, so he can say, 'I as a Tibetan.' And then at another level, that person can have another identity in which monkhood and ethnic origin may not play any important role. He can think, 'I as a human being.' So you can see different perspectives within each person's individual identity.

"What this indicates is that when we conceptually relate to something, we are capable of looking at one phenomenon from many different angles. And the capacity to see things from different angles is quite selective; we can focus on a particular angle, a particular aspect of that phenomenon, and adopt a particular perspective. This capacity becomes very important when we seek to identify and eliminate certain negative aspects of ourselves or enhance positive traits. *Because of this capacity to adopt a different perspective, we can isolate parts of ourselves that we seek to eliminate and do battle with them.*

"Now, in further examining this subject, a very important question arises: Although we may engage in combat with anger, hatred, and the other negative states of mind, what guarantee or assurance do we have that it is possible to gain victory over them?

"When speaking of these negative states of mind, I should point out that I am referring to what are called *Nyon Mong* in Tibetan, or *Klesha* in Sanskrit. This term literally means that which afflicts from within. That's a long term, so it is often translated as 'delusions.' The very etymology of the Tibetan word *Nyon Mong* gives you a sense that it is an emotional and cognitive event that spontaneously afflicts your mind, destroys your peace of mind, or brings about a disturbance within your psyche when it arises. If we pay close enough attention, it's easy to recognize the afflictive nature of these 'delusions' simply because they have this tendency to destroy our calmness and presence of mind. But it's much more difficult to find out whether we can overcome them. That is a question that directly relates to the whole idea of whether it is possible to attain the

◆

full realization of our spiritual potential. And that is a very serious and difficult question.

"So, what grounds do we have to accept that these afflictive emotions and cognitive events, or 'delusions,' can be ultimately rooted out and eliminated from our minds? In Buddhist thought, we have three principal premises or grounds on which we believe that that can happen.

"The first premise is that all 'deluded' states of mind, all afflictive emotions and thoughts, are essentially distorted, in that they are rooted in misperceiving the actual reality of the situation. No matter how powerful, deep down these negative emotions have no valid foundation. They are based on ignorance. On the other hand, all the positive emotions or states of mind, such as love, compassion, insight, and so on have a solid basis. When the mind is experiencing these positive states, there is no distortion. In addition, these positive factors are grounded in reality. They can be verified by our own experience. There is a kind of grounding and rootedness in reason and understanding; this is not the case with afflictive emotions like anger and hatred. On top of that, all these positive states of mind have the quality that you can enhance their capacity and increase their potential to a limitless degree, if you regularly practice them through training and constant familiarity . . ."

I interrupted, "Can you explain a bit more what you mean by the positive states of mind having a 'valid basis,' and the negative states of mind having 'no valid basis'?"

He clarified, "Well, for example, compassion is considered a positive emotion. In generating compassion, you start by recognizing that you do not want suffering and that you have a right to have happiness. This can be verified or validated by your own experience. You then recognize that other people, just like yourself, also do not want to suffer and they have the right to have happiness. This becomes the basis of your beginning to generate compassion.

"Essentially, there are two kinds of emotions or states of mind: positive and negative. One way of categorizing these emotions is in terms of understanding that the positive emotions are those which can be justified, and the negative emotions are those which cannot be justified. For instance, earlier we discussed the topic of desire, how there can be positive desires and negative desires. Desire for one's basic necessities to be met is a positive kind of desire. It is justifiable. It is based on the fact that we all exist and have the right to survive. And in order to survive, there are certain things that we require, certain needs that have to be met. So that kind of desire has a valid foundation. And, as we discussed, there are other types of desire that are negative, like excessive desire and greed. Those kinds of desires are not based on valid reasons, and often just create trouble and complicate one's life. Those kinds of desires are simply based on a feeling of discontentment, of wanting more, even though the things we want aren't really necessary. Those kinds of desires have no solid reasons behind them. So, in this way we can say that the positive emotions have a firm and valid foundation, and the negative emotions lack this valid foundation."

The Dalai Lama continued his examination of the human mind, dissecting the workings of the mind with the same scrutiny that a botanist might use in classifying species of rare flowers.

"Now this brings us to the second premise on which we base the claim that our negative emotions can be rooted out and eliminated. *This premise is based on the fact that our positive states of mind can act as antidotes to our negative tendencies and delusory states of mind. So, the second premise is that as you enhance the capacity of these antidotal factors, the greater their force, the more you will be able to reduce the force of the mental and emotional afflictions,* the more you will be able to reduce the influences and effects of these things.

"When talking about eliminating negative states of mind, there is one point that should be born in mind. Within Buddhist practice, the cultivation of certain specific positive mental qualities such as patience, tolerance, kindness, and so on can act as specific antidotes to negative states of mind such as anger, hatred, and attachment. Applying antidotes such as love and compassion can significantly reduce the degree or influence of the mental and emotional afflictions, but since they seek to eliminate only certain specific or individual afflictive emotions, in some sense they can be seen as only partial measures. These afflictive emotions, such as attachment and hatred, are ultimately rooted in ignorance—misconception of the true nature of reality. Therefore, there seems to be a consensus among all Buddhist traditions that in order to *fully* overcome all of these negative tendencies, one must apply the antidote to ignorance—the 'Wisdom factor.' This is indispensable. The 'Wisdom factor' involves generating insight into the true nature of reality.

"So, within the Buddhist tradition, we not only have specific antidotes for specific states of mind, for example, patience and tolerance act as specific antidotes to anger and hatred, but we also have a general antidote—insight into the ultimate nature of reality—that acts as an antidote to *all* of the negative states of mind. It is similar to getting rid of a poisonous plant: you can eliminate the harmful effects by cutting off the specific branches and leaves, or you can eliminate the entire plant by going to the root and uprooting it."

Concluding his discussion about the possibility of eliminating our negative mental states, the Dalai Lama explained, "The third premise is that the essential nature of mind is pure. It is based on the belief that the underlying basic subtle consciousness is untainted by the negative emotions. Its nature is pure, a state which is referred to as the 'mind of Clear Light.' That basic nature of the mind is also called Buddha Nature. So, since the negative emotions are not an intrinsic part of this Buddha Nature, there is a possibility to eliminate them and purify the mind.

"So it is on these three premises that Buddhism accepts that the mental and emotional afflictions ultimately can be eliminated through deliberately cultivating antidotal forces like love, compassion, tolerance, and forgiveness, and through various practices such as meditation."

The idea that the underlying nature of the mind is pure and we have the capacity to completely eliminate our negative patterns of thinking was a topic that I had heard the Dalai Lama speak of before. He had compared the mind to a glass of muddy water; the afflictive mental states were like the "impurities" or the mud, which could be removed to reveal the underlying "pure" nature of the water. This seemed a little abstract, so moving on to more practical concerns, I interrupted.

"Let's say that one accepts the possibility of eliminating one's negative emotions, and even begins to take steps in that direction. From our discussions, however, I sense that it would take tremendous effort to eradicate this dark side—tremendous study, contemplation, constant application of antidotal factors, intensive meditation practices, and so on. That might be appropriate for a monk or someone who can devote a lot of time and attention to these practices. But what about an ordinary person, with a family and so on, who may not have the time or opportunity to practice these intensive techniques? For them, wouldn't it be more appropriate to simply try to control their afflictive emotions, to learn to live with them and manage them properly, rather than to try to completely eradicate them? It's like patients with diabetes. They may not have the means of a complete cure, but by watching their diet, taking insulin, and so on, they can control the disease and prevent the symptoms and the negative sequelae of the disease."

"Yes, that's the way!" he enthusiastically responded. "I agree with you. Whatever steps, however small, one can take towards learning to reduce the influence of the negative emotions can be very helpful. It can definitely help one live a happier and more satisfying life. However, it is also possible for a layperson to attain high levels of spiritual realization—someone who has a job, a family, a sexual relationship with one's spouse, and so on. And not only that, but there have been people who didn't start serious practice until later in life, when they were in their forties, fifties, or even eighties, and yet they were able to become great highly realized masters."

"Have you personally met many individuals who you feel may have achieved these high states?" I inquired.

"I think that's very, very difficult to judge. I think that true sincere practitioners never show off these things." He laughed.

Many in the West turn to religious beliefs as a source of happiness, yet the Dalai Lama's approach is fundamentally different from many Western religions in that it relies more heavily on reasoning and training the mind than on faith. In some respects, the Dalai Lama's approach resembles a mind science, a system that one could apply in much the same way as people utilize psychotherapy. But what the Dalai Lama suggests goes further. While we're used to the idea of using psychotherapeutic techniques such as behavior therapy to attack specific bad habits— smoking, drinking, temper flares—we are not accustomed to cultivating positive attributes—love, compassion, patience, generosity—as weapons against all negative emotions and mental states. The Dalai Lama's method for achieving happiness is based on the revolutionary idea that negative mental states are not an intrinsic part of our minds; they are transient obstacles that obstruct the expression of our underlying natural state of joy and happiness.

Most traditional schools of Western psychotherapy tend to focus on adjusting to one's neurosis rather than a complete overhaul of one's entire outlook. They explore the individual's personal history, relationships, day-to-day experiences (including dreams and fantasies), and even the relationship with the therapist in an attempt to resolve the patient's internal conflicts, unconscious motives, and psychological dynamics that may be contributing to his or her problems and unhappiness. The goal is to achieve healthier coping strategies, adjustment, and amelioration of symptoms, rather than directly training the mind to be happy.

The most distinguishing feature of the Dalai Lama's method of training the mind involves the idea that *positive states of mind can act as direct antidotes to negative states of mind.* In looking for parallels to this approach in modern behavioral science, cognitive therapy perhaps comes closest. This form of psychotherapy has become increasingly popular over the past few decades and has been proven to be very effective in treating a wide variety of common problems, particularly mood disorders such as depression and anxiety. Modern cognitive therapy, developed by psychotherapists such as Dr. Albert Ellis and Dr. Aaron Beck, is based on the idea that our upsetting emotions and maladaptive behaviors are caused by distortions in thinking and irrational beliefs. The therapy focuses on helping the patient systematically identify, examine, and correct these distortions in thinking. The corrective thoughts, in a sense, become an antidote to the distorted thinking patterns that are the source of the patient's suffering.

For example, a person is rejected by another and responds with excessive feelings of hurt. The cognitive therapist first helps the person identify the underlying irrational belief: for example, "I must be loved and approved of by almost every significant person in my life at all times, or if not it's horrible and I'm unworthy." The therapist then presents the person with evidence that challenges this unrealistic belief. Although this approach may seem superficial, many studies have shown that cognitive therapy works. In depression, for instance, cognitive therapists argue that it is one's negative self-defeating thoughts that underlie the depression. In much the same way that Buddhists view all afflictive emotions as distorted, cognitive therapists view these negative depression-generating thoughts as "essentially distorted." In depression, thinking can become distorted by viewing events in all-or-nothing terms or overgeneralizing (e.g., if you lose a job or fail a class, you automatically think, "I'm a total failure!") or by selectively perceiving only certain events (e.g., three good things and two bad things may happen in one day, but the depressed person ignores the good and focuses only on the bad). So in treating the depression, with the help of the therapist the patient is encouraged to monitor the automatic arising of negative thoughts (e.g., "I'm completely worthless") and actively correct these distorted thoughts by gathering information and evidence that contradict or disprove it (e.g., "I have worked hard to raise two children," "I have a talent for singing," "I have been a good friend," "I have held down a difficult job," etc.). Investigators have proven that by replacing these distorted modes of thinking with accurate information, one can bring about a change in one's feelings and improve one's mood.

The very fact that we can change our emotions and counteract negative thoughts by applying alternative ways of thinking lends support to the Dalai Lama's position that we can overcome our negative mental states through the application of the "antidotes," or the corresponding positive mental states. And when this fact is combined with recent scientific evidence that we can change the structure and function of the brain by cultivating new thoughts, then the idea that we can achieve happiness through training of the mind seems a very real possibility.

Chapter 13

DEALING WITH ANGER
AND HATRED

If one comes across a person who has been shot by an arrow, one does not spend time wondering about where the arrow came from, or the caste of the individual who shot it, or analyzing what type of wood the shaft is made of, or the manner in which the arrowhead was fashioned. Rather, one should focus on immediately pulling out the arrow.

—*Shakyamuni, the Buddha*

We turn now to some of the "arrows," the negative states of mind that destroy our happiness, and their corresponding antidotes. All negative mental states act as obstacles to our happiness, but we begin with anger, which seems to be one of the biggest blocks. It is described by the Stoic philosopher Seneca as "the most hideous and frenzied of all the emotions." The destructive effects of anger and hatred have been well documented by recent scientific studies. Of course, one doesn't need scientific evidence to realize how these emotions can cloud our judgment, cause feelings of extreme discomfort, or wreak havoc in our personal relationships. Our personal experience can tell us that. But in recent years, great inroads have been made in documenting the harmful physical effects of anger and hostility. Dozens of studies have shown these emotions to be a significant cause of disease and premature death. Investigators such as Dr. Redford Williams at Duke University and Dr. Robert Sapolsky at Stanford University have conducted studies that demonstrate that anger, rage, and hostility are particularly damaging to the cardiovascular system. So much evidence has mounted about the harmful effects of hostility, in fact, that it is now considered a major risk factor in heart disease, at least equal to, or perhaps greater than, the traditionally recognized risk factors such as high cholesterol or high blood pressure.

So, once we accept the harmful effects of anger and hatred, the next question becomes: how do we overcome it?

On my first day as a psychiatric consultant to a treatment facility, I was being shown to my new office by a staff member when I heard blood-curdling screams reverberating down the hall . . .

"I'm angry. . ."

"Louder!"

"I'M ANGRY!"

"LOUDER! SHOW IT TO ME. LET ME SEE IT!"

"I'M ANGRY!! I'M ANGRY!! I HATE YOU!!! I HATE YOU!!"

It was truly frightening. I remarked to the staff member that it sounded as if there was a crisis that needed urgent attention.

"Don't worry about it," she laughed. "They're just having a group therapy session down the hall—helping the patient get in touch with her anger."

◆

Later that day, I met with the patient privately. She appeared drained.

"I feel *so relaxed*," she said, "that therapy session really worked. I feel as if I've gotten all my anger out."

In our next session the following day, however, the patient reported, "Well, I guess I didn't get all my anger out after all. Right after I left here yesterday, as I was pulling out of the parking lot some jerk almost cut me off . . . and I was *furious!* And I kept cursing that jerk under my breath all the way home. I guess I still need a few more of those anger sessions to get the rest of it out."

In setting out to conquer anger and hatred, the Dalai Lama begins by investigating the nature of these destructive emotions.

"Generally speaking," he explained, "there are many different kinds of afflictive or negative emotions, such as conceit, arrogance, jealousy, desire, lust, closed-mindedness, and so on. But out of all these, hatred and anger are considered to be the greatest evils because they are the greatest obstacles to developing compassion and altruism, and they destroy one's virtue and calmness of mind.

"In thinking about anger, there can be two types. One type of anger can be positive. This would be mainly due to one's motivation. There can be some anger that is motivated by compassion or a sense of responsibility. Where anger is motivated by compassion, it can be used as an impetus or a catalyst for a positive action. Under these circumstances, a human emotion like anger can act as a force to bring about swift action. It creates a kind of energy that enables an individual to act quickly and decisively. It can be a powerful motivating factor. So, sometimes that kind of anger can be positive. All too often, however, even though that kind of anger can act as a kind of protector and bring one extra energy, that energy is also blind, so it is uncertain whether it will become constructive or destructive in the end.

"So, even though under rare circumstances some kinds of anger can be positive, generally speaking, anger leads to ill feeling and hatred. And, as far as hatred is concerned, it is never positive. It has no benefit at all. It is always totally negative.

"We cannot overcome anger and hatred simply by suppressing them. *We need to actively cultivate the antidotes to hatred: patience and tolerance.* Following the model that we spoke of earlier, in order for you to be able to successfully cultivate patience and tolerance you need to generate enthusiasm, a strong desire to seek it. The stronger your enthusiasm, the greater your ability to withstand the hardships that you encounter in the process. When you are engaged in the practice of patience and tolerance, in reality, what is happening is you are engaged in a combat with hatred and anger. Since it is a situation of combat, you seek victory, but you also have to be prepared for the possibility of losing that battle. So while you are engaged in combat, you should not lose sight of the fact that in the process, you will confront many problems. You should have the ability to withstand these hardships. Someone who gains victory over hatred and anger through such an arduous process is a true hero.

"It is with this in mind that we generate this strong enthusiasm. Enthusiasm results from learning about and reflecting upon

◆

the beneficial effects of tolerance and patience, and the destructive and negative effects of anger and hatred. And that very act,
that very realization in itself, will create an affinity towards feelings of tolerance and patience and make you feel more cautious
and wary of angry and hateful thoughts. Usually, we don't
bother much about anger or hatred, so it just comes. But once
we develop a cautious attitude towards these emotions, that
reluctant attitude itself can act as a preventative measure against
anger or hatred.

"The destructive effects of hatred are very visible, very obvious and immediate. For example, when a very strong or force-
ful thought of hatred arises within you, at that very instant, it
totally overwhelms you and destroys your peace of mind; your
presence of mind disappears completely. When such intense
anger and hatred arises, it obliterates the best part of your
brain, which is the ability to judge between right and wrong,
and the long-term and short-term consequences of your
actions. Your power of judgment becomes totally inoperable;
it can no longer function. It is almost like you have become
insane. So, this anger and hatred tends to throw you into a
state of confusion, which just serves to make your problems
and difficulties so much worse.

"Even at the physical level, hatred brings about a very ugly,
unpleasant physical transformation of the individual. At the
very instant when strong feelings of anger or hatred arise, no
matter how hard the person tries to pretend or adopt a digni-
fied pose, it is very obvious that the person's face looks con-
torted and ugly. There is a very unpleasant expression, and the
person gives out a very hostile vibration. Other people can

sense it. It is almost as if they can feel steam coming out of that person's body. So much so, that not only are human beings capable of sensing it, but even animals, pets, would try to avoid the person at that instant. Also, when a person harbors hateful thoughts, they tend to collect inside the person, and this can cause things like loss of appetite, loss of sleep, and certainly make the person feel more tense and uptight.

"For reasons such as these, hatred is compared to an enemy. This internal enemy, this inner enemy, has no other function than causing us harm. It is our true enemy, our ultimate enemy. It has no other function than simply destroying us, both in the immediate term and in the long term.

"This is very different from an ordinary enemy. Although an ordinary enemy, a person whom we regard as an enemy, may engage in activities that are harmful to us, at least he or she has other functions; that person has got to eat, and that person has got to sleep. So he or she has many other functions and therefore cannot devote twenty-four hours a day of his or her existence to this project of destroying us. On the other hand, hatred has no other function, no other purpose, than destroying us. So, by realizing this fact, we should resolve that we will never give an opportunity for this enemy, hatred, to arise within us."

"In dealing with anger, what do you think about some of the methods of Western psychotherapy, which encourage expressing one's anger?"

"Here, I think we have to understand that there may be different situations," the Dalai Lama explained. "In some cases, people harbor strong feelings of anger and hurt based on something done to them in the past, an abuse or whatever, and that feeling is kept bottled up. There is a Tibetan expression that says that if there is any sickness in the conch shell, you can clear it by blowing it out. In other words, if anything is blocking the conch shell, just blow it out, and it will be clear. So similarly here, it is possible to imagine a situation in which, due to the bottling up of certain emotions or certain feelings of anger, it may be better to just let it out and express it.

"However, I believe that generally speaking, anger and hatred are the type of emotions which, if you leave them unchecked or unattended, tend to aggravate and keep on increasing. If you simply get more and more used to letting them happen and just keep expressing them, this usually results in their growth, not their reduction. So, I feel that the more you adopt a cautious attitude and actively try to reduce the level of their force, the better it is."

"So, if you feel that expressing or releasing our anger isn't the answer, then what is?" I inquired.

"Now, first of all, feelings of anger and hatred arise from a mind that is troubled by dissatisfaction and discontent. So you can prepare ahead of time by constantly working toward building inner contentment and cultivating kindness and compassion. This brings about a certain calmness of mind that can help prevent anger from arising in the first place. And then when a situation does arise that makes you angry, you should directly confront your anger and analyze it. Investigate what factors have given rise to that particular instance of anger or hatred. Then, analyze further, seeing whether it is an appropriate response and especially whether it is constructive or destructive. And you make an effort to exert a certain inner discipline and restraint, actively combating it by applying the antidotes: coun-teracting these negative emotions with thoughts of patience and tolerance."

The Dalai Lama paused, then with his customary pragmatism, added, "Of course, in working towards overcoming anger and hatred, at the initial stage you may still experience these nega-tive emotions. But there are different levels; if it's a mild degree of anger, then at that moment you can attempt to directly con-front it and combat it. However, if it's a very strong negative emotion that develops, then, at that moment, it might be very difficult to challenge or to face it. If that is the case, then at that moment it may be best to simply try to forget about it. Think of something else. Once your mind is a little bit calmed down, then you can analyze; you can reason." In other words, I reflected, he was saying, "Take a time out."

He went on. "In seeking to eliminate anger and hatred, the intentional cultivation of patience and tolerance is indispens-able. You could conceive of the value and importance of patience and tolerance in these terms: Insofar as the destruc-tive effects of angry and hateful thoughts are concerned, you cannot get protection from these from wealth. Even if you are a millionaire, you are still subject to the destructive effects of anger and hatred. Nor can education alone give you a guaran-tee that you will be protected from these effects. Similarly, the law cannot give you such guarantees or protection. Even nu-clear weapons, no matter how sophisticated the defense sys-tem may be, cannot give you the protection or defense from these effects . . ."

The Dalai Lama paused to gather momentum, then concluded in a clear, firm voice, *"The only factor that can give you refuge or protection from the destructive effects of anger and hatred is your practice of tolerance and patience."*

Once again, the Dalai Lama's traditional wisdom is completely consistent with the scientific data. Dr. Dolf Zillmann at the University of Alabama has conducted experiments demonstrating that angry thoughts tend to create a state of physiological arousal that makes us even more prone to anger. Anger builds on anger, and as our state of arousal increases, we are more easily triggered by anger-provoking environmental stimuli.

If left unchecked, anger tends to escalate. So, how do we go about diffusing our anger? As the Dalai Lama suggests, giving vent to anger and rage has very limited benefits. The therapeutic expression of anger as a means of catharsis seems to have originated from Freud's theories of emotion, which he saw as operating on a hydraulic model: when pressure builds, it must be released. The idea of getting rid of our anger by giving vent to it has some dramatic appeal and in a way might even sound like fun, but the problem is that this method simply does not work. Many studies over the past four decades have consistently shown that the verbal and physical expression of our anger does nothing to dispel it and just makes things worse. Dr. Aaron Siegman, a psychologist and anger researcher at the University of Maryland, believes, for instance, that it is just this kind of repeated expression of anger and rage that triggers the internal arousal systems and biochemical responses that are most likely to cause damage to our arteries.

While giving vent to our anger clearly isn't the answer, neither is ignoring our anger or pretending it isn't there. As we discussed in Part III, avoidance of our problems does not make
them go away. So, what's the best approach? Interestingly, the
consensus among modern anger researchers such as Dr. Zillmann and Dr. Williams, is that methods similar to the Dalai
Lama's appear to be most effective. Since general stress lowers
the threshold for what may trigger anger, the first step is preventative: cultivating an inner contentment and calmer state of
mind, as recommended by the Dalai Lama, can definitely help.
And when anger does occur, research has shown that actively
challenging, logically analyzing, and reappraising the thoughts
that trigger the anger can help dissipate it. There is also experimental evidence suggesting that the techniques that we discussed earlier, such as shifting perspective or looking at different
angles of a situation, can also be very effective. Of course, these
things are often easier to do at lower or moderate levels of anger,
so practicing early intervention before thoughts of anger and
hatred escalate can be an important factor.

Because of their vast importance in overcoming anger and
hatred, the Dalai Lama spoke in some detail on the meaning and
value of patience and tolerance.

"In our day-to-day life experiences, tolerance and patience
have great benefits. For instance, developing them will allow us
to sustain and maintain our presence of mind. So if an individual possesses this capacity of tolerance and patience, then, even
in spite of living in a very tense environment, which is very

frantic and stressful, so long as the person has tolerance and patience, the person's calmness and peace of mind will not be disturbed.

"Another benefit of responding to difficult situations with patience rather than giving in to anger is that you protect yourself from potential undesirable consequences that might come about if you reacted with anger. If you respond to situations with anger and hatred, not only does it not protect you from the injury or harm that has already been done to you—the injury and harm has already taken place—but on top of that, you create an additional cause for your own suffering in the future. However, if you respond to an injury with patience and tolerance, then although you may face temporary discomfort and hurt, you will still avoid the potentially dangerous long-term consequences. By sacrificing small things, by putting up with small problems or hardships, you will be able to forgo experiences or sufferings that can be much more enormous in the future. To illustrate, if a convicted prisoner could save his life by sacrificing his arm as a punishment, wouldn't that person feel grateful for the opportunity? By putting up with that pain and suffering of having an arm cut off, the person would be saving himself or herself from death, which is a greater suffering."

"To the Western mind," I observed, "patience and tolerance are certainly considered virtues, but when you are directly beset by others, when someone is actively harming you, responding with 'patience and tolerance' seems to have a flavor of weakness, of passivity."

Shaking his head in disagreement, the Dalai Lama said, "Since patience or tolerance comes from an ability to remain firm and steadfast and not be overwhelmed by the adverse situations or conditions that one faces, one should not see tolerance or patience as a sign of weakness, or giving in, but rather as a sign of strength, coming from a deep ability to remain firm. Responding to a trying situation with patience and tolerance rather than reacting with anger and hatred involves active restraint, which comes from a strong, self-disciplined mind.

"Of course, in discussing the concept of patience, as in most other things, there can be positive and negative kinds of patience. Impatience isn't always bad. For instance, it can help you take action to get things done. Even in your daily chores, like cleaning your room, if you have too much patience, you might move too slowly and get little done. Or, impatience to gain world peace—that certainly can be positive. But in situations that are difficult and challenging, patience helps maintain your willpower and can sustain you."

Becoming increasingly animated as he moved more deeply into his investigation of the meaning of patience, the Dalai Lama added, "I think that there is a very close connection between humility and patience. Humility involves having the capacity to take a more confrontational stance, having the capacity to retaliate if you wish, yet deliberately deciding not to do so. That is what I would call genuine humility. I think that true tolerance or patience has a component or element of self-discipline and restraint—the realization that you could have acted otherwise, you could have adopted a more aggressive approach, but decided not to do so. On the other hand, being forced to adopt a certain passive response out of a feeling of helplessness or incapacitation—that I wouldn't call genuine humility. That may be a kind of meekness, but it isn't genuine tolerance.

"Now when we talk about how we should develop tolerance towards those who harm us, we should not misunderstand this to mean that we should just meekly accept whatever is done against us." The Dalai Lama paused, then laughed. "Rather, if necessary, the best, the wisest course, might be to simply run away—run miles away!"

"You can't always avoid being harmed by running away . . ."

"Yes, that's true," he replied. "Sometimes, you may encounter situations that require strong countermeasures. I believe, however, that you can take a strong stand and even take strong countermeasures out of a feeling of compassion, or a sense of concern for the other, rather than out of anger. One of the reasons why there is a need to adopt a very strong countermeasure against someone is that if you let it pass—whatever the harm or the crime that is being perpetrated against you—then there is a danger of that person's habituating in a very negative way, which, in reality, will cause that individual's own downfall and is very destructive in the long run for the individual himself or herself. Therefore a strong countermeasure is necessary, but with this thought in mind, you can do it out of compassion and concern for that individual. For example, so far as our own dealings with China are concerned, even if there is a likelihood of some feeling of hatred arising, we deliberately check ourselves and try to reduce that, we try to consciously develop a feeling of compassion towards the Chinese. And I think that countermeasures can ultimately be more effective without feelings of anger and hatred.

◆

"Now, we've explored methods of developing patience and tolerance and letting go of anger and hatred, methods such as using reasoning to analyze the situation, adopting a wider perspective, and looking at other angles of a situation. *An end result, or a product of patience and tolerance, is forgiveness. When you are truly patient and tolerant, then forgiveness comes naturally.*

"Although you may have experienced many negative events in the past, with the development of patience and tolerance it is possible to let go of your sense of anger and resentment. If you analyze the situation, you'll realize that the past is past, so there is no use continuing to feel anger and hatred, which do not change the situation but just cause a disturbance within your mind and cause your continued unhappiness. Of course, you may still remember the events. Forgetting and forgiving are two different things. There's nothing wrong with simply remembering those negative events; if you have a sharp mind, you'll always remember," he laughed. "I think the Buddha remembered everything. But with the development of patience and tolerance, it's possible to let go of the negative feelings associated with the events."

MEDITATIONS ON ANGER

In many of these discussions, the Dalai Lama's primary method of overcoming anger and hatred involved the use of reasoning and analysis to investigate the causes of anger, to combat these harmful mental states through understanding. In a sense, this approach can be seen as using logic to neutralize anger and hatred and to cultivate the antidotes of patience and tolerance. But that wasn't his only technique. In his public talks he supplemented his discussion by presenting instruction on these two simple yet effective meditations to help overcome anger.

Meditation on Anger: Exercise 1

"Let us imagine a scenario in which someone who you know very well, someone who is close or dear to you, is in a situation in which he or she loses his or her temper. You can imagine this occurring either in a very acrimonious relationship or in a situation in which something personally upsetting is happening. The person is so angry that he or she has lost all his or her mental composure, creating very negative vibrations, even going to the extent of beating himself or herself up or breaking things.

"Then, reflect upon the immediate effects of the person's rage. You'll see a physical transformation happening to that person. This person whom you feel close to, whom you like, the very sight of whom gave you pleasure in the past, now turns into this ugly person, even physically speaking. The reason why I think you should visualize this happening to someone else is because it is easier to see the faults of others than to see your own faults. So, using your imagination, do this meditation and visualization for a few minutes.

"At the end of that visualization, analyze the situation and relate the circumstances to your own experience. See that you yourself have been in this state many times. Resolve that 'I shall never let myself fall under the sway of such intense anger and hatred, because if I do that, I will be in the same position. I will also suffer all these consequences, lose my peace of mind, lose my composure, assume this ugly physical appearance,' and so on. So once you make that decision, then for the last few minutes of the meditation focus your mind on that conclusion; without further analysis, simply let your mind remain on your resolution not to fall under the influence of anger and hatred."

Meditation on Anger: Exercise 2

"Let us do another meditation using visualization. Begin by visualizing someone whom you dislike, someone who annoys you, causes a lot of problems for you, or gets on your nerves. Then, imagine a scenario in which the person irritates you, or does something that offends you or annoys you. And, in your imagination, when you visualize this, let your natural response follow; just let it flow naturally. Then see how you feel, see whether that causes the rate of your heartbeat to go up, and so on. Examine whether you are comfortable or uncomfortable; see if you immediately become more peaceful or if you develop an uncomfortable mental feeling. Judge for yourself; investigate. So for a few minutes, three or four minutes perhaps, judge, and experiment. And then at the end of your investigation, if you discover that 'Yes, it is of no use to allow that irritation to develop. Immediately I lose my peace of mind,' then say to yourself, 'In the future, I will never do that.' Develop that determination. Finally, for the last few minutes of the exercise, place your mind single-pointedly upon that conclusion or determination. So that's the meditation."

The Dalai Lama paused for a moment, then looking around

the room of sincere students preparing to practice this meditation, he laughed, and added, "I think if I had the cognitive faculty, ability, or the clear awareness to be able to read other people's minds, then there would be a great spectacle here!"

There was a ripple of laughter in the audience, which quickly died down as his listeners started the meditation, beginning the serious business of doing battle with their anger.

Chapter 14

DEALING WITH ANXIETY AND
BUILDING SELF-ESTEEM

I t is estimated that in the course of a lifetime at least one in four Americans will suffer from a debilitating degree of anxiety or worry severe enough to meet the criteria for the medical diagnosis of an anxiety disorder. But even those who never suffer from a pathological or disabling state of anxiety will, at one time or another, experience excessive levels of worry and anxiety that serve no useful purpose and do nothing but undermine their happiness and interfere with their ability to accomplish their goals.

The human brain is equipped with an elaborate system designed to register the emotions of fear and worry. This system serves an important function—it mobilizes us to respond to danger by setting in motion a complex sequence of biochemical and physiological events. The adaptive side of worry is that it allows us to anticipate danger and take preventative action. So, some types of fears and a certain amount of worry can be healthy. However, feelings of fear and anxiety can persist and even escalate in the absence of an authentic threat, and when these emotions grow out of proportion to any real danger they become maladaptive. Excessive anxiety and worry can, like anger and hatred, have devastating effects on the mind and body, becoming the source of much emotional suffering and even physical illness.

On a mental level, chronic anxiety can impair judgment, increase irritability, and hinder one's overall effectiveness. It can also lead to physical problems including depressed immune function, heart disease, gastrointestinal disorders, fatigue, and muscle tension and pain. Anxiety disorders, for instance, have even been shown to cause stunted growth in adolescent girls.

In seeking strategies to deal with anxiety, we must first recognize, as the Dalai Lama will point out, that there may be many factors contributing to the experience of anxiety. In some cases, there may be a strong biological component. Some people seem to have a certain neurological vulnerability to experiencing states of worry and anxiety. Scientists have recently discovered a gene that is linked to people who are prone to anxiety and negative thinking. Not all cases of toxic worry are genetic in origin, however, and there is little doubt that learning and conditioning play a major role in its etiology.

But, regardless of whether our anxiety is predominantly physical or psychological in origin, the good news is that there is something we can do about it. In the most severe cases of anxiety, medication can be a useful part of the treatment regimen. But most of us who are troubled by nagging day-to-day worries and anxiety will not need pharmacological intervention. Experts in the field of anxiety management generally feel that a multidimensional approach is best. This would include first ruling out an underlying medical condition as the cause of our anxiety. Working on improving our physical health through proper diet and exercise can also be helpful. And, as the Dalai Lama has emphasized, cultivating compassion and deepening our connection with others can promote good mental hygiene and help combat anxiety states.

In searching for practical strategies to overcome anxiety, however, there is one technique that stands out as particularly effective: cognitive intervention. This is one of the main methods used by the Dalai Lama to overcome daily worries and anxiety. Applying the same procedure used with anger and hatred, this technique involves actively challenging the anxiety-generating thoughts and replacing them with well-reasoned positive thoughts and attitudes.

Because of the pervasiveness of anxiety in our culture, I was eager to bring up the subject with the Dalai Lama and learn how he deals with it. His schedule was particularly busy that day, and I could feel my own anxiety level rising as, moments before our interview, I was informed by his secretary that we would have to cut our conversation short. Feeling pressed for time and worrying that we wouldn't be able to address all the topics I wanted to discuss, I sat down quickly and began, reverting to my intermittent tendency to try to elicit simplistic answers from him.

"You know, fear and anxiety can be a major obstacle to achieving our goals, whether they are external goals or inner growth. In psychiatry we have various methods of dealing with these things, but I'm curious, from your standpoint, what's the best way to overcome fear and anxiety?"

Resisting my invitation to oversimplify the matter, the Dalai Lama answered with his characteristically thorough approach.

"In dealing with fear, I think that we first need to recognize that there are many different types of fear. Some kinds of fear are very genuine, based on valid reasons, fear of violence or fear of bloodshed, for example. We can see that these things are very bad. Then there's fear about the long-term negative consequences of our negative actions, fear of suffering, fear of our negative emotions such as hatred. I think these are the right kinds of fears; having these kinds of fears bring us onto the right path, bring us closer to becoming a warmhearted person." He stopped to reflect, then mused, "Although in a sense these are kinds of fears, I think perhaps that there may be some difference between fearing these things and the mind's seeing the destructive nature of these things . . ."

He ceased speaking again for several moments, and appeared to be deliberating, while I stole furtive glances at my watch. Clearly he didn't feel the same time crunch that I did. Finally, he continued speaking in a leisurely manner.

"On the other hand, some kinds of fears are our own mental creations. These fears may be based mainly on mental projection. For example, there are very childish fears," he laughed, "like when we were young and passed through a dark place, especially some of the dark rooms in the Potala,* and became afraid—that was based completely on mental projection. Or, when I was young, the sweepers and people looking after me always warned me that there was an owl that caught young children and consumed them!" the Dalai Lama laughed even harder. "And I really believed them!"

"There are other types of fear based on mental projection," he continued. "For example, if you have negative feelings, because of your own mental situation, you may project those feelings onto another, who then appears as someone negative and hostile. And as a result, you feel fear. That kind of fear, I think, is related to hatred and comes about as a sort of mental creation. So, in dealing with fear, you need to first use your faculty of reasoning and try to discover whether there is a valid basis for your fear or not."

I asked, "Well, rather than an intense or focused fear of a specific individual or situation, many of us are plagued by more of an ongoing diffuse worry about a variety of day-to-day problems. Do you have any suggestions about how to handle that?"

Nodding his head, he replied, "One of the approaches that I

---

*The Potala was the traditional winter palace of the Dalai Lamas, and a symbol of the religious and historical heritage of Tibet. Originally built by the Tibetan King Song-tsen Gampo in the seventh century, it was later destroyed and not rebuilt until the seventeenth century by the fifth Dalai Lama. The current structure rises a majestic 440 feet from the summit of the "Red Hill" in Lhasa. It is over a quarter mile long, thirteen stories high, and filled with over a thousand chambers, assembly halls, shrines, and chapels.

personally find useful to reduce that kind of worry is to cultivate the thought: *If the situation or problem is such that it can be remedied, then there is no need to worry about it.* In other words, if there is a solution or a way out of the difficulty, then one needn't be overwhelmed by it. The appropriate action is to seek its solution. It is more sensible to spend the energy focusing on the solution rather than worrying about the problem. *Alternatively, if there is no way out, no solution, no possibility of resolution, then there is also no point in being worried about it, because you can't do anything about it anyway.* In that case, the sooner you accept this fact, the easier it will be on you. This formula, of course, implies directly confronting the problem. Otherwise you won't be able to find out whether or not there is a resolution to the problem."

"What if thinking about that doesn't help alleviate your anxiety?"

"Well, you may need to reflect on these thoughts a bit more and reinforce these ideas. Remind yourself of it repeatedly. Anyway, I think that this approach can help reduce anxiety and worry, but that doesn't mean it always will work. If you are dealing with ongoing anxiety, I think you need to look at the specific situation. There are different types of anxieties and different causes. For example, some types of anxiety or nervousness could have some biological causes; for instance, some people tend to get sweaty palms, which according to the Tibetan medical system could indicate an imbalance of subtle energy levels. Some types of anxiety, just like some types of depression for instance, may have biological roots, and for these medical treatment may be useful. So in order to deal with the anxiety effectively, you need to look at the kind it is and the cause.

◆

"So, just like fear, there can be different types of anxiety. For example, one type of anxiety, which I think may be common, could involve fear of appearing foolish in front of others or fear that others might think badly of you . . ."

"Have you ever experienced that kind of anxiety or nervousness?" I interrupted.

The Dalai Lama broke into a robust laugh, and without hesitation he responded, "Oh yes!"

"Can you give an example?"

He thought for a moment, then said, "Now, for instance, in 1954 in China, on the first day of meeting with Chairman Mao Zedong, and also another occasion in meeting with Chou En-lai. In those days I wasn't fully aware of the proper protocol and convention. The usual procedure for a meeting was to start with some casual talk and then proceed to the discussion of business. But on that occasion I was so nervous that the moment I sat down, I just jumped right into business!" The Dalai Lama laughed at the memory. "I remember that afterwards my translator, a Tibetan communist who was very reliable and my great, great friend, looked at me and started laughing and teasing me about it.

"I think that even these days, just before a public talk or teachings are about to start, I always feel a little bit of anxiety, so some of my attendants usually say, 'If that's the case, then why did you accept the invitation to give teachings in the first place?' " He laughed again.

"So how do you personally deal with that kind of anxiety?" I asked.

With a querulous and unaffected tone in his voice he said quietly, "I don't know . . ." He paused, and we sat in silence for a long time, as once again he seemed to carefully consider and reflect. At last he said, "I think having proper motivation and honesty are the keys to overcoming those kinds of fear and anxiety. So, if I am anxious before giving a talk, I'll remind myself that the main reason, the aim of giving the lecture, is to be of at least some benefit to the people, not for showing off my knowledge. So, those points which I know, I'll explain. Those points which I do not understand properly—then it doesn't matter; I just say, 'For me, this is difficult.' There's no reason to hide or to pretend. From that standpoint, with that motivation, I don't have to worry about appearing foolish or care about what others think of me. *So, I've found that sincere motivation acts as an antidote to reduce fear and anxiety.*"

"Well, sometimes the anxiety involves more than just appearing foolish in front of others. It's more of a fear of failure, a feeling of being incompetent . . ." I reflected for a moment, considering how much personal information to reveal.

The Dalai Lama listened intently, silently nodding as I spoke. I'm not sure what it was. Maybe it was his attitude of sympathetic understanding, but before I knew it, I had shifted from discussing broad general issues to soliciting his advice about dealing with my own fears and anxieties.

"I don't know . . . sometimes with my patients for instance . . . some are very difficult to treat—cases in which it isn't a matter of making a clear-cut diagnosis like depression or some other illness that is easily remedied. There are some patients with severe personality disorders, for instance, who don't respond to medication and have failed to make much progress in psychotherapy despite my best efforts. Sometimes I just don't know what to do with these people, how to help them. I can't seem to get a grasp on what's going on with them. And it makes me feel immobilized, sort of helpless," I complained. "It makes me feel incompetent, and that really creates a certain kind of fear, of anxiety."

He listened solemnly, then asked in a kindly voice, "Would you say that you're able to help 70 percent of your patients?"

"At least that," I replied.

Patting my hand gently, he said, "Then I think that there's no problem here. If you were able to help only 30 percent of your patients, then I might suggest that you consider another profession. But I think you're doing fine. In my case people also come to me for help. Many are looking for miracles, for miraculous cures, and so on, and of course I can't help everybody. But I think the main thing is motivation—to have a sincere motivation to help. Then you just do the best you can, and you don't have to worry about it.

"So, in my case also there are of course some situations that are tremendously delicate or serious, and such a heavy responsibility. I think the worst is when people place too much trust or belief in me, in circumstances in which some things are beyond my capability. In such cases, sometimes anxiety, of course, develops. Here, once again, we return to the importance of motivation. Then, I try to remind myself as far as my own motivation is concerned, I am sincere, and I tried my best. With a sincere motivation, one of compassion, even if I made a mistake or failed, there is no cause for regret. For my part I did my best. Then, you see, if I failed, it was because the situation was beyond my best efforts. So that sincere motivation removes fear and gives you self-confidence. On the other hand, if your underlying motivation is to cheat someone, then if you fail, you really become nervous. But if you cultivate a compassionate motivation, if you fail, then there's no regret.

"So, again and again, I think that proper motivation can be a sort of protector, shielding you against these feelings of fear and anxiety. Motivation is so important. In fact all human action can be seen in terms of movement, and the mover behind all actions is one's motivation. If you develop a pure and sincere motivation, if you are motivated by a wish to help on the basis of kindness, compassion, and respect, then you can carry on any kind of work, in any field, and function more effectively with less fear or worry, not being afraid of what others think or whether you ultimately will be successful in reaching your goal. Even if you fail to achieve your goal, you can feel good about having made the effort. But with a bad motivation, people can praise you or you can achieve goals, but you still will not be happy."

In discussing the antidotes to anxiety, the Dalai Lama offers two remedies, each working on a different level. The first involves actively combating chronic rumination and worry by applying a counteractive thought: reminding oneself, *If there is a solution to the problem, there is no need to worry. If there is no solution, there is no sense in worrying either.*

The second antidote is a more broad-spectrum remedy. It involves the transformation of one's underlying motivation. There is an interesting contrast between the Dalai Lama's approach to human motivation and that of Western science and psychology. As we previously discussed, researchers who have studied human motivation have investigated normal human motives, looking at both instinctual and learned needs and drives. At this level, the Dalai Lama has focused on developing and using learned drives to enhance one's "enthusiasm and determination." In some respects, this is similar to the view of many conventional Western "motivation experts," who also seek to boost one's enthusiasm and determination to accomplish goals. But the difference is that the Dalai Lama seeks to build determination and enthusiasm to engage in more wholesome behaviors and eliminate negative mental traits, rather than emphasizing the achievement of worldly success, money, or power. And perhaps the most striking difference is that whereas the "motivational speakers" are busy fanning the flames of *already existing* motives for worldly success, and the Western theorists are preoccupied with categorizing standard human motives, the Dalai Lama's primary interest in human motivation lies in *reshaping and changing* one's underlying motivation to one of compassion and kindness.

In the Dalai Lama's system of training the mind and achieving happiness, *the closer one gets to being motivated by altruism, the more fearless one becomes in the face of even extremely anxiety-provoking circumstances.* But the same principle can be applied in smaller ways, even when one's motivation is less than completely altruistic. Standing back and simply making sure that you mean no harm and that your motivation is sincere can help reduce anxiety in ordinary daily situations.

Not long after the above conversation with the Dalai Lama, I had lunch with a group of people that included one young man whom I had not met before, a college student at a local university. During lunch, someone asked how my series of discussions

◆

with the Dalai Lama were going, and I recounted the conversation about overcoming anxiety. After quietly listening to me describe the idea of "sincere motivation as an antidote to anxiety," the student confided that he had always been painfully shy and very anxious in social situations. In thinking about how he might apply this technique in overcoming his own anxiety, the student muttered, "Well, all that's pretty interesting. But I guess the hard part is always having this lofty motivation of kindness and compassion."

"I suppose that's true," I had to admit.

The general conversation turned to other subjects, and we finished our lunch. I happened to run into the same college student the following week at the same restaurant.

Approaching me in a cheerful manner, he said, "You remember we were talking about motivation and anxiety the other day? Well, I tried it out and it really works! There's this girl who works at a department store in the mall whom I've seen a lot of times; I've always wanted to ask her out, but I don't know her and I've always felt too shy and anxious, so I've never even talked to her. Well, the other day I went in again, but this time I started thinking about my motivation for asking her out. My motivation, of course, is that I'd like to date her. But behind that is just the wish that I could find someone whom I can love and who will love me. When I thought about it, I realized that there is nothing wrong with that, that my motivation was sincere; I didn't wish any harm to her or myself, but only good things. Just keeping that in mind, and reminding myself of it a few times, seemed to help somehow; it gave me the courage to strike up a conversation with her. My heart was still pounding, but I feel great that at least I was able to get up the nerve to speak with her."

"I'm glad to hear that," I said. "What happened?"

"Well, as it turns out, she already has a steady boyfriend. I was a bit disappointed, but it's okay. It just felt good that I was able to overcome my shyness. And it made me realize that if I make sure that there's nothing wrong with my motivation and keep that in mind, it could help the next time I'm in the same situation."

HONESTY AS AN ANTIDOTE TO LOW SELF-ESTEEM OR INFLATED SELF-CONFIDENCE

A healthy sense of self-confidence is a critical factor in achieving our goals. This holds true whether our goal is to earn a college degree, build a successful business, enjoy a satisfying relationship, or train the mind to become happier. Low self-confidence inhibits our efforts to move ahead, to meet challenges, and even to take some risks when necessary in the pursuit of our objectives. Inflated self-confidence can be equally hazardous. Those who suffer from an exaggerated sense of their own abilities and accomplishments are continuously subject to frustration, disappointment, and rage when reality intrudes and the world doesn't validate their idealized view of themselves. And they are always precariously close to sinking into depression when they fail to live up to their own idealized self-image. In addition, these individuals' grandiosity often leads to a sense of entitlement and a kind of arrogance that distances them from others and prevents emotionally satisfying relationships.

◆

Finally, overestimating their abilities can lead to taking dangerous risks. As inspector Dirty Harry Callahan, in a philosophical
frame of mind, tells us in the film *Magnum Force* (while watching
the overconfident villain blow himself up), "A man's gotta know
his limitations."

In the Western psychotherapeutic tradition, theorists have
related both low and inflated self-confidence to disturbances in
people's self-image and have searched for the roots of these disturbances in people's early upbringing. Many theorists see poor
self-image and inflated self-image as two sides of the same coin,
conceptualizing people's inflated self-image, for instance, as an
unconscious defense against underlying insecurities and negative feelings about themselves. Psychoanalytically oriented psychotherapists in particular have formulated elaborate theories of
how distortions in self-image occur. They explain how the self-
image is formed as people internalize feedback from the environment. They describe how people develop their concepts of
who they are by incorporating explicit and implicit messages
about themselves from their parents and how distortions can
occur when early interactions with their caregivers are neither
healthy nor nurturing.

When disturbances in self-image are severe enough to cause
significant problems in their lives, many of these people turn to
psychotherapy. Insight-oriented psychotherapists focus on
helping the patients gain an understanding of the dysfunctional
patterns in their early relationships that were the cause of the
problem and provide appropriate feedback and a therapeutic
environment where the patients can gradually restructure and
repair their negative self-image. On the other hand, the Dalai

Lama focuses on "pulling out the arrow" rather than spending time wondering who shot it. Instead of wondering why people have low self-esteem or inflated self-confidence, he presents a method of directly combating these negative states of mind.

In recent decades, the nature of "the self" was one of the most researched topics in the field of psychology. In the "me decade" of the 1980s, for instance, thousands of articles appeared each year, exploring issues related to self-esteem and self-confidence. With this in mind, I addressed the subject with the Dalai Lama.

"In one of our other conversations you spoke of humility as a positive trait, and how it is linked with the cultivation of patience and tolerance. In Western psychology, and our culture in general, it seems that being humble is largely overlooked in favor of developing qualities like high levels of self-esteem and self-confidence. In fact, in the West there's a lot of importance placed on these attributes. I was just wondering—do you feel that Westerners sometimes tend to put too much emphasis on self-confidence, that it's kind of overindulgent or too self-absorbed?"

"Not necessarily," the Dalai Lama replied, "although the subject can be quite complicated. For example, the great spiritual practitioners are those who have made a pledge, or developed the determination, to eradicate all of their negative states of mind in order to help to bring ultimate happiness to all sentient beings. They have this kind of vision and aspiration. This requires a tremendous sense of self-confidence. And this self-confidence can be very important because it gives you a certain boldness of mind that helps you accomplish great goals. In a way, this may

◆

seem like a kind of arrogance, although not in a negative way. It is based on sound reasons. So, here, I would consider them to be very courageous—I would consider them to be heroes."

"Well, for a great spiritual master what may appear on the surface to be a form of arrogance may in fact be a kind of self-confidence and courage," I allowed. "But for normal people, under everyday circumstances, the opposite is more likely to occur—someone appears to have strong self-confidence or high self-esteem, but it can be in reality simply arrogance. I understand that according to Buddhism, arrogance is categorized as one of the 'basic afflicted emotions.' In fact, I've read that according to one system, they list seven different types of arrogance. So, avoiding or overcoming arrogance is considered very important. But so is having a strong sense of self-confidence. There seems to be a fine line between them sometimes. How can you tell the difference between them and cultivate one while reducing the other?"

"Sometimes it's quite difficult to distinguish between confidence and arrogance," he conceded. "Maybe one way of distinguishing between the two is to see whether or not it is sound. One can have a very sound or very valid sense of superiority in relation to someone else, which could be very justified and which could be valid. And then there could also be an inflated sense of self which is totally groundless. That would be arrogance. So in terms of their phenomenological state, they may seem similar . . . ."

"But, an arrogant person *always* feels that they have a valid basis of . . ."

"That's right, that's right," the Dalai Lama acknowledged.

◆

"So, then how can you distinguish between the two?" I inquired.

"I think sometimes it can be judged only in retrospect, either by the individual or from a third person's perspective." The Dalai Lama paused, then joked, "Maybe the person should go to the court to find out if it is a case of inflated pride or arrogance!" He laughed.

"In making the distinction between conceit and valid self-confidence," he went on, "one could think in terms of the consequences of one's attitude—conceit and arrogance generally lead to negative consequences whereas a healthy self-confidence leads to more positive consequences. So, here when we are dealing with 'self-confidence' you need to look at what is the underlying sense of 'self.' I think one can categorize two types. One sense of self, or 'ego,' is concerned only with the fulfillment of one's self-interest, one's selfish desires, with complete disregard for the well-being of others. The other type of ego or sense of self is based on a genuine concern for others, and the desire to be of service. In order to fulfill that wish to be of service, one needs a strong sense of self, and a sense of self-confidence. This kind of self-confidence is the kind that leads to positive consequences."

"Earlier," I noted, "I think you mentioned that one way to help reduce arrogance or pride, if a person acknowledged pride as a fault and wished to overcome it, was to contemplate one's suffering—reflecting on all the ways we are subject to or prone to suffering, and so on. Besides contemplating one's suffering, are there any other techniques or antidotes to work with pride?"

He said, "One antidote is to reflect upon the diversity of disciplines that you may have no knowledge of. For example, in the modern educational system you have a multitude of disciplines. So by thinking about how many fields you are ignorant of, it may help you overcome pride."

The Dalai Lama stopped speaking, and, thinking that was all he had to say on the subject, I started looking through my notes to move on to a new topic. He suddenly resumed speaking in a reflective tone, "You know, we've been talking about developing a healthy self-confidence . . . *I think perhaps honesty and self-confidence are closely linked.*"

"Do you mean being honest with yourself about what your capabilities are and so on? Or do you mean being honest with others?" I asked.

"Both," he replied. "The more honest you are, the more open, the less fear you will have, because there's no anxiety about being exposed or revealed to others. So, I think that the more honest you are, the more self-confident you will be . . ."

"I'm interested in exploring a bit more about how you personally deal with the issue of self-confidence," I said. "You've mentioned that people seem to come to you and expect you to perform miracles. They seem to put so much pressure on you and have such high expectations. Even if you have a proper underlying motivation, doesn't this still cause you to feel a certain lack of confidence in your abilities?"

"Here, I think you have to keep in mind what you mean when you say either 'lack of confidence' or 'possessing confidence' with regard to a particular act or whatever it may be. In order for you to have a lack of confidence in something, it implies that you have a kind of belief that you can do it, that, generally speaking, it is within your scope. And then if something is within your scope and you can't do it, you begin to feel, 'Oh, you know, maybe I'm not good enough or competent enough or up to it' or something along those lines. However, for me to realize that I cannot per-form miracles—that does not lead to loss of confidence, because I never believed myself to have that capacity in the first place. I don't expect myself to be able to perform functions like the fully enlightened Buddhas—to be able to know everything, perceive everything, or do the right thing at any and all times. So when people come to me and ask me to heal them or perform a miracle or something like that, instead of making me feel a lack of confi-dence, it just makes me feel quite awkward.

"I think that, generally, being honest with oneself and others about what you are or are not capable of doing can counteract that feeling of lack of self-confidence.

"But then, now for example, in handling the situation with China, sometimes I feel a lack of self-confidence. But usually I consult about such a situation with officials and in some cases nonofficials. I ask my friends their opinion and then discuss the matter. Since many of the decisions are taken on the basis of dis-cussions with various people and not just taken rashly, any deci-sion that is taken then makes me feel quite confident and there's no sense of regret for having taken that course."

Fearless and honest self-appraisal can be a powerful weapon against self-doubt and low self-confidence. The Dalai Lama's belief that this kind of honesty can act as an antidote to these negative states of mind has in fact been confirmed by a number of recent studies that clearly show that those who have a realistic and accurate view of themselves tend to like themselves better and have more confidence than those with poor or inaccurate self-knowledge.

Over the years, I've often witnessed the Dalai Lama's illustrating how self-confidence comes from being honest and straightforward about one's abilities. It came as quite a surprise to me when I first heard him say in front of a large audience simply "I don't know" in response to a question. Unlike what I was used to with academic lecturers or those who set themselves up as authorities, he admitted his lack of knowledge without embarrassment, qualifying statements, or attempting to appear that he knew something by skirting the issue.

In fact, he seemed to take a certain delight when confronted with a difficult question for which he had no answer and often joked about it. For example, one afternoon in Tucson, he had been commenting on one verse of Shantideva's *Guide to the Bodhisattva's Way of Life* that was particularly complex in its logic. He struggled with it for a while, got mixed up, then burst out laughing, saying:

"I'm confused! I think it's better just to leave it. Now, in the next verse . . ."

In response to appreciative laughter from the audience, he laughed even harder, commenting, "There is a particular expression for this approach. The expression is it's like an old person eating—an old person with very poor teeth. The soft things you eat; the hard things, you just leave." Still laughing, he said, "So we'll leave it at that for today." He never wavered in that moment from his own supreme confidence.

◆

REFLECTING ON OUR POTENTIAL AS
AN ANTIDOTE TO SELF-HATRED

On one trip to India in 1991, two years before the Dalai Lama's visit to Arizona, I briefly met with him at his home in Dharamsala. That week he had been meeting daily with a distinguished group of Western scientists, physicians, psychologists, and meditation teachers, in an attempt to explore the mind-body connection and understand the relationship between emotional experience and physical health. I met with the Dalai Lama late one afternoon, after one of his sessions with the scientists. Toward the end of our interview, the Dalai Lama asked, "You know this week I've been meeting with these scientists?"

"Yes . . ."

"Something came up this week which I found very surprising. This concept of 'self-hatred.' You are familiar with that concept?"

"Definitely. A fair proportion of my patients suffer from it."

"When these people were speaking about it, at first I wasn't certain if I was understanding the concept correctly," he laughed. "I thought, 'Of course we love ourselves! How can a person hate himself or herself?' Although I thought that I had some understanding about how the mind works, this idea of hating oneself was completely new to me. The reason why I found it quite unbelievable is that practicing Buddhists work very hard trying to overcome our self-centered attitude, our selfish thoughts and motives. From this viewpoint I think we love and cherish ourselves too much. So to think of the possibility of

◆

283

someone not cherishing oneself, and even hating oneself, was quite, quite unbelievable. As a psychiatrist, can you explain this concept for me, how it occurs?"

I briefly described for him the psychological view of how self-hatred arises. I explained how our self-image is shaped by our parents and upbringing, how we pick up implicit messages about ourselves from them as we grow and develop, and I outlined the specific conditions that create a negative self-image. I went on to detail the factors that exacerbate self-hatred, such as when our behavior fails to live up to our idealized self-image, and described some of the ways that self-hatred can be culturally reinforced, particularly in some women and minorities. While I was discussing these things, the Dalai Lama continued to nod thoughtfully with a quizzical expression on his face, as if he were still having some difficulty grasping this strange concept.

Groucho Marx once quipped, "I'd never join any club that would have me for a member." Broadening this kind of negative self-view into an observation about human nature, Mark Twain said, "No man, deep down in the privacy of his own heart, has any considerable respect for himself." And taking this pessimistic view of humanity and incorporating it into his psychological theories, the humanistic psychologist Carl Rogers once claimed, "Most people despise themselves, regard themselves as worthless and unlovable."

There is a popular notion in our society, shared by most contemporary psychotherapists, that self-hatred is rampant within Western culture. While it certainly exists, fortunately it may not be as widespread as many believe. It certainly is a common problem among those who seek psychotherapy, but sometimes psychotherapists in clinical practice have a skewed view, a tendency to base their general view of human nature on those few individuals who walk into their offices. Most of the data based on experimental evidence, however, have established the fact that often people tend to (or at least want to) see themselves in a favorable light, rating themselves as "better than average" in almost any survey asking about subjective and socially desirable qualities.

So, while self-hatred may not be as universal as commonly thought, it can still be a tremendous obstacle for many people. I was as surprised by the Dalai Lama's reaction as he was by the concept of self-hatred. His initial response alone can be very revealing and healing.

There are two points related to his remarkable reaction that warrant examination. The first point is simply that he was unfamiliar with the existence of self-hatred. The underlying assumption that self-hatred is a widespread human problem leads to an impressionistic sense that it is a deeply ingrained feature of the human psyche. But the fact that it is virtually unheard of within entire cultures, in this case the Tibetan culture, strongly reminds us that this troubling mental state, like all of the other negative mental states that we have discussed, *is not an intrinsic part of the human mind.* It is not something that we are born with, irrevocably saddled with, nor is it an indelible characteristic of our nature. It can be removed. This realization alone can serve to weaken its power, give us hope, and increase our commitment to eliminate it.

The second point related to the Dalai Lama's initial reaction was his response, "*Hate* oneself? Of course, we *love* ourselves!" For those of us who suffer from self-hatred or know someone who does, this response may seem incredibly naive at first glance. But on closer investigation, there may be a penetrating truth to his response. Love is difficult to define, and there may be different definitions. But one definition of love, and perhaps the most pure and exalted kind of love, is an utter, absolute, and unqualified wish for the happiness of another individual. It is a heartfelt wish for the other's happiness regardless of whether he does something to injure us or even whether we like him. Now, deep in our hearts, there's no question that every one of us wants to be happy. *So, if our definition of love is based on a genuine wish for someone's happiness, then each of us does in fact love himself or herself—every one of us sincerely wishes for his or her own happiness.* In my clinical practice I've sometimes encountered the most extreme cases of self-hatred, to the point where the person experiences recurrent thoughts of suicide. But even in these most extreme cases, the thought of death is ultimately based on the individual's wish (distorted and misguided though it may be) to *release her- or himself* from suffering, not cause it.

So perhaps the Dalai Lama was not far off the mark in his belief that all of us have an underlying self-love, and this idea suggests a powerful antidote to self-hatred: we can directly counteract thoughts of self-contempt by reminding ourselves that no matter how much we may dislike some of our charac-

◆

teristics, underneath it all we wish ourselves to be happy, and that is a profound kind of love.

On a subsequent visit to Dharamsala, I returned to the subject of self-hatred with the Dalai Lama. By then he had familiarized himself with the concept and had begun developing methods for combating it.

"From the Buddhist point of view," he explained, "being in a depressed state, in a state of discouragement, is seen as a kind of extreme that can clearly be an obstacle to taking the steps necessary to accomplish one's goals. A state of self-hatred is even far more extreme than simply being discouraged, and this can be very, very dangerous. For those engaged in Buddhist practice, the antidote to self-hatred would be to reflect upon the fact that all beings, including oneself, have Buddha Nature—the seed or potential for perfection, full Enlightenment—no matter how weak or poor or deprived one's present situation may be. So those people involved in Buddhist practice who suffer from self-hatred or self-loathing should avoid contemplating the suffering nature of existence or the underlying unsatisfactory nature of existence, and instead they should concentrate more on the positive aspects of one's existence, such as appreciating the tremendous potential that lies within oneself as a human being. And by reflecting upon these opportunities and potentials, they will be able to increase their sense of worth and confidence in themselves."

Raising my now-standard question from the perspective of a non-Buddhist, I asked, "Well, what would be the antidote for someone who may not have heard of the concept of Buddha Nature or who may not be a Buddhist?"

"One thing in general that we could point out to such people is that we are gifted as human beings with this wonderful human intelligence. On top of that, all human beings have the capacity to be very determined and to direct that strong sense of determination in whatever direction they would like to use it. There is no doubt of this. So if one maintains an awareness of these potentials and reminds oneself of them repeatedly until it becomes part of one's customary way of perceiving human beings—including oneself—then this could serve to help reduce feelings of discouragement, helplessness, and self-contempt."

The Dalai Lama stopped for a moment, then proceeded with a probing inflection which suggested that he was still actively exploring, continuously engaging in a process of discovery.

"I think that here there might be some sort of parallel to the way we treat physical illnesses. When doctors treat someone for a specific illness, not only do they give antibiotics for the specific condition, but they also make sure that the person's underlying physical condition is such that he or she can take antibiotics and tolerate them. So in order to ensure that, the doctors make sure, for instance, that the person is generally well nourished, and often they may also have to give vitamins or whatever to build the body. So long as the person has that underlying strength in his or her body, then there is the potential or capacity within the body to heal itself from the illness through medication. *Similarly, so long as we know and maintain an awareness that we have this marvelous gift of human intelligence and a capac-*

◆

ity to develop determination and use it in positive ways, in some sense we have this underlying mental health. An underlying strength, that comes from realizing we have this great human potential. This realization can act as a sort of built-in mechanism that allows us to deal with any difficulty, no matter what situation we are facing, without losing hope or sinking into self-hatred."

Reminding ourselves of the great qualities we share with all human beings acts to neutralize the impulse to think we're bad or undeserving. Many Tibetans do this as a daily meditation practice. Perhaps that's the reason why in Tibetan culture self-hatred never took hold.

Part V

CLOSING REFLECTIONS ON LIVING A SPIRITUAL LIFE

Chapter 15

BASIC SPIRITUAL VALUES

The art of happiness has many components. As we've seen, it begins with developing an understanding of the truest sources of happiness and setting our priorities in life based on the cultivation of those sources. It involves an inner discipline, a gradual process of rooting out destructive mental states and replacing them with positive, constructive states of mind, such as kindness, tolerance, and forgiveness. In identifying the factors that lead to a full and satisfying life, we conclude with a discussion of the final component—spirituality.

There is a natural tendency to associate spirituality with religion. The Dalai Lama's approach to achieving happiness has been shaped by his years of rigorous training as an ordained Buddhist monk. He is also widely regarded as a preeminent Buddhist scholar. For many, however, it is not his grasp of complex philosophical issues that offers the most appeal but rather his personal warmth, humor, and down-to-earth approach to life. During the course of our conversations, in fact, his basic humanness seemed to override even his primary role as a Buddhist monk. Despite his shaved head and striking maroon robes, despite his position as one of the most prominent religious figures in the world, the tone of our conversations was simply of one human being to another, discussing the problems that we all share.

In helping us understand the true meaning of spirituality, the Dalai Lama began by distinguishing between spirituality and religion:

"I believe that it is essential to appreciate our potential as human beings and recognize the importance of inner transformation. This should be achieved through what could be called a process of mental development. Sometimes, I call this having a spiritual dimension in our life.

"There can be two levels of spirituality. One level of spirituality has to do with our religious beliefs. In this world, there are so many different people, so many different dispositions. There are five billion human beings and in a certain way I think we need five billion different religions, because there is such a large variety of dispositions. I believe that each individual should embark upon a spiritual path that is best suited to his or her mental disposition, natural inclination, temperament, belief, family, and cultural background.

"Now, for example, as a Buddhist monk, I find Buddhism to be most suitable. So, for myself, I've found that Buddhism is best. But that does not mean Buddhism is best for everyone. That's clear. It's definite. If I believed that Buddhism were best for everyone, that would be foolish, because different people have different mental dispositions. So, the variety of people calls for a variety of religions. The purpose of religion is to benefit people, and I think that if we only had one religion, after a while it would cease to benefit many people. If we had a restaurant, for instance, and it only served one dish—day after day, for every meal—that restaurant wouldn't have many customers left after a while. People need and appreciate diversity in their food because there are so many different tastes. In the same way, religions are meant to nourish the human spirit. And I think we can learn to celebrate that diversity in religions and develop a deep appreciation of the variety of religions. So certain people may find Judaism, the Christian tradition, or the Islamic tradition to be most effective for them. Therefore, we must respect and appreciate the value of all the different major world religious traditions.

"All of these religions can make an effective contribution for the benefit of humanity. They are all designed to make the individual a happier person, and the world a better place. However, in order for the religion to have an impact in making the world a better place, I think it's important for the individual practitioner to sincerely practice the teachings of that religion. One must integrate the religious teachings into one's life, wherever one is, so one can use them as a source of inner strength. And one must gain a deeper understanding of the religion's ideas, not just on an intellectual level but with a deep feeling, making them part of one's inner experience.

"I believe that one can cultivate a deep respect for all the different religious traditions. One reason to respect these other traditions is that all of these traditions can provide an ethical framework which can govern one's behavior and have positive effects. For instance, in the Christian tradition a belief in God can provide one with a coherent and clear-cut ethical framework which can govern one's behavior and way of life—and it can be a very powerful approach because there is a certain intimacy created in one's relationship with God, and the way to demonstrate one's love of God, the God who created you, is by showing love and compassion to one's fellow human beings.

"I believe that there are many similar reasons to respect other religious traditions as well. All major religions, of course, have provided tremendous benefit for millions of human beings throughout many centuries in the past. And even at this very moment, millions of people still get a benefit, get some kind of inspiration, from these different religious traditions. It is clear. And in the future also, these different religious traditions will give inspiration to millions of coming generations. That is a fact. So therefore, it is very, very important to realize that reality and respect other traditions.

"I think that one way of strengthening that mutual respect is through closer contact between those of different religious faiths—personal contact. I have made efforts over the past few years to meet and have dialogues with, for example, the Christian community and the Jewish community, and I think that some really positive results have come of this. Through this kind of closer contact we can learn about the useful contributions that these religions have made to humanity and find useful aspects of the other traditions that we can learn from. We may even discover methods and techniques that we can adopt in our own practice.

"So, it is essential that we develop closer bonds among the various religions; through this we can make a common effort for the benefit of humanity. There are so many things that divide humanity, so many problems in the world. Religion should be a remedy to help reduce the conflict and suffering in the world, not another source of conflict.

"We often hear people say that all human beings are equal. By this we mean that everyone has the obvious desire of happiness. Everybody has the right to be a happy person. And everyone has the right to overcome suffering. So if someone is deriving happiness or benefit from a particular religious tradition, it becomes important to respect the rights of others; thus we must learn to respect all these major religious traditions. That is clear."

During the Dalai Lama's week of talks in Tucson, the spirit of mutual respect was more than just wishful thinking. Those of many different religious traditions were found among the audience, including a sizable representation of Christian clergy. Despite the differences in traditions, a peaceful and harmonious atmosphere pervaded the room. It was palpable. There was a spirit of exchange as well, and no little curiosity among the non-Buddhists present about the Dalai Lama's daily spiritual practice. This curiosity prompted one listener to ask:

"Whether one is a Buddhist or of a different tradition, practices such as prayer seem to be emphasized. Why is prayer important for a spiritual life?"

The Dalai Lama answered, "I think prayer is, for the most part, a simple daily reminder of your deeply held principles and convictions. I, myself, repeat certain Buddhist verses every morning. The verses may look like prayers, but they are actually reminders. Reminders of how to speak to others, how to deal with other people, how to deal with problems in your daily life, things like that. So, for the most part, my practice involves reminders—reviewing the importance of compassion, forgiveness, all these things. And, of course, it also includes certain Buddhist meditations about the nature of reality, and also certain visualization practices. So, in my own daily practice, my own daily prayers, if I go leisurely, it takes about four hours. It's quite long."

The thought of spending four hours a day in prayer prompted another listener to ask, "I'm a working mother with small children, with very little free time. For someone who is really busy, how does one find the time to do these kinds of prayers and meditation practices?"

"Even in my case, if I wish to complain, I can always complain about lack of time," the Dalai Lama remarked. "I'm very busy. However, if you make the effort, you can always find some time, say, in the early morning. Then, I think there are some times like the weekend. You can sacrifice some of your fun," he laughed. "So at least, I think daily, say a half an hour. Or if you make the effort, try hard enough, perhaps you may be able to find, let us say, thirty minutes in the morning and thirty minutes in the evening. If you really think about it, maybe it is possible to figure out a way of getting some time.

◆

"However, if you think seriously about the true meaning of spiritual practices, it has to do with the development and training of your mental state, attitudes, and psychological and emotional state and well-being. You should not confine your understanding of spiritual practice to terms of some physical activities or verbal activities, like doing recitations of prayers and chanting. If your understanding of spiritual practice is limited to only these activities, then, of course, you will need a specific time, a separate allotted time to do your practice—because you can't go around doing your daily chores, like cooking and so on, while reciting mantras. That could be quite annoying to people around you. However, if you understand spiritual practice in its true sense, then you can use all twenty-four hours of your day for your practice. *True spirituality is a mental attitude that you can practice at any time.* For example, if you find yourself in a situation in which you might be tempted to insult someone, then you immediately take precautions and restrain yourself from doing that. Similarly, if you encounter a situation in which you may lose your temper, immediately you are mindful and say, 'No, this is not the appropriate way.' That actually is a spiritual practice. Seen in that light, you will always have time.

"This reminds me of one of the Tibetan Kadampa masters, Potowa, who said that for a meditator who has a certain degree of inner stability and realization, every event, every experience you are exposed to comes as a kind of a teaching. It's a learning experience. This I think is very true.

"So, from this perspective, even when you are exposed to, for instance, disturbing scenes of violence and sex, like in TV and films, there is a possibility to view them with an underlying mindfulness of the harmful effects of going to extremes. Then, instead of being totally overwhelmed by the sight, rather you can take these scenes as a kind of an indicator of the damaging nature of unchecked negative emotions—something from which you can learn lessons."

But learning lessons from old reruns of *The A-Team* or *Melrose Place* is one thing. As a practicing Buddhist, however, the Dalai Lama's personal spiritual regimen certainly includes features unique to the Buddhist path. In describing his daily practice, for instance, he mentioned it includes Buddhist meditations on the nature of reality, as well as certain visualization practices. While in the context of this discussion he mentioned these practices only in passing, over the years I've had an opportunity to hear him discuss these topics at length—his talks comprising some of the most complex discussions I've ever heard on *any* subject. His talks on the nature of reality were filled with labyrinthine philosophical arguments and analyses; his descriptions of Tantric visualizations were inconceivably intricate and elaborate—meditations and visualizations whose objective seemed to be to construct within one's imagination a sort of holographic atlas of the universe. He had spent a lifetime engaged in the study and practice of these Buddhist meditations. It was with this in mind, knowing the monumental scope of his efforts, that I asked him:

"Can you describe the practical benefit or impact these spiritual practices have had on your day-to-day life?"

The Dalai Lama was silent for several moments, then quietly

replied, "Although my own experience may be very little, one thing that I can say for certain is that I feel that through Buddhist training, I feel that my mind has become much more calm. That's definite. Although the change has come about gradually, perhaps centimeter by centimeter," he laughed, "I think that there has been a change in my attitude towards myself and others. Although it's difficult to point to the precise causes of this change, I think that it has been influenced by a realization, not full realization, but a certain feeling or sense of the underlying fundamental nature of reality, and also through contemplating subjects such as impermanence, our suffering nature, and the value of compassion and altruism.

"So, for example, even when thinking about those Communist Chinese who inflicted great harm on some of the Tibetan people—as a result of my Buddhist training I feel a certain compassion towards even the torturer, because I understand that the torturer was in fact compelled by other negative forces. Because of these things and my Bodhisattva vows and commitments, even if a person committed atrocities, I simply cannot feel or think that because of their atrocities they should experience negative things or not experience a moment of happiness.* The Bodhisattva vow has helped me develop this attitude; it has been very useful, so naturally I love this vow.

---

*In the Bodhisattva vow, the spiritual trainee affirms his intention to become a Bodhisattva. A Bodhisattva, literally translated as the "awakening warrior," is one who, out of love and compassion, has attained a realization of *Bodhicitta*, a mental state characterized by the spontaneous and genuine aspiration to attain full Enlightenment in order to be of benefit to all beings.

"This reminds me of one senior chant master who is staying at Namgyal Monastery. He was in Chinese prisons as a political prisoner and in labor camps for twenty years. Once I asked him what was the most difficult situation he faced when he was in prison. Surprisingly, he said that he felt the greatest danger was of losing compassion for the Chinese!

"There are many such stories. For example, three days ago I met a monk who spent many years in Chinese prisons. He told me that he was twenty-four years old at the time of the 1959 Tibetan uprising. At that time he joined the Tibetan forces in Norbulinga. He was caught by the Chinese and put in prison along with three brothers who were killed there. Two other brothers were also killed. Then his parents died in a labor camp. But he told me that when he was in prison, he reflected on his life until then and concluded that even though he had spent his entire life as a monk at Drepung Monastery, until that time he felt that he was not a good monk. He felt that he had been a stupid monk. At that moment he made a pledge that now that he was in prison, he would try to be a genuinely good monk. So as a result of his Buddhist practices, because of this training of the mind, he was able to remain mentally very happy even if he was in physical pain. Even when he underwent torture and severe beatings, he was able to survive it and still feel happy by viewing it as a cleansing of his past negative Karma.

"So, through these examples, one can really appreciate the value of incorporating spiritual practices within one's everyday life."

Thus, the Dalai Lama added the final ingredient of a happier life—the spiritual dimension. Through the teachings of the

Buddha, the Dalai Lama and many others have found a meaningful framework that enables them to endure and even tran-
scend the pain and suffering that life sometimes brings. And as
the Dalai Lama suggests, each of the world's major religious traditions can offer the same opportunities to help one achieve a
happier life. The power of faith, generated on a widespread scale
by these religious traditions, is interwoven in the lives of millions. That deep religious faith has sustained countless people
through difficult times. Sometimes it operates in small quiet
ways, sometimes in profound transformative experiences. Every
one of us, at some time during our lives, has no doubt witnessed
that power operate on a family member, a friend, or an acquaintance. Occasionally, examples of the sustaining power of faith
find their way onto the front pages. Many are familiar, for
instance, with the ordeal of Terry Anderson, an ordinary man
who was suddenly kidnapped off the street in Beirut one morning in 1985. A blanket was thrown over him, he was shoved into
a car, and for the next seven years he was held as a hostage by
Hezbollah, a group of Islamic fundamentalist extremists. Until
1991 he was imprisoned in damp, filthy basements and small
cells, blindfolded and chained for extended periods, enduring
regular beatings and harsh conditions. When he was finally
released, the world turned its eyes toward him and found a man
overjoyed to be returned to his family and his life but with surprisingly little bitterness and hatred toward his captors. When
questioned by reporters about the source of his remarkable
strength, he identified faith and prayer as significant factors that
helped him endure his ordeal.

The world is filled with such examples of the ways in which

religious faith offers concrete help in times of trouble. And extensive recent surveys seem to confirm the fact that religious faith can substantially contribute to a happier life. Those conducted by independent researchers and polling organizations (such as the Gallup company) have found that religious people report feeling happy and satisfied with life more often than nonreligious people. Studies have found that not only is faith a predictor of self-reports of feelings of well-being, but a strong religious faith also appears to help individuals deal more effectively with issues such as aging or coping with personal crises and traumatic events. In addition, statistics show that families of those with strong religious belief often have lower rates of delinquency, alcohol and drug abuse, and ruined marriages. There is even some evidence to suggest that faith may have benefits for people's physical health—even for those with serious illnesses. There have, in fact, been literally hundreds of scientific and epidemiologic studies establishing a link between strong religious faith, lower death rates, and improved health. In one study, elderly women with strong religious beliefs were able to walk farther after hip surgery than those with fewer religious convictions, and they were also less depressed following the surgery. A study done by Ronna Casar Harris and Mary Amanda Dew at the University of Pittsburgh Medical Center found that heart-transplant patients with strong religious beliefs have less difficulty coping with postoperative medical regimens and display better long-term physical and emotional health. In another, conducted by Dr. Thomas Oxman and his colleagues at Dartmouth Medical School, it was found that patients over the age of fifty-five who underwent open-heart surgery for coronary artery or heart valve disease and who had taken refuge in their religious beliefs were three times more likely to survive than those who did not.

The benefits of a strong religious faith sometimes come about as a direct product of certain specific doctrines and beliefs of a particular tradition. Many Buddhists, for instance, are helped to endure their suffering as a result of their firm belief in the doctrine of Karma. In the same way, those who have an unshakable faith in God are often able to withstand intense hardship because of their belief in an omniscient and loving God—a God whose plan may be obscure to us at present but One who, in His wisdom, will ultimately reveal His love for us. With faith in the teachings of the Bible, they can take comfort in verses such as Romans 8:28: "All things work together for the good to them that love God, to them who are called according to His purpose."

Although some of the rewards of faith may be based on specific doctrines unique to a particular religious tradition, there are other strength-giving features of a spiritual life that are common to all religions. Involvement in *any* religious group can create a feeling of belonging, communal ties, a caring connection with fellow practitioners. It offers a meaningful framework in which one can connect and relate with others. And it can give one a feeling of acceptance. Strongly held religious beliefs can give one a deep sense of purpose, providing meaning for one's life. These beliefs can offer hope in the face of adversity, suffering, and death. They can help one adopt an eternal perspective that allows one to get outside of oneself when overwhelmed by life's daily problems.

Although all these potential benefits are available to those who choose to practice the teachings of an established religion, it is clear that having a religious belief alone is no guarantee of happiness and peace. For example, at the very same moment Terry Anderson sat chained in a cell demonstrating the finest attributes of religious faith, just outside his cell raged mass violence and hatred demonstrating the very worst attributes of religious faith. For years in Lebanon, various sects of Muslims were at war with Christians and Jews, fueled by violent hatred on all sides and resulting in unspeakable atrocities committed in the name of faith. It's an old story, and one that has been told too often throughout history and repeated too often in the modern world.

Because of this potential to breed divisiveness and hatred, it is easy to lose faith in religious institutions. This has led some religious figures such as the Dalai Lama to try to distill those elements of a spiritual life that can be universally applied by any individual to enhance his or her happiness, regardless of religious tradition or whether he or she believes in religion.

Thus, with a tone of complete conviction, the Dalai Lama concluded his discussion with his vision of a truly spiritual life:

"So, in speaking of having a spiritual dimension to our lives, we have identified our religious beliefs as one level of spirituality. Now regarding religion, if we believe in any religion, that's good. But even without a religious belief, we can still manage. In some cases, we can manage even better. But that's our own individual right; if we wish to believe, good! If not, it's all right.

But then there's another level of spirituality. That is what I call *basic spirituality*—basic human qualities of goodness, kindness, compassion, caring. Whether we are believers or nonbelievers, this kind of spirituality is essential. I personally consider this second level of spirituality to be more important than the first, because no matter how wonderful a particular religion may be, it will still only be accepted by a limited number of human beings, only a portion of humanity. But as long as we are human beings, as long as we are members of the human family, *all* of us need these basic spiritual values. Without these, human existence remains hard, very dry. As a result, none of us can be a happy person, our whole family will suffer, and then, eventually, society will be more troubled. So, it becomes clear that cultivating these kinds of basic spiritual values becomes crucial.

"In seeking to cultivate these basic spiritual values, I think we need to remember that out of the, say, five billion human beings on this planet, I think perhaps one or two billion are very sincere, genuine believers in religion. Of course, when I refer to sincere believers, I'm not including those people who simply say, for example, 'I am Christian' mainly because their family background is Christian but in daily life may not consider very much about the Christian faith or actively practice it. So excluding these people, I believe that there are perhaps only around one billion who sincerely practice their religion. That means that four billion, the majority of the people on this earth, are nonbelievers. So we must still find a way to try to improve life for this majority of the people, the four billion people who aren't involved in a specific religion—ways to help them become good human beings, moral people, without any

◆

religion. Here I think that education is crucial—instilling in people a sense that compassion, kindness, and so on are the basic good qualities of human beings, not just a matter of religious subjects. I think earlier we spoke at greater length about the prime importance of human warmth, affection, and compassion in people's physical health, happiness, and peace of mind. This is a very practical issue, not religious theory or philosophical speculation. It is a key issue. And I think that this is in fact the essence of all the religious teachings of the different traditions. But it remains just as crucial for those who choose not to follow any particular religion. For those people, I think we can educate them and impress upon them that it's all right to remain without any religion but be a good human being, a sensible human being, with a sense of responsibility and commitment for a better, happier world.

"In general, it is possible to indicate your particular religious or spiritual way of life through external means, such as wearing certain clothes, or having a shrine or altar in your house, or doing recitations and chanting, and so on. There are ways of demonstrating that externally. However, these practices or activities are secondary to your conducting a truly spiritual way of life, based on the basic spiritual values, because it is possible that all of these external religious activities can still go along with a person's harboring a very negative state of mind. But true spirituality should have the result of making a person calmer, happier, more peaceful.

"All of the virtuous states of mind—compassion, tolerance, forgiveness, caring, and so on—these mental qualities are genuine Dharma, or genuine spiritual qualities, because all of these internal mental qualities cannot coexist with ill feelings or negative states of mind.

"So, engaging in training or a method of bringing about inner discipline within one's mind is the essence of a religious life, an inner discipline that has the purpose of cultivating these positive mental states. Thus, whether one leads a spiritual life depends on whether one has been successful in bringing about that disciplined, tamed state of mind and translating that state of mind into one's daily actions."

The Dalai Lama was due to attend a small reception held in honor of a group of donors who had been strong supporters of the Tibetan cause. Outside the reception room a large crowd had gathered in anticipation of his appearance. By the time of his arrival the crowd had become quite dense. Among the onlookers I saw a man whom I had noticed a couple of times during the week. He was of indeterminate age, although I would have guessed middle twenties, maybe early thirties, tall and very thin. Notable for his disheveled appearance, he, however, had caught my attention because of his expression, one that I had frequently seen among my patients—anxious, profoundly depressed, in pain. And I thought I noticed slight repetitive involuntary movements of the musculature around his mouth. "Tardive dyskinesia," I had silently diagnosed, a neurological condition caused by chronic use of antipsychotic medication. "Poor guy," I thought at the time but quickly forgot about him.

As the Dalai Lama arrived, the crowd condensed, pressing forward to greet him. The security staff, most of them volunteers, struggled to hold back the advancing mass of people and clear a path to the reception room. The troubled young man whom I had seen earlier, now with a somewhat bewildered expression, was crushed forward by the crowd and pushed to the edge of the clearing made by the security team. As the Dalai Lama made his way through, he noticed the man, broke free from the mooring of the security crew, and stopped to talk to him. The man was startled at first and began to speak very rapidly to the Dalai Lama, who spoke a few words in return. I couldn't hear what they were saying, but I saw that as the man spoke, he started to become visibly more agitated. The man was saying something, but instead of responding, the Dalai Lama spontaneously took the man's hand between his, patted it gently, and for several moments simply stood there silently nodding. As he held the man's hand firmly, looking into his eyes, it seemed as if he were unaware of the mass of people around him. The look of pain and agitation suddenly seemed to drain from the man's face and tears ran down his cheeks. Although the smile that surfaced and slowly spread across his features was thin, a look of comfort and gladness appeared in the man's eyes.

The Dalai Lama has repeatedly emphasized that inner discipline is the basis of a spiritual life. It is the fundamental method of achieving happiness. As he explained throughout this book, from his perspective inner discipline involves combating negative states of mind such as anger, hatred, and greed, and cultivating positive states such as kindness, compassion, and tolerance. He also has pointed out that a happy life is built on a foundation of a calm, stable state of mind. The practice of inner discipline can include formal meditation techniques that are intended to help stabilize the mind and achieve that calm state. Most spiritual traditions include practices that seek to quiet the mind, to put us more in touch with our deeper spiritual nature. At the conclusion of the Dalai Lama's series of public talks in Tucson, he presented instruction on one meditation designed to help us begin to quiet our thoughts, observe the underlying nature of the mind, and thus develop a "stillness of mind."

Looking out over the assembly, he began to speak in his characteristic manner as if, instead of addressing a large group, he was personally instructing each individual in the audience. At times he was still and focused, at times more animated, choreographing his instruction with subtle head nods, hand gestures, and gentle rocking motions.

MEDITATION ON THE NATURE OF THE MIND

"The purpose of this exercise is to begin to recognize and get a feel for the nature of our mind," he began, "at least on a conventional level. Generally, when we refer to our 'mind,' we are talking about an abstract concept. Without having a direct experience of our mind, for example, if we are asked to identify the mind, we may be compelled to merely point to the brain. Or, if we are asked to define the mind, we may say it is something that has the capacity to 'know,' something that is 'clear' and 'cognitive.' But without having directly grasped the mind through meditative practices, these definitions are just words. It's important to be able to identify the mind through direct experience, not just as an abstract concept. So the purpose of this exercise is to be able to *directly* feel or grasp the conventional nature of the mind, so when you say the mind has qualities of 'clarity' and 'cognition,' you will be able to identify it through experience, not just as an abstract concept.

"This exercise helps you to deliberately stop the discursive thoughts and gradually remain in that state for longer and longer duration. As you practice this exercise, eventually you will get to a feeling as if there is nothing there, a sense of vacuity. But if you go farther, you eventually begin to recognize the underlying nature of the mind, the qualities of 'clarity' and 'knowing.' It is similar to having a pure crystal glass full of water. If the water is pure, you can see the bottom of the glass, but you still recognize that the water is there.

"So, today, let us meditate on nonconceptuality. This is not a mere state of dullness, or a blanked-out state of mind. Rather, what you should do is, first of all, generate the determination that 'I will maintain a state without conceptual thoughts.' The way in which you should do that is this:

"Generally speaking, our mind is predominantly directed towards external objects. Our attention follows after the sense experiences. It remains at a predominantly sensory and conceptual level. In other words, normally our awareness is directed towards physical sensory experiences and mental concepts. But in this exercise, what you should do is to withdraw your mind inward; don't let it chase after or pay attention to sensory objects. At the same time, don't allow it to be so totally withdrawn that there is a kind of dullness or lack of mindfulness. You should maintain a very full state of alertness and mindfulness, and then try to see the natural state of your consciousness—a state in which your consciousness is not afflicted by thoughts of the past, the things that have happened, your memories and remembrances; nor is it afflicted by thoughts of the future, like your future plans, anticipations, fears, and hopes. But rather, try to remain in a natural and neutral state.

"This is a bit like a river that is flowing quite strongly, in which you cannot see the riverbed very clearly. If, however, there was some way you could stop the flow in both directions, from where the water is coming and to where the water is flowing, then you could keep the water still. That would allow you to see the base of the river quite clearly. Similarly, when you are able to stop your mind from chasing sensory objects and thinking about the past and future and so on, and when you can free your mind from being totally 'blanked out' as well, then you will begin to see underneath this turbulence of the thought processes. There is an underlying stillness, an underlying clarity of the mind. You should try to observe or experience this . . .

"This can be very difficult at the initial stage, so let us begin to practice from this very session. At the initial stage, when you begin to experience this underlying natural state of consciousness, you might experience it in the form of some sort of 'absence.' This is happening because we are so habituated to understanding our mind in terms of external objects; we tend to look at the world through our concepts, images, and so on. So when you withdraw your mind from external objects, it's almost as if you can't recognize your mind. There's a kind of absence, a kind of vacuity. However, as you slowly progress and get used to it, you begin to notice an underlying clarity, a luminosity. That's when you begin to appreciate and realize the natural state of the mind.

"Many of the truly profound meditative experiences must come on the basis of this kind of stillness of mind. . . . Oh," the Dalai Lama laughed, "I should warn that in this type of meditation, since there is no specific object to focus on, there is a danger of falling asleep.

"So, now let us meditate . . .

"To begin, first do three rounds of breathing, and focus your attention simply on the breath. Just be aware of inhaling, exhaling, and then inhaling, exhaling—three times. Then, start the meditation."

The Dalai Lama removed his glasses, folded his hands in his lap, and remained motionless in meditation. Total silence pervaded the hall, as fifteen hundred people turned inward, in the solitude of fifteen hundred private worlds, seeking to still their thoughts and perhaps catch a glimpse of the true nature of their own mind. After five minutes, the silence was cracked but not broken as the Dalai Lama began to chant softly, his voice low and melodic, gently leading his listeners from their meditation.

At the close of the session that day, as always, the Dalai Lama folded his hands together, bowed to his audience out of affection and respect, rose, and made his way through the surrounding crowd. His hands remained clasped together and he continued to bow as he left the room. As he walked through the dense crowd he bowed so low, in fact, that for anyone who stood more than a few feet away, it was impossible to see him. He appeared to be lost in a sea of heads. From a distance one could still detect his path, however, from the subtle shift in the crowd's movement as he passed along. It was as if he had ceased to be a visible object and had simply become a felt presence.

ACKNOWLEDGMENTS

This book would not exist without the efforts and kindness of many people. First, I would like to extend my heartfelt thanks to Tenzin Gyatso, the fourteenth Dalai Lama, with deep gratitude for his boundless kindness, generosity, inspiration, and friendship. And to my parents, James and Bettie Cutler, in loving memory, for providing the foundation for my own path to happiness in life.

My sincere thanks extends to many others:

To Dr. Thupten Jinpa for his friendship, his help in editing the Dalai Lama's portions of this book, and his critical role in acting as interpreter for the Dalai Lama's public talks and many of our private conversations. Also to Lobsang Jordhen, the Ven. Lhakdor, for acting as interpreter for a number of my conversations with the Dalai Lama in India.

To Tenzin Geyche Tethong, Rinchen Dharlo, and Dawa Tsering, for their support and assistance in many ways over the years.

To the many people who worked so hard to assure that the Dalai Lama's 1993 visit to Arizona was a rewarding experience for so many others: to Claude d'Estree, Ken Bacher, and the board and staff of Arizona Teachings, Inc., to Peggy Hitchcock and the board of Arizona Friends of Tibet, to Dr. Pam Willson and those who helped organize the Dalai Lama's address at Arizona State University, and to the dozens of dedicated volunteers for their tireless efforts on behalf of all those who attended the Dalai Lama's teachings in Arizona.

To my extraordinary agents, Sharon Friedman and Ralph Vicinanza, and their wonderful staff, for their encouragement, kindness, dedication, help in many aspects of this project, and hard work above and beyond the call of duty. I owe them a special debt of gratitude.

To those who provided invaluable editorial assistance, insight, and expertise, as well as personal support during the lengthy writing process: to Ruth Hapgood for her skillful efforts in editing earlier versions of the manuscript, to Barbara Gates and Dr. Ronna Kabatznick for their indispensable help in wading through voluminous material and focusing and organizing that material into a coherent structure, and to my very talented editor at Riverhead, Amy Hertz, for believing in the project and helping shape the book into its final form. Also to Jennifer Repo and the hard-working copy editors and staff at Riverhead Books. I would also like to extend warm thanks to those who helped transcribe the Dalai Lama's public talks in Arizona, type the transcripts of my conversations with the Dalai Lama, and type parts of the earliest versions of the manuscript.

In closing, my profound thanks:

To my teachers.

To my family and the many friends who have enriched my life in more ways than I can express: to Gina Beckwith Eckel, Dr. David Weiss and Daphne Atkeson, Dr. Gillian Hamilton, Helen Mitsios, David Greenwalt, Dale Brozosky, Kristi Ingham Espinasse, Dr. David Klebanoff, Henrietta Bernstein, Tom Minor, Ellen Wyatt Gothe, Dr. Gail McDonald, Larry Cutler, Randy Cutler, Lori Warren, and with special thanks and deep appreciation to Candee and Scott Brierley—and to other friends whom I may have failed to mention here by name, but whom I hold in my heart with continued love, gratitude, and respect.

SELECTED TITLES
BY HIS HOLINESS
THE DALAI LAMA

The following works are listed alphabetically by title.

The Dalai Lama: A Policy of Kindness, compiled and edited by Sidney Piburn. Ithaca: Snow Lion Publications, 1990.

A Flash of Lightning in the Dark of Night—A Guide to the Bodhisattva's Way of Life, by H.H. the Dalai Lama. Boston: Shambhala Publications, 1994.

The Four Noble Truths, by H.H. the Dalai Lama. Translated by Dr. Thupten Jinpa, edited by Dominique Side. London: Thorsons, 1998.

Freedom in Exile—The Autobiography of the Dalai Lama, by H.H. the Dalai Lama. New York: HarperCollins, 1991.

The Good Heart—A Buddhist Perspective on the Teachings of Jesus, by H.H. the Dalai Lama. Boston: Wisdom Publications, 1996.

Kindness, Clarity, and Insight, by H.H. the Dalai Lama. Jeffrey Hopkins, translator and editor; Elizabeth Napper, co-editor. Ithaca: Snow Lion Publications, 1984.

The World of Tibetan Buddhism, by H.H. the Dalai Lama. Translated, edited, and annotated by Dr. Thupten Jinpa. Boston: Wisdom Publications, 1995.

3174